THE **COMPLETE IDIOT'S GUIDE** TO

Crowdsourcing

by Aliza Sherman

ALPHA

A member of Penguin Group (USA) Inc.

To my husband, Greg Risdahl, with love and thanks.

ALPHA BOOKS

Published by the Penguin Group

Penguin Group (USA) Inc., 375 Hudson Street, New York, New York 10014, USA

Penguin Group (Canada), 90 Eglinton Avenue East, Suite 700, Toronto, Ontario M4P 2Y3, Canada (a division of Pearson Penguin Canada Inc.)

Penguin Books Ltd., 80 Strand, London WC2R 0RL, England

Penguin Ireland, 25 St. Stephen's Green, Dublin 2, Ireland (a division of Penguin Books Ltd.)

Penguin Group (Australia), 250 Camberwell Road, Camberwell, Victoria 3124, Australia (a division of Pearson Australia Group Pty. Ltd.)

Penguin Books India Pvt. Ltd., 11 Community Centre, Panchsheel Park, New Delhi—110 017, India

Penguin Group (NZ), 67 Apollo Drive, Rosedale, North Shore, Auckland 1311, New Zealand (a division of Pearson New Zealand Ltd.)

Penguin Books (South Africa) (Pty.) Ltd., 24 Sturdee Avenue, Rosebank, Johannesburg 2196, South Africa

Penguin Books Ltd., Registered Offices: 80 Strand, London WC2R 0RL, England

Copyright © 2011 by Aliza Sherman Risdahl

International Standard Book Number: 978-1-61564-092-8
Library of Congress Catalog Card Number: 2010919339

13 12 11   8 7 6 5 4 3 2 1

Interpretation of the printing code: The rightmost number of the first series of numbers is the year of the book's printing; the rightmost number of the second series of numbers is the number of the book's printing. For example, a printing code of 11-1 shows that the first printing occurred in 2011.

Printed in the United States of America

Note: This publication contains the opinions and ideas of its author. It is intended to provide helpful and informative material on the subject matter covered. It is sold with the understanding that the author and publisher are not engaged in rendering professional services in the book. If the reader requires personal assistance or advice, a competent professional should be consulted.

The author and publisher specifically disclaim any responsibility for any liability, loss, or risk, personal or otherwise, which is incurred as a consequence, directly or indirectly, of the use and application of any of the contents of this book.

Most Alpha books are available at special quantity discounts for bulk purchases for sales promotions, premiums, fund-raising, or educational use. Special books, or book excerpts, can also be created to fit specific needs.

For details, write: Special Markets, Alpha Books, 375 Hudson Street, New York, NY 10014.

Publisher: *Marie Butler-Knight*
Associate Publisher: *Mike Sanders*
Executive Managing Editor: *Billy Fields*
Senior Acquisitions Editor: *Paul Dinas*
Senior Development Editor: *Phil Kitchel*
Senior Production Editor: *Kayla Dugger*

Copy Editor: *Christine Hackerd*
Cover Designer: *Rebecca Batchelor*
Book Designers: *William Thomas, Rebecca Batchelor*
Indexer: *Johnna VanHoose Dinse*
Layout: *Brian Massey*
Proofreader: *John Etchison*

Contents

Introduction

You're busy. You have a lot on your plate. You need assistance getting everything done. Maybe you've been outsourcing some work or hiring part-time help. There are new, fast, affordable ways to get things done—ways that take advantage of how connected we all are to the Internet, and that utilize the new communications, technology, and social tools at our disposal.

Crowdsourcing is a process, or set of processes, that leverages the Internet and our ability to gather groups—or crowds—of people online to get something done. You'll soon find out that what we can get done through crowdsourcing can run the gamut from verifying information to designing a tattoo to raising money for a startup business.

Crowdsourcing has forever changed the way we look at work and the way we do it. It's an understatement to say that crowdsourcing is a new process and is still undergoing major changes and growth. By the time you read this book, the definition of crowdsourcing will have morphed and expanded even further than it had since 2006 when writer Jeff Howe first used the term in an article for *Wired* magazine. There will be new crowdsourcing terms, companies, services, and sites that will continue to expand on what you'll find in this book.

How This Book Is Organized

More than anything, this book is a starting point for understanding the many facets of crowdsourcing. You'll learn the nuts and bolts of tapping into crowds in an organized manner to embark on your first crowdsourcing project or campaign.

In **Part 1, Crowdsourcing Your Way to Results,** you'll learn how crowdsourcing evolved from other forms of working and collaborating online. You'll also gain insight into how crowds gather and react, and why people join crowds to work, to provide input, or for other organized activities.

In **Part 2, Crowdsourcing for Feedback and Input,** you'll see that not all crowdsourcing involves getting work done. You can get feedback from crowds gathered online, or bring your own crowd together to provide input. Building your own crowd community takes time, and the steps and considerations of undertaking your own community building are outlined in this part.

In **Part 3, Crowdsourcing on Social Networks,** you'll learn how to tap into your connections on social networks like Facebook and LinkedIn and on microblogs like Twitter. Each network has its own set of features for communicating that can be leveraged to different degrees for crowdsourcing endeavors. Tapping into your own networks can satisfy some of your crowdsourcing needs, but I'll tell you about their potential limitations.

In **Part 4, Harnessing Crowds for Work,** you'll learn about companies specifically focused on providing you with work-related services through their proprietary crowdsourcing platforms. You'll also learn about crowd competitions such as design contests and other creative and collaborative platforms for sourcing design and creative work. Not only will you discover ways to cast a wide net to source a crowd for experts, but you'll also learn how to gather your customers and collect their input to help you improve what you do.

In **Part 5, More Ways to Crowdsource,** you'll see that crowdsourcing isn't limited to technical tasks. You can run the gamut from translation to traffic reporting. You'll learn how major corporations are using crowdsourcing principles to tap into customers for ideas and innovations.

In addition, I have provided a glossary as well as some resources to help you begin crowdsourcing. There are ways to leverage crowdsourcing technology and social networks to raise funds for organizations and causes, for creative projects, and even for companies. The interconnected communications and tools of crowdsourcing platforms can facilitate organizing crowds to take actions in their communities or around the world.

Extras

Throughout the book, you'll find the following sidebars that highlight information I want to be sure you catch.

DEFINITION

In these sidebars, you'll find clear, user-friendly explanations of crowdsourcing terms and concepts.

BEST PRACTICES

These sidebars provide tips to best leverage crowdsourcing tools and tactics.

PITFALLS

Check these sidebars for potential mistakes to avoid or challenges you might need to overcome to have a successful crowdsourcing campaign.

DULY NOTED

These sidebars highlight important information to consider when you're preparing for and actually conducting crowdsourcing activities.

Acknowledgments

I couldn't have written this book without the help and support of my family and friends and my business partners Monique Elwell and Steven Jackson and the team at Conversify. I spoke with many entrepreneurs who are innovating what crowdsourcing is becoming and who provided me with invaluable information for this book; the list of these individuals includes, but is not limited to: Lukas Biewald and the helpful folks at CrowdFlower, Matt Johnston of uTest, David Bratvold of Prova, Brandon Evans and Matt Listro of Crowdtap, Kyle Hawke of Whinot, James DeJulio and Justin J. Carter of Tongal, Shelley Kuipers of Chaordix, Philip Letts of blur Group, Neil Takemoto of CoolTown Beta Communities, Klaus Speidel of Hypios, Matthew Heim of NineSigma, and Alex Edelstein of CloudCrowd.

Special thanks to my Twitter friends, Facebook friends, LinkedIn connections, and HelpaReporter.com, all part of generous crowds, who let me tap into them often to lead me to additional resources and experts for my book. Heartfelt thanks to my agent, Katelynn Lacopo at BookEnds, LLC, and my patient editor, Paul Dinas at Alpha Books.

Special Thanks to the Technical Reviewer

The Complete Idiot's Guide to Crowdsourcing was reviewed by an expert who double-checked the accuracy of what you'll learn here, to help us ensure that this book gives you everything you need to know about crowdsourcing. Special thanks are extended to Clinton Bonner.

Trademarks

All terms mentioned in this book that are known to be or are suspected of being trademarks or service marks have been appropriately capitalized. Alpha Books and Penguin Group (USA) Inc. cannot attest to the accuracy of this information. Use of a term in this book should not be regarded as affecting the validity of any trademark or service mark.

Crowdsourcing Your Way to Results

In Part 1, you'll discover the origins of the term "crowdsourcing" and learn why people participate as members of crowds that produce work or provide input. I lay out some of the basic mechanics of "do-it-yourself" crowdsourcing—what works and what doesn't—and how to manage crowdsourcing campaigns.

It's nice to have options, so I lay out some resources, including companies that provide crowdsourcing-related services, in case you don't want to handle crowdsourcing activities directly.

Crowdsourcing Gets Things Done

Chapter

1

In This Chapter

- Definitions of crowdsourcing
- Reasons for crowdsourcing
- Common types of crowdsourcing
- Some concerns about crowdsourcing

You've heard the adage, "Two heads are better than one." What about dozens or hundreds or thousands of heads working together on a single problem? What about reaching out to dozens, hundreds, or thousands of people who could perform tasks to complete a project? Imagine if the world was at your fingertips, and you could tap into vast labor pools and collective minds with the click of a button. Today, it's not so far-fetched to reach out beyond your immediate network—beyond even your physical location—to find workers and thinkers to help you get things done.

With the advent of the Internet and the web, you can access the world through your keyboard and online connections. You can communicate around the world with relative speed and ease. With specialized websites, you can reach out to crowds of people, manage their input and output, and even pay them for their work. With new technological tools, you can leverage the power of many to crowdsource.

A Brief History of Crowdsourcing

"Crowdsourcing" is a term used for the first time in 2006 by Jeff Howe, a writer for *Wired* magazine. Howe described new opportunities cropping up due to our interconnected world, vast online communities, and cutting-edge communications tools. Howe made a distinction between crowdsourcing and outsourcing.

Outsourcing means you hire and pay an individual or a firm outside your company to work on something you don't want to or can't handle on your own. For example, when you need to make a lot of sales calls, and you farm that work out to a tele-marketing firm, you are outsourcing the work. Other commonly outsourced work includes customer service call centers and technical support; these complex tasks often require specialized training and skills.

Crowdsourcing involves reaching beyond yourself or your company to get something done. Usually, the people you can reach out to are not part of an organized business entity. Rather, they are independent workers who can either perform work individually or be brought together for a specific project. They are willing and able to perform small, repetitive tasks separately, or they may collaborate as an ad-hoc team.

If you needed help reading through comments on your Facebook page to determine whether they are positive, negative, or neutral, you can post your project on a crowdsourcing site. Workers around the globe can take on your project—no matter how small or tedious—and take small payments in exchange for their work. In other cases, crowds can be used to work on more complex projects, such as identifying bugs in software code. By applying collective intelligence and skills, groups can solve problems and complete work more quickly and efficiently than relying on a single person. Not all crowdsourcing work is cheap, but in some cases a job that costs $15 per hour when completed by an intern can cost only $7 total when completed by *crowdworkers*.

> **DEFINITION**
>
> A **crowdworker** is someone who performs a task as part of a crowdsourced project or participates in a crowdsourcing campaign.

Ways to Crowdsource

Crowdsourcing mostly falls into the following three categories:

1. Work

2. Input

3. Organizing

Work is any task that needs to be done, especially small or tedious tasks that are part of a larger project. A majority of crowdsourced work is handled online. *Input* is anything from feedback and opinions to ideas, answers, and solutions. *Organizing* means bringing people together in an organized way to take action or fund something—to combine efforts or money to get something done.

There are multiple terms to express different configurations of crowdsourcing:

- **One-sourcing:** Reaching out to crowds to find a specific individual who has the skills to complete less skill-intensive tasks.
- **Expert-sourcing:** Similar to one-sourcing, but you are seeking someone with highly specialized skills or talents.
- **Team-sourcing:** Reaching out to crowds and using a vetting process to identify specific individuals who will work with you as a team.
- **Wide-sourcing:** Another word for crowdsourcing; reaching out to many, without the connotation of randomness.
- **Mob-sourcing:** Casting a wide net to engage a large number of people, without requiring specialized skills.

These terms are relatively new, and are often created by different companies as they establish business models around some variation of crowdsourcing.

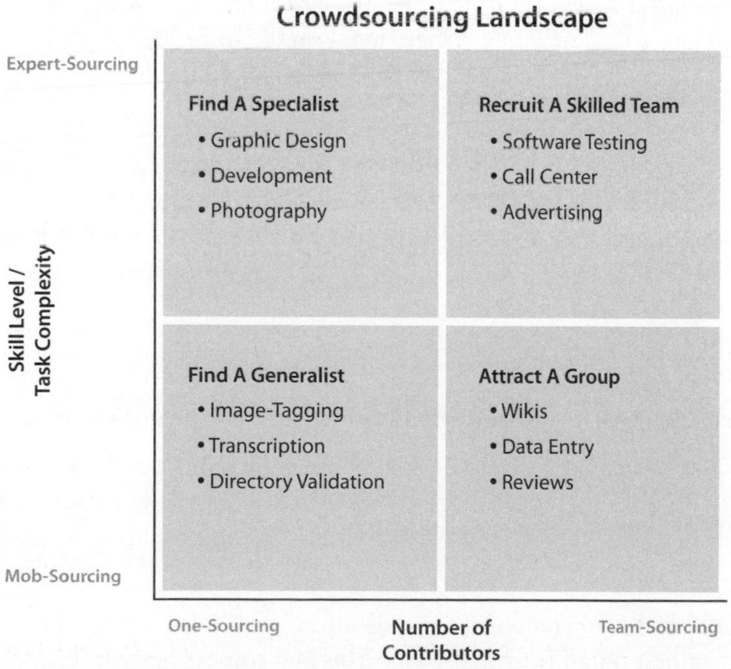
Crowdsourcing Landscape
Expert-Sourcing
Find A Specialist
• Graphic Design
• Development
• Photography
Recruit A Skilled Team
• Software Testing
• Call Center
• Advertising
Skill Level / Task Complexity
Find A Generalist
• Image-Tagging
• Transcription
• Directory Validation
Attract A Group
• Wikis
• Data Entry
• Reviews
Mob-Sourcing
One-Sourcing
Number of Contributors
Team-Sourcing

You can crowdsource based on the number of contributors and the skill level you are seeking, or by task complexity.

(Courtesy of uTest)

Communities of Crowdsourcing

The Internet makes it easy for people to gather in online communities, creating crowds that may be ripe for crowdsourcing. Usually, online communities form simply because of shared interests, but sometimes communities form with the express purpose of providing work or input; these are organized crowd communities.

Most crowdsourcing efforts are widely distributed and are a diverse collection of people. Crowdworkers operate as individuals—or are tapped individually from a larger group—and come together for specific work or tasks. Crowd communities can work as a group or be the pool from which you connect with an individual or a set of individuals to help you get something done.

Sourcing work or input from crowds can be either a free or fee-based arrangement. To capitalize on crowdsourcing opportunities, some companies are launching websites or online platforms with the express purpose of building crowd communities and offering crowdsourcing services. Some of these companies offer "self-service" crowdsourcing tools so you can manage your own crowdsourcing activities on their sites, such as Amazon's Mechanical Turk, or they offer consulting services so you can hire them and access their crowdsourcing tools and crowds, such as Chaordix. These companies make money either by taking a cut of fees you pay to crowdworkers through their site or fees you pay directly to them for strategic crowdsourcing services.

You can gather your own crowds online to carry out crowdsourcing campaigns. There are many web-based tools you can use to build online communities, not to mention social networks. You probably already have a following of people you know on Facebook and Twitter. You may already be crowdsourcing online and not even realize it!

How Does Crowdsourcing Happen?

Have you ever e-mailed a group of friends for input on a personal issue? Have you ever e-mailed your employees to get their input on a problem your company is facing? Have you ever asked your friends or followers for their advice via Facebook, Twitter, or other social network?

Before you even heard the term "crowdsource," you were already crowdsourcing in some way—albeit on an informal basis. You had something you needed to do or a question you needed answered or a problem you wanted solved, and you used Internet communications to reach out for help. Reaching out brought you the answer you sought, the solution to your problem, or simply helped you get something done. In an organic way, you were crowdsourcing. Perhaps you've sent out an e-mail to family members that included a link to a survey asking them to cast a vote or provide input on a family vacation or reunion. Or perhaps you've used a site such as Punchbowl. com to create a list of all the things you need to throw a party and then invite your friends via e-mail to go to the site and select what they can bring. The site removes each item from the list as friends volunteer to take care of them. In this case, you've crowdsourced the fixings for a party.

Most likely you reached out only so far because you didn't really need a lot of people to provide input. With fewer people involved, sorting through answers is easy enough. You probably received feedback on your query faster than you could have if you did all the thinking on your own. Today, crowdsourcing happens in more deliberate ways, tapping into larger and farther-flung pools of workers and thinkers. You can still crowdsource in smaller circles, but you can gain greater time- and cost-saving benefits by reaching out to bigger crowds.

The Upsides of Crowdsourcing

You can use the Internet and online tools to identify, connect with, and manage groups of people who can do something you cannot do alone. Perhaps you can do something on your own, but there are benefits to having others do it for you instead. Here are some of the benefits of crowdsourcing:

- **Cost savings:** Instead of paying large fees to contractors or consultants, you can get similar work done through a crowd that provides labor for less pay.

- **Time savings:** By reaching out to a crowd, you can more easily find an answer, get an idea, or source a design, saving you hours of research.

- **Built-in market research:** If you use a crowd as your sounding board or collaborative platform for a new product, you're also getting valuable input from the very people who might end up buying the finished product.

- **Increased productivity bandwidth:** You only have so many workers. By tapping a crowd properly, you can bolster your productivity over a time period.

- **Customer loyalty:** When you reach out to consumers and ask them what they think or need, you engender a greater connection with customers or potential customers.

Crowdsourcing can be more affordable than hiring independent contractors to do the work or provide you with the input you need. The intention of crowdsourcing, however, is not to take advantage of other people, but rather to create mutually beneficial opportunities and relationships.

Potential Pitfalls Sourcing Crowds

As with anything that provides benefits, crowdsourcing has potential downsides. Too many variables can complicate an otherwise simple process. When you hire someone to do work, they are a somewhat known entity; you can get references, run a background check, and speak to or meet with the person or a representative of the company you are hiring. When you crowdsource, you may never see your workers, and you may barely interact with them on an individual level.

If not managed properly, crowdsourcing can cause project bloat. What if you aren't satisfied with the outcome? You might have to add more steps or repeat steps in your crowdsourcing process, which adds time and potential costs. There's no guarantee that working directly with a consultant or contractor will give you stellar results; if not managed properly, crowdsourcing can increase the possibility of inconsistent outcomes. Using more than one person to complete a task or verify work can help reduce errors that might otherwise occur with a single person at work.

Without vetting or checks and balances in place, you may also have accountability and quality-control issues. In many crowdsourcing situations, there is no contract in place to which the crowd members must adhere. Throwing something out to the crowd and expecting good results can be a recipe for disaster. Planning carefully, and choosing reputable companies or well-regarded crowdsourcing sites, can help minimize the potential negatives.

In some cases, crowdsourcing is frowned upon or perceived as unfair to crowdworkers. Since the advent of crowdsourced design contests, for example, some outspoken designers began the "No-Spec Movement," arguing that producing design work on speculation without a guarantee of pay takes unfair advantage of designers. Keep in mind the sensitivities around crowdsourcing and always respect your crowd community to get the benefits of crowdsourcing while avoiding potential backlash.

Crowdsourcing Applications

Knowing which tools and websites to use can make all the difference when you are launching a crowdsourcing campaign. You can turn to a crowd of people for input or output in many areas of both work and life. Crowdsourcing isn't limited to work, although it's is often the first application that comes to mind. Wikipedia—a reasonable place to look for a definition of crowdsourcing—starts by calling it "the act of outsourcing tasks traditionally performed by an employee or contractor to a large group of people or community (a crowd), through an open call." Crowdsourcing takes its lead from the *open-source* movement, but instead of involving voluntary participation, crowdsourcing often involves some form of motivation ranging from payment to credit and recognition.

DEFINITION

Open source is a philosophy and attitude of openness, with voluntary participation. Open-source technology projects involve revealing a product's source code and allowing other programmers to rework, enhance, and improve it for a continually improving product or complementary products.

Wikipedia's basic crowdsourcing definition is widely agreed upon, but the principles of crowdsourcing can be applied in many ways; it doesn't always have to involve work or tasks. Crowdsourcing simply entails participation from members of a crowd or community.

Don't limit how you think about applying crowdsourcing principles to a problem or project. Ask yourself, "How could I benefit from additional input or support?" and you may find new reasons to leverage a crowd. Knowing what you want to crowdsource will guide you to the correct crowdsourcing category and the tools, sites, and resources you need to use.

Crowds for Work

You can break down most projects into a series of discrete tasks. You can tap into crowds to get individuals to perform some of these tasks for you, from aggregating information to analyzing data to verifying calculations. You can think of this form of work as *micro-labor*. If you can provide directions, data, and materials online, people can access and work on your project remotely.

DEFINITION

Micro-labor refers to work that is broken down into smaller parts or a work process that consists of tiny or compact tasks, usually to complete a bigger task or project.

You can use crowdsourcing to send small pieces of a project out to a crowd; for example, you could ask a crowd to size hundreds of digital images. Also, you can use crowdsourcing to identify a single contractor or small team to perform complex tasks, such as designing your company logo. You can find one person out of many to handle a job through crowd competitions or contests—as they are sometimes called—in which you put your project request onto a site that organizes competitions and where members of a crowd bid on your project or provide work on spec. If you're getting a logo designed, you can use a site that reaches an online designers community that holds bidding competitions for design jobs.

Crowds can also work for you in the customer service area. As more consumers turn to the web for reviews, advice, and even help with products, companies are tapping into their core customers' loyalty and willingness to assist new customers. Managing customer service–oriented crowds involves organizing, moderating, and vetting to ensure top-quality information is disseminated. You can also tap into your community of customers to develop a comprehensive frequently asked questions (FAQ) document by asking your customers to contribute questions and even suggested answers; then you can aggregate, edit, and publish the results.

Crowds for Input

Not every task begins or ends with tangible materials. You can turn to crowds to help you generate ideas. Many companies reach out to their existing and potential customers to obtain ideas to help improve their existing products or to generate ideas for new products. When you ask customers what they want, it enables you to produce products that fill an actual need and have a pool of buyers already primed and ready to buy. Individuals who make up crowds can also work together on projects in an interactive format to provide crowd collaboration.

How many times have you been looking for input about something you're working on or an idea you've come up with, but your own circle of friends and colleagues don't have the expertise—or the time—to work through the issues with you? That's a perfect time to turn to a crowd that is ready, willing, and able to give you feedback. You can survey crowds of people with a particular expertise or base your crowd choices on particular demographics, such as gender, age, or psychographics (such as women who travel a lot for business or men who golf often).

DULY NOTED

T-shirt company Threadless (http://threadless.com) was founded in 2000 on the premise of crowdsourcing, even though the term hadn't yet been coined. Co-founders Jake Nickell and Jacob DeHart began a t-shirt design contest that has grown into a multimillion-dollar business. Each month, the company invites people to submit t-shirt designs to the Threadless website. The Threadless community votes on their favorite submissions. The winning designs are then produced by the company.

The winning designers get $2,000, plus free t-shirts printed with their design. Everyone else on the site—and the general public—can buy the new designs at premium prices, usually between $18 and $25. Threadless not only gets crowd input on new products, but also on design selection. The company has a built-in community of buyers who are chomping at the bit to purchase the shirts as soon as they are produced!

If you've developed something, such as a website redesign, a software product, or even a physical product, you can use crowds to test what you've created to make sure it works. In software and application development, this is called "beta testing," but you can apply the principles of beta testing to anything that needs pre-launch testing.

Crowds can also help you troubleshoot and solve problems. Post a problem to a crowd of scientists, and you may get solutions to a problem with the new skin-care products you're developing. Share a scripting error with a crowd of programmers, and they may help you debut a computer program.

Crowds for Organizing

Businesses and nonprofit organizations can use crowdsourcing principles to motivate crowds of people to take action. Typical outreach can involve calling or e-mailing individuals to bring them together, and then trying to coordinate the crowd, communicate a consistent message, and track their activities. With crowdsourcing tools, you can manage the entire process from outreach to management to measurement.

There is something to be said for reaching out to crowds for fundraising. Whether you run a nonprofit organization and are looking for more efficient ways to increase donations, or you're a startup company looking for innovative ways to get funded, crowdsourcing can bring the power of crowds to bring in money.

You still need to have proper financial and legal systems in place before you ask for money. There are new tools to help you expand your reach and allow you to raise smaller sums of money from a greater number of people.

The Co-Creation Debate

Some people feel crowdsourcing is not necessarily the best approach to creating something or solving a problem. Although some believe there is great value in connecting and exchanging ideas with a larger group of people, they are concerned that the excitement of applying crowdsourcing to a project may lead you away from more traditional solutions based in sound and proven processes.

Traditionally you'd look for a designer through references, review their portfolio, and then work with them one-on-one to develop a logo. If you need a logo, is asking a crowd of designers to participate in a collaborative design process or competition the best solution? Some people—particularly some designers—think not, because crowdsourcing may seem unfair to designers who produce work but may not be compensated fairly, or at all.

If you have a problem that needs solving, should you hire a consultant well versed in working on similar problems, or can you get the same quality of work from a crowd of people online? There is no definitive right or wrong answer; every case has different variables, needs, and standards.

The stronger debates over co-creation tend to come from scientific communities, in which research has widely accepted steps that don't often include tackling problems via crowd input—even if they are crowds made up of scientists. A major concern is the potential harm to the integrity of the scientific process, because of the challenges of approaching a problem with crowd input.

The more heads that come together to collaborate or co-create, the more challenges you face in managing the process and organizing the input. You also need to make sure in advance that the crowd you're tapping into consists of people with the appropriate skills, experience, or profile to suit your needs. If you use ad-hoc crowds or sites that aggregate crowds for crowdsourcing purposes, you may not have the same vetting ability that you may have if you hire someone directly after carefully reviewing their resumé. Some crowdsourcing sites, such as Tongal, help you manage the collaborative creation process through a series of contests, bringing together people with the right skills for each task—from coming up with a logo and tagline, to writing a script for a video spot, to producing an actual video. See Chapter 16 for more information about Tongal.

Power in Numbers

Crowdsourcing is appealing and useful because of the speed with which you can get things done in comparison to the traditional approaches. If you're a designer with three sketches for a dress and you want to know which one will sell better, there are many different ways you can try to determine this:

- Hire a research firm and perform expensive market research.

- Ask customers, family, friends, co-workers, and colleagues.

- Mail a survey to customers and potential customers.

- Survey people on your website.

- Send an e-mail survey to your list of contacts.

- Post electronic versions of the three sketches to your Facebook page and ask for "likes" and comments.

- Join a community and marketplace such as FashionStake.com where the general public can fund and pre-order designs from your collection.

With the exception of the first option, all these ways involve seeking input from a large number of people—not just from people you know, but also from those you don't. Casting a wider net can give you a broader picture of what the "masses" think, feel, need, or prefer.

Some tools for reaching out to others are more familiar than others, such as e-mails and websites. Sites now exist to carry out a myriad of highly specific crowdsourcing efforts, including input on fashion design. Putting technology to use to obtain input from a crowd can be as simple as sending out an e-mail and asking people you know for answers. It can be as complex as gathering a large number of people through newer communications tools, including social networks and topic- or task-specific crowdsourcing communities.

Through crowdsourcing, you can gather exponentially more responses than if you reach out to only your own immediate circle of contacts. Technology is essential to almost all crowdsourcing. With more input comes challenges—including organizing data and managing workers—so you need to pick the right tools to harness the power of crowds.

The Least You Need to Know

- Don't limit your crowdsourcing to work-related applications; consider getting input from larger groups of people on other areas of your life, too.

- Keep in mind the sensitive nature of crowdsourcing and respect your crowd community to avoid potential backlash.

- Use crowdsourcing to cast a wider net, so you can get feedback from people beyond your own contacts.

- You need proper systems in place in advance of implementing crowdsourcing, such as having the appropriate financial and legal systems for raising money from a crowd.

The Psychology of Crowds

In This Chapter

- Identifying crowds by demographics and psychographics
- Reasons people become crowdworkers
- Understanding the dynamics and expectations of crowds
- Crowdsourcing incentives and payments

There's a lot of psychology in crowdsourcing. Crowds are made up of people, and each person has his or her own personality and way of thinking. Putting people together can affect the ways people think. An entire branch of psychology looks at how crowds think and act differently than individuals, and is called, predictably, "crowd psychology." This branch is part of a larger study called "social psychology," which is focused on relationships between individuals and groups.

The theories of crowds and crowd behavior have been examined by many of the prominent thinkers of the last century, including Carl Jung and Sigmund Freud. Early theories of crowd psychology posit that, in a crowd, an individual's thought processes, reactions, and actions are melded with others so he or she might behave differently than if the individual were alone. This idea goes beyond the subtle influence of peer pressure and actually defines changes that can occur in an individual's mind. In some cases, the individuals are not aware they are behaving out of character.

The Brains of Crowds

Crowd psychology can impact crowdsourcing efforts. Crowds gathered online in a virtually shared space can have different dynamics than crowds of people who are in a physically shared space. Understanding a little bit about the psychology of online crowds can help when you are turning to a crowd for something, especially for honest feedback and opinions.

The idea that "two heads are better than one" is not a hard-and-fast rule. It stands to reason that if you bring a lot of people together—especially diverse people—they will come to a richer, more nuanced and considered conclusion than a single person, but there are definitely cases in which this simply is not true.

In the report "Optimally Interacting Minds," which appeared in *Science* magazine in August 2010, researchers came to the conclusion that a group's ability is as strong as its weakest link. Therefore, if everyone in a crowd has the same or similar set of skills, the results of bringing them all together to work on something may be successful. But if members of the crowd are lacking in some way—and it might not be in skills, but rather in assets, such as a poor Internet connection—these individuals' weaknesses could weaken the whole group. A weaker crowd may mean weaker results.

Who's in Your Crowd?

Knowing your crowd can help you better identify weaknesses before you begin sourcing the entire group. In crowdsourcing, you can't actually get to know every member of your diverse and dispersed crowd, but you can conduct some preliminary surveys based on fixed sets of criteria to get to know them better.

When you are dealing with people, there are many different ways to survey, classify, and group them. People are commonly classified by demographics. The term *demographics* comes from the Greek words *demos*, meaning "people," and *graphie*, meaning "writing." Advertisers and marketers have used demographics since the 1960s to better define and segment television audiences. Even governments slice and dice populations using demographical data.

PITFALLS

Don't be too rigid in surveying or classifying your crowd. Most people will self-select correctly, according to your crowd campaign description or project brief. You could miss out on valuable input by controlling your crowd too closely.

Common demographics categories used by marketers include …

- Gender

- Ethnicity

- Age

- Income

- Education

- Geographic location

Another common way to classify people is by psychographics, which are more subjective and variable. Whereas demographics are concrete and objective, psychographics cover the more personal aspects of individuals, such as …

- Personalities

- Attitudes

- Opinions

- Interests

- Values

- Lifestyles

Establishing clear-cut classifications for better defining your crowd before you engage them in a crowdsourcing activity can help you arrive at your preferred outcomes. Diversity can be beneficial for some types of crowdsourcing, but ultimately you want to bring people together or reach out to crowds that are best suited to respond to your queries or to carry out your tasks.

Why People Sign On

People who participate in crowdsourcing—also known as crowdworkers—fall into two main categories: those who deliberately seek out opportunities to be part of organized crowds through sites that assemble and manage crowds, and those who join online communities based on their interests and then participate in crowdsourcing activities with their fellow community members. In a way, there are deliberate crowdworkers who seek out crowd-powered projects, and there are accidental crowd-workers who didn't initially realize they'd be part of a crowdsourcing effort but who ultimately opt to participate.

What motivates people to become part of a crowd to provide input or perform work? There is no single reason.

Generating Income

Not everyone engages in crowdsourcing activities to make money, but there are sites and systems in place where crowdworkers get paid for their input or output, even if the tasks are very small. Being paid in *micro-transactions* may seem like an effort in futility, but if someone is a dedicated crowdworker, those small amounts of money can easily add up to a meaningful sum.

 DEFINITION

Micro-transactions, also called micropayments, are financial exchanges that involve very small amounts of money. These transactions usually take place online. The online payments company PayPal, for example, defines a micropayment as anything under $12.

In some cases, crowdworkers are located in countries where a few U.S. dollars per day or week could make a significant impact on their household incomes and livelihoods. By crowdsourcing, you may be supplementing one person's income while providing an entire living to another.

Believe it or not, some people perform work tasks or participate in other types of crowdsourcing activities to earn virtual money, such as game currency for online games. Many popular online gaming sites, virtual worlds, and applications—such as Farmville, World of Warcraft, and Second Life—run on game currencies.

The crowdsourcing labor site CrowdFlower provides an option to run virtual currency payments through a site called Gambit, to pay crowdworkers who perform tasks on your projects. In some cases, virtual currency can be converted into real money, but most gamers and virtual world enthusiasts just use their virtual currency for their favorite games. Other gamers get paid for their crowdsourcing work in real money but keep it in a separate account as their gaming slush fund, converting the real money into gaming money as needed. Still others use virtual currency on a site called SwagBucks, where you can accumulate virtual SwagBucks and trade them for actual products from t-shirts to kitchen mixers.

Building a Portfolio

In many industries, portfolios are the workers' calling cards. In the design field, for example, aspiring designers showcase their work with an online or offline portfolio. Some designers are caught in a Catch-22: they are seeking design jobs to build a work portfolio, but they must show a portfolio to get a job. Without design jobs, they can't easily build a work portfolio. That's where crowdsourcing competitions can come in.

A designer can be connected to design jobs through crowdsourced design competitions, and build a portfolio from his or her submissions. If his or her design is chosen as a winning submission, the designer gets additional kudos, recognition, and a payment—or "prize"—of some kind. If a design project is collaborative, each member of the design team can claim participation in the finished project—another example of work for the members' portfolios. Some crowdworkers' resumés may mention prizes they've won, or peer or client ratings they've received on crowdsourcing sites, to demonstrate their skills.

DULY NOTED

Brian Ghidinelli used to work in the design field and had experience with outsourcing work. Recently, when he was looking to update a logo for a company he had established, he decided to turn to crowdsourcing to get it done. He used a relatively small amount of money—$300—to source design ideas through a design crowdsourcing site called Crowdspring. He provided a brand guide, a design brief, and other specifications and requirements for the logo he was seeking. He posted his support materials and design references, and then began receiving submissions.

He found a logo he liked, but not until he had participated actively in the submissions process, giving very specific and critical feedback to each submitter. He treated the crowdsourcing project as a collaboration and attributes his success in getting the right logo to his ongoing dialogue with the designers.

Working Virtually

As workforces move from shared physical locations to distributed or virtual settings, virtual crowdsourcing begins to make sense for work. The very nature of crowdsourcing lends itself to an online approach. Some people choose to become crowdworkers because it allows them to bring their skills and experiences from the traditional workplace setting to a virtual work environment, so they can benefit from the flexibility and adjustable time commitments crowdsourcing offers.

Take a stay-at-home mom who wants to work from home for only a few hours a day—such as during her infant's nap time—and do work that leverages her skills in sales, customer service, or communications. She can become part of a pool of skilled workers who receive work through a crowdsourcing model. The contact-center industry has identified this kind of "at home talent" as a valuable asset. Companies such as LiveOps put into place intricate, technology-based systems to manage many virtual workers to provide skilled services to their clients. LiveOps pools together the skills and availabilities of their dispersed and distributed workers through a web-based proprietary system, so that their clients receive a seamless delivery of call-center services.

As a LiveOps contractor, a stay-at-home mom can set her own hours and choose from the clients and types of products and services with which LiveOps works, and then she can receive specialized training. LiveOps routes calls to her based on her interests, training, and availability. The calls she cannot field go to others in the arge pool of workers.

Overcoming Limitations

In some cases, getting out of one's location isn't a question of preference but circumstance. Online crowdsourced projects offer an opportunity for homebound or even bedbound individuals to build skills, generate income, or just stay sharp. Retirees make excellent crowdworkers, and can benefit from crowdsourcing's flexibility. Given their years of work experience and potentially extensive skills, retirees have a lot to offer.

Gaining New Work Opportunities

Some workers use crowdsourcing to get more exposure and identify new work opportunities, particularly in markets where they might not otherwise gain a foothold. For example, many designers who participate in design-focused crowd contests for U.S.-based companies are from other parts of the world. They not only have a chance to work with a company in the states, but also they can establish longer-term client relationships beyond the contest. In turn, companies can identify fresh talent through crowdsourcing sites and contests.

DULY NOTED

Looking to give back? You can give work to refugees through an iPhone app called Give Work, a project created by crowdsourcing sites Samasource and CrowdFlower.

Internet-based jobs can provide income to people in developing countries or rural areas where there is limited access to work opportunities. The crowdsourcing company Samasource has a website and system that organizes and manages computer-based work projects. Samasource provides work to marginalized people worldwide, such as refugees in refugee camps in Kenya and women in rural Afghanistan. Some of the work provided through Samasource includes data entry, Internet-based research, audio transcription, and video captioning. You can read more about Samasource, and how to use the site for your own projects, in Chapter 14.

What Crowds Expect

In an open-source model, participants expect open information exchange and often participate for less tangible reasons than monetary compensation. These individuals may participate in hopes of enhancing their reputation and recognition amongst peers. They may also contribute to have a hand in improving a product or developing a new product related to the source, or simply to achieve the satisfaction of solving a problem no one else can.

In crowdsourcing, crowd members can have more concrete expectations. Some crowd members participate solely for payment, and the sites where they work have built-in monetary components as motivation and compensation. Understanding what motivates your crowd and what they expect from your crowdsourcing campaign is critical for both immediate and ongoing success.

If you plan on crowdsourcing more than once, make sure you foster a reputation for offering compelling projects and fair motivators. Be honest and forthright in your communications and your commitments. Use reputable crowdsourcing sites or partner with crowdsourcing service providers who have solid track records. Crowdsourcing service providers are companies that act as a middleman or facilitator between clients and crowds, and manage crowdsourcing projects and campaigns from beginning to end.

Most crowdsourcing sites have a built-in system to secure the money you've committed to your campaign in an escrow account, and to release it to crowdworkers as they complete their work. This mechanism keeps you honest and ensures that crowd members are compensated as dictated by the campaign structure.

Incentives for Crowds

Do you have to pay people to participate in your crowdsourcing campaign? The short answer is no. Not every crowdsourcing project or campaign must result in payment. The longer answer is that it depends on your campaign, your crowd, your goals, and the kinds of outcomes you hope to achieve.

Someone performing work to provide you with a completed task or finished product clearly calls for different compensation than requesting feedback on a product. Even the type of task you are asking a crowdworker to perform can dictate whether or not you should pay, or how much to pay. You would expect to pay someone tagging photographs less than someone retouching photographs, but more than someone counting photographs.

Keep in mind that, in some cases, adding incentives to your campaign can skew the results. In formal surveying, offering an incentive can invalidate your results. You can't be sure whether someone has participated in your campaign just to win a prize or accept a reward, rather than to provide honest, candid input. Knowing when and how to provide an incentive can require an educated guess, in addition to a good working knowledge of formal or academic data collection.

Monetary Motivation

When you are seeking individuals who can provide "real" work—such as idea generation, transcription, translation, image manipulation, logo design … you name it—such crowdsourcing projects customarily include monetary compensation. On most popular and reputable crowdsourcing sites, payment or money awards are built right into their systems.

The average payment amount or prize varies from site to site and job to job. On some sites, you can get a logo for $175. On others, a logo price is $300. Crowdsourcing sites may encourage you to offer more than a suggested minimum price, and even correlate the price you offer with the estimated number of submissions you will receive. More money means more motivation—which can translate to more submissions.

In-Kind Consideration

When you are conducting a more informal crowdsourcing campaign, you may find that offering something small can mean a lot to your crowd. Providing a product sample, discount coupon, or some other token could be an unexpected bonus to the ad-hoc crowd.

Offering a prize to a random winner culled from your crowd members may spur more responses to your campaign. Few things online seem to get people more excited than a free offer. If you decide to give a prize to a random winner in the form of a sweepstakes, make sure you've researched the best way to set up your giveaway. You should have written rules that explain how you will select a winner randomly. Check with a lawyer to make sure you've got the legal side of giveaways covered.

> **DULY NOTED**
>
> If you have your crowd members' names in a numbered list and want to pick someone at random, you can use a site like Random.org to generate a random number. Your winner is the person who corresponds with that number. This works best with smaller crowds, and only if you have a way to assign a number to each member.

Consider offering some form of in-kind compensation. Don't forget that some people consider gaming or virtual currency an acceptable form of payment. To avid gamers, virtual money is just as good as real money.

Reputation Enhancement

Although money and freebies seem like obvious forms of compensation for crowd members or crowdworkers, some people participate in crowdsourcing projects and campaigns to build their reputation. Coders are known to participate in crowd-sourced troubleshooting exercises just to be the one to find the most software bugs or the one to solve a puzzling code error faster than his or her peers.

Others participate in crowdsourcing to be a part of creating something. Sometimes a pat on the back, a feather in his or her cap, or an acknowledgment from the crowd is all one needs to feel like the work was worth doing. Some crowdsourcing sites employ game-based tactics and tools, such as scoreboards, badges, and levels of achievement so crowdworkers can "compete," work to improve their rankings, and sport badges to demonstrate their skills.

Understanding Crowd Influence

In traditional focus groups, a potential challenge is the tendency for participants to be influenced by other group members and to not express their true feelings and opinions. If you are using crowdsourcing for feedback, be aware that when you bring like-minded people together and they are aware of the actions of other crowd members, they may be inclined to provide feedback in line with others.

You can put mechanisms in place to help avoid potentially skewed results that stem from crowd members being swayed to respond similarly to those around them. Try using online surveys, questionnaires, and polls, for example, and collect answers privately before sharing results with participants. This approach ensures that individual crowd members won't adjust their answers to fit in with the rest of the crowd. You can choose when and how to reveal the collective input.

The Least You Need to Know

- You can conduct some preliminary surveys to get to know your crowd better.
- Understanding what motivates your crowd and what they expect from participating in your crowdsourcing campaign is critical for both immediate and ongoing success.
- If you plan on crowdsourcing more than once, make sure you foster a reputation for offering compelling projects and fair motivators.
- In some cases, adding incentives to your campaign can skew and invalidate results, such as with formal surveying.
- When you have "real" work that must be completed, crowdsourcing customarily involves monetary compensation.

Defining Your Projects

Chapter

3

In This Chapter

- Articulating goals and objectives
- Understanding project pieces and processes
- Determining crowdsourcing costs
- Deciding to crowdsource

With a better understanding of the different categories of crowdsourcing, and how and why crowds are willing to participate, you can turn your focus to yourself. Look more closely at your needs to make sure crowdsourcing is right for what you're trying to achieve.

Crowdsourcing is not suitable for every project—not every problem needs a crowd to solve it. By taking systematic steps to better assess your needs, you can see clearly whether there is a good case for crowdsourcing rather than for traditional processes (such as hiring a consultant).

Let's Get Started

As with any project, you need to go through a discovery process, so you can put together a plan that gets you from Point A to Point B. To get the most out of crowdsourcing, you have to articulate what you need done. Then you can match the job, project, or campaign to the right sites, resources, tools, and crowds to help you crowdsource.

When completing an assessment of your needs, the following questions must be addressed:

- Will crowdsourcing save you time?

- Will crowdsourcing save you money?

- Can crowdsourcing provide you with the outcome you need?

- Do you have the right tools to manage your crowdsourcing project?

To answer these questions, you need to start at the beginning: the reason you are considering crowdsourcing in the first place. Remember: saving time or money may not be the most important criteria—they just happen to be common ways people assess the value of doing something one way rather than another.

Specifying Your Goals

When doing any kind of strategic planning, start with setting your goals. A goal is an overarching, broad thing you are trying to achieve as opposed to an objective, which is a more tangible, measurable, and actionable thing.

> **BEST PRACTICES**
>
> As with any business process, crowdsourcing requires strategic planning, research, and careful assessment before you can start the actual process. Shortcuts now could cost you in the long run.

Goals can be very large and broad, such as "become a national name brand in the category of natural cereals." You can list your objectives for getting you to that goal, including writing a business plan for your cereal company; developing an all-natural cereal; conducting cereal taste tests; developing a branding strategy for your cereal; creating a marketing plan to launch your cereal; building relationships with local and national retailers who can carry your cereal; and so on.

As you can see, the list of steps to achieving a business goal can go on and on, but it all starts with what you are trying to achieve. Clearly articulate your overarching goal to help determine whether crowdsourcing is the route you need to get something done. Here are some common business goals:

- Launch a new software product or website.

- Improve a product or service offering.

- Complete a large project despite limited internal resources.

- Raise funds for something.

- Solve a problem.

- Identify a contractor to complete a project.

You can then break down each goal into objectives that directly outline how you are going to achieve the larger goal.

Clear Objectives Rule

If goals are broad, objectives are narrow. Given the preceding goals, here are some corresponding objectives where crowdsourcing might fit in:

- Launch a new software product or website: Complete beta testing for the software or website.

- Improve a product or service offering: Obtain consumer feedback for a product or service.

- Complete a large project despite limited internal resources: Complete smaller tasks within the larger project.

- Raise funds for something: Pool together resources.

- Solve a problem: Obtain diverse input toward a solution.

- Identify a contractor to complete a project: Identify the right individual for the task.

As you move your focus from the goal you ultimately want to achieve to the objective or objectives that will get you there, you'll see you have even further to go to define what you need.

Breaking Down Your Tasks

Each objective you come up with to achieve your goals will probably consist of several or many steps. If you want to beta test your new website, you still need to break that objective into more granular pieces.

Let's look more closely at launching a new website and how you can crowdsource your site's beta testing. Saying "I need help beta testing my new site" doesn't clearly define what you want. You must break down "beta testing" into specific steps:

1. Identify what skills are needed to beta test the site properly.

2. Identify the computer systems, online connections, browsers, and other software required to properly conduct testing.

3. List what you want tested, such as checks for broken images and links on every page and running through the entire shopping cart system to check for bugs.

4. Articulate any special steps that the testers must take, such as having dozens of people accessing your site at the same time to see how it handles simultaneous requests.

5. Specify how testers should submit their feedback, and provide or use the appropriate tools to manage data.

6. Determine how you will handle information regarding broken links and images and bugs.

7. Make arrangements for follow-up testing until your site is bug-free, all the links work, and the images are intact.

You should break down every objective you list into its smallest parts or steps before you begin crowdsourcing. Until you can clearly articulate what you are trying to achieve and the steps you need to take, you won't be able to properly determine whether crowdsourcing is a viable solution. If you decide to go with crowdsourcing, you can potentially work on parts of your project while other tasks are being crowdsourced to condense time to completion.

Crunching the Numbers

Can crowdsourcing save you money? Yes and no. Saving money should not be your main reason for outsourcing, but effective crowdsourcing can save both time and money. Crowdsourcing isn't meant to be a free way to get something done; it's meant to be a way to do things that allows you to leverage the power of many instead of just a few.

PITFALLS

Thinking of crowdsourcing as a free way to get work done can lead you to make bad decisions regarding how and where you crowdsource. Pick sites by how reputable they are, not how cheap.

In business, the bottom line often rules the decisions we make. In some cases, you need to be able to prove to yourself or your boss that crowdsourcing has some tangible benefits to your company or organization, such as cutting down on costs.

The Cost of Traditional Labor

As you assess the cost of crowdsourcing, you need to look at the cost of doing the same task using more traditional means. If you have work that must be done, chances are there are people you could hire directly to complete the work. If you don't already know, find out the going rate for getting the work done through traditional channels.

Say you are looking for someone to convert 1,000 images from tiff format to jpeg, and you know you can hire an intern at $9 per hour to do this work. Next, you need to determine approximately how long the work will take. Converting images can take anywhere from one to three minutes per photograph (depending on the worker's familiarity with photo conversion software). Your formula for calculating cost is: the total number of images (1,000) divided by the number of images that can be converted in an hour (in this case, between 20 and 60) multiplied by the worker's hourly rate ($9). If your intern does the work, which requires minimal skill but good attention to detail, you can spend between $150 and $450.

If you use crowdsourcing, however, you may get the task completed by crowdworkers for 10¢ per image or less. You're now looking at a total cost of $100 or less for the same work, because this particular kind of work doesn't rely on quality. You can have set parameters for converting images from one format to another, and you will have consistent quality regardless of who does the work or what kind of computer he or she uses.

Opportunity Costs

You do so many small tasks every day to complete larger projects or just to get something done. How many of those tasks could be done by someone else, freeing you up to do more important work—work that brings in more income? Learning to identify the tasks you can hand off, and then actually delegating them, can be challenging for anyone. You may think you are the only one who can do something, but the truth is lower-level tasks and work can be handled by almost anyone with the minimum skills to do the work.

Going back to the image-conversion example, what if you weren't even thinking about hiring an intern to do the work and were going to do it yourself? Now you need to calculate the costs in an entirely different way. You may think that you are saving money by doing it yourself or that doing it yourself equals "free."

> **DULY NOTED**
>
> Crowdsourcing is not, as a rule, fast. Choosing to crowdsource just to save time may get you into trouble. Crowdsourcing should be less about speed and more about leveraging the right resources for each task.

Here's how you calculate the cost of doing it yourself. Start with your hourly wage—say, $80 per hour. Now run through the same calculation as before: the total number of images (1,000) divided by the number of images that can be converted in an hour (20 and 60) multiplied by $80. The cost of completing this task if you do it is now $1,333 to $4,000. Sure, you don't have to pay yourself to do the work, but if you do the image conversions yourself, you are spending 16 to 50 hours working on those instead of other projects. If you work for yourself, you're spending valuable time on menial tasks that you can get others to do. If someone else is paying you, they are wasting company resources.

It may not feel like you are losing money directly, but your time is money, so wasting your time adds up to losses for you and your company.

The Cost of Not Getting the Work Done

There are costs to getting work done, costs when you miss opportunities because you do the work, and then there are the costs of not doing the work at all. Clearly you are exploring crowdsourcing as a way to get things done because you actually have something that must be done. But how many times have you sat on tasks and not gotten around to them?

In the case of the image conversions, you can immediately see the effects of not completing the work. If you have 1,000 images in tiff format and you don't convert them to jpeg, you can't upload them to your website. Without your images online, you won't be able to properly display your work and get more clients for your stock photography business.

The cost of not doing something can have a major impact.

Additional Cost Benefits

By deciding to crowdsource one task, you could also identify additional tasks that can be crowdsourced that can save you both time and money. For example, in the process of analyzing the cost of getting your images converted, you may also have identified another potential crowdsourcing task: uploading the 1,000 images to your website. Chances are, this work can't be done in bulk, but it does consist of straightforward steps that anyone with basic FTP and HTML skills can handle.

Crowdsourcing can save you even more time and money in the long run because your images can be converted and uploaded in the next 24 hours for less money than if you paid an intern to do it. During that time, you can work in parallel, making sales calls or producing other work that generates more immediate revenues.

Envisioning Your Outcome

When considering crowdsourcing, knowing what you want to ultimately achieve helps guide your decision-making process. Of course you want great results, but what exactly does "great" mean to you? In some cases, such as translations or editing, accuracy is key.

In other cases, speed might be mission-critical, such as quickly culling the Internet for your company name and sorting mentions by positive, negative, and neutral so you can get the results to your company's board of directors. If you need feedback on a product, you want honesty and clarity, and you want the feedback to be actionable (meaning you can do something about it if you choose to do so).

Crowdsourcing can produce varying degrees of quality. Sometimes the work is done quickly, and sometimes it takes longer than expected. Understanding where you want to get to at the end of your crowdsourcing campaign sets the stage for how you'll get there.

Confirming You Should Crowdsource

When thinking about your project in detail, you should be evaluating based on quality, speed, and cost—including the hidden costs of doing the work in-house. Once you've done this, you should have a better sense of whether crowdsourcing can help you with the work you have at hand.

For task-related projects, ask yourself: Can this task be done by someone else? Does this task require minimal or a very clear set of skills? Is this task something that can be automated yet still requires human intelligence to do?

Not all tasks can or should be automated, but neither do they all require highly skilled workers. For information-gathering projects, ask yourself: Does the input need to come from more than my immediate connections? Will I get better or more useful results if I cast a wide net? Do I need responses from diverse individuals?

If you answer yes to all or most of those questions—in the case of either work or input—you can be pretty confident that crowdsourcing is a good option for you.

Managing Your Expectations

If you're looking to crowdsource for consumer feedback for a product or service, you need to determine the specific kind of feedback you're seeking. Do you need highly skilled individuals, or are you looking for consumers who have no specialized skills but might be the potential target market for your product?

Say you are looking for feedback on a DVD you've produced to help toddlers learn the alphabet. The DVD isn't selling as well as your DVD that teaches toddlers their numbers. Is there a product flaw or weakness? Are you targeting children too young? Do you need teachers or moms to review your DVD?

You don't have to choose both teachers and moms—you might want to do two separate campaigns, reaching out to two distinct crowds and then comparing the results.

If you choose moms instead of teachers, you need to manage your expectations, because the input you receive may differ from an academic crowd. Understand what you are asking for and from whom you are asking it, so you can be receptive to the outcomes you'll get.

Short-Term and Long-Term Success

You may have already envisioned your outcome, such as an accurate translation or the speedy retrieval and sorting of online mentions of your company name, but what constitutes success to you? Short-term success is that you receive accurate translation of a document at an affordable price and in a reasonable amount of time. How will you know that the translation was good? You won't know until either you or someone else reviews it, or you use it and get further feedback on it.

Consider the case of gathering and sorting mentions of your company to provide that information in time for a board meeting. If you get the information and it looks good, and you make the deadline for getting the data to your board of directors, was crowdsourcing a success? What if the next day a board member discovers a critical mention of your company that was overlooked in the information you provided? Now what?

At what stage will you feel crowdsourcing was successful? When you get the work back? When you assess the results or at some step further down the road? Crowdsourcing is not an exact science, particularly because it often involves variables, including people with different skill levels handling disparate pieces of a whole. Make sure to consider these variables. Reputable crowdsourcing companies consider quality control and stand by the work their system provides to varying degrees. Establish, from the outset, the quality of work you are willing to accept, and use the appropriate tools and resources available to you to get the results you can call a success.

Picking Your Crowdsourcing Solutions

There are a myriad of companies developing tools and launching sites you can use to crowdsource. Some companies act as middlemen to crowds or crowdsourcing service providers. These highly specialized companies offer a menu of services to manage the crowdsourcing process for you.

Barring sourcing a crowd on your own, how do you find and choose the right companies, sites, or tools to get something done?

The Right Companies and Sites

You can use an established company that has a website and other tools to help you with crowdsourcing activities. You need to assess what they can do for you. You can do so by using a set of criteria to help determine how and where you'll crowdsource.

Like any assessment process for identifying who you will hire or what tools you will use to get something done, the larger criteria for determining what companies or sites you should use for crowdsourcing are as follows:

- **Referrals:** What do others recommend for getting the work done?

- **Reputation:** What are you hearing from others or what can you find online about the company or site that speaks to their quality of work and the way they work?

- **Track record:** What tangible results can the company point to that demonstrate their ability to deliver?

- **Testimonials:** What are their customers saying? Will the company provide you with customer contacts so you can ask them additional questions?

- **Core competencies:** What category of crowdsourcing does the company or site specialize in, and does it suit your needs?

- **Core crowd:** What type of crowd does the company or site gather? Do they cover the right skills, demographics, or psychographics for your needs?

Even as you seek the best solutions for crowdsourcing, you can use crowdsourcing principles to identify the right companies and sites. You can e-mail your colleagues or post questions to your favorite social network and glean answers from your social crowd.

Fee Versus Free

Price can be an issue and sometimes even a barrier. As you shop around for the right crowdsourcing site to use, you may be keeping your immediate budget in mind, but you should also remember the adage "you get what you pay for." Paying less money initially could end up costing you more in the long run.

Some crowdsourcing sites display prices set to projects or campaigns, and those prices are viewable by the public. Crowd competition sites present projects as open calls for submissions and a winning submission is chosen via the site. Everyone knows up front what the prize or reward is, and that amount is established by the client or the person who is using the crowd competition site to get something done.

Here's a comparison of reward or prize amounts to give a sense of the wide range of costs associated with crowd competitions and challenge sites:

Range of Prizes on Crowd Competition Sites

Site	Service Type	Approximate Prize Range
Guerra-Creativa	Design	$75–$1,000
SquadHelp	Branding/Marketing	$50–$350
99Designs	Design	$100–$2,500
Crowdspring	Design	$200–$13,000*
Prova	Ad Creative	$200–$10,000*
Tongal	Ad Creative incl. video	$450–$15,000*

Note: Larger sums might include prizes for several winners, including a first place winner.

You can hire a crowdsourcing services provider, a company that incorporates the crowdsourcing process into their service offerings or that helps you manage your crowdsourcing process. Fees for these companies can range from hundreds to thousands of dollars. You may find that more automated crowdsourcing options with "self-serve" technology and tools, such as Amazon's Mechanical Turk, can be more cost-effective than crowdsourcing systems managed by people, such as CastingWords, for audio transcription. CastingWords taps into the Mechanical Turk workforce for their transcribers, but adds fees for their expertise and management of the crowd-workers. Options with human managers and overseers in place can deliver higher quality but will cost more to use.

Quality Assurance Controls

A reputable crowdsourcing site puts a great deal of effort toward quality assurance because their business depends on satisfied and repeat customers, as well as a reputation for quality work. There are a number of different ways sites ensure quality of work performed by their crowdworkers.

- **Peer review:** Cloudcrowd allows their workers to review and rate one another's work.

- **Credibility score:** Cloudcrowd translates peer review into a scoring system. Other crowdsourcing companies measure the amount of work accepted by clients to rate a worker.

- **Redundancy:** CrowdFlower provides the same task to several different workers, based on each worker's accuracy score. The most accurate results are gleaned through automated statistical analysis.

- **Credentialing:** Cloudcrowd offers credentialing for crowdworkers to ensure work quality.

- **Oversight:** Samasource uses a volunteer labor force to perform human-powered quality assurance checks.

- **Validators:** CrowdFlower has systems in place to automate validations of data such as phone numbers, currencies, and e-mail addresses.

Some crowdsourcing sites offer 100 percent guarantees on successful project outcomes based on the work submitted by their crowds, and claim very few refund requests. Most people involved with crowdsourcing agree that the most important factor regarding quality assurance is starting out with and communicating clearly what you need done.

Projects You Shouldn't Crowdsource

When crowdsourcing work, your greatest success comes when you have a black and white situation. Projects with gray areas aren't good candidates for crowdsourcing. For crowdsourcing, tasks must have clear and verifiable answers. A task such as "verify that a website is a company's official site and not a Yellow Pages online listing" is verifiable. "Determine whether a website is effective" is too fuzzy to bring back quality responses or results. "Translate 100 tweets" is a task that can be crowdsourced through sites like Mechanical Turk and CrowdFlower. "Translate a novel" probably won't work.

If the work doesn't have a clear right or wrong answer, a company like CrowdFlower won't recommend crowdsourcing for the job, despite all their highly technical and refined quality assurance techniques—developed, managed, and optimized by a team of over a dozen engineers. Any work in which the results aren't definable is not likely to be successful on CrowdFlower.

Not all crowdsourcing involves work, and not all crowdsourcing must be black and white. If you are crowdsourcing ideas or opinions, there is plenty of room for shades of gray and varying responses. But if you are thinking of using crowdsourcing for ideas and opinions, think twice before putting highly sensitive, confidential, or high-stakes projects out there where everything you're doing as a business banks on the results.

There are times and places where crowdsourcing can be suitable for getting something done, but don't try to give a project to a crowd just because you read about it in an article. Do your homework first and make sure crowdsourcing is a strategic fit for what you're trying to achieve.

The Least You Need to Know

- Not every project is suitable for crowdsourcing. Assess your needs first, and make sure you don't need to use traditional processes or hire a consultant.
- Start with identifying what you are trying to achieve and articulate your over-arching goal to help determine whether your goal can be accomplished with crowdsourcing.
- Break down every objective into its smallest parts or steps before you begin crowdsourcing.
- The best way to assure quality is to clearly communicate what you need done and how, so you have benchmarks to more easily assess the quality of the work once it's completed.

Do-It-Yourself Crowdsourcing

In This Chapter

- Using tools for manual crowdsourcing
- Assessing response rates
- Finding places to crowdsource
- Discovering the crowdsourcing process

You've decided you want to crowdsource entirely from scratch. You're not going to use any websites or tools designed specifically to handle crowdsourcing processes and activities, because the work you need done doesn't require a formal system with high levels of quality assurance built in.

Doing your own crowdsourcing can be as easy or as complex as the work you need to do. The best kind of crowdsourcing to do on your own is gathering manageable amounts of data or input from the crowd, which you can then collect in a repository of some kind and cull through. Keep in mind that the more steps you require to get your work done, the more moving parts you'll need to track. Do-it-yourself crowdsourcing is easiest to manage when you have only a single task or very few tasks with simpler outcomes.

Your Do-It-Yourself Toolkit

Doing your own crowdsourcing means you have to first determine what your project entails and then break the project down into smaller pieces. Then you need to be prepared to manage every step of the process, which can be a daunting task. There is a reason why people use sites and tools to manage the crowdsourcing process; there are a lot of moving parts that require a lot of planning, coordinating, managing, and tracking.

Crowdsourcing basic tasks and simple projects reduces the burden of coordination, but it still requires a clear system with the appropriate tools to facilitate the process. You need to be able to streamline your crowdsourcing activities without skimping on quality controls. You also need to make sure you can communicate your project or task to your crowd properly and are able to organize and analyze the outcomes of your crowdsourcing efforts.

Using Forms and Spreadsheets

The first tools you want to put into place are your data-gathering and collection tools. In their simplest forms, these are web-based forms with which you can direct your crowd to provide their input, and spreadsheets that provide a file format that makes it easy to import and export the data you collect.

You can certainly use Excel spreadsheets—or any other popular spreadsheet software—to import, view, and manage data. Unfortunately, most spreadsheet software is missing an element critical to any crowdsourcing campaign: a bi-directional connection to the Internet. On its own, an Excel spreadsheet is a static place to put, sort, and read data. Without a means for collecting that data in the first place—from a crowd, no less—a spreadsheet is limited in its overall usefulness to online crowdsourcing.

A handy online solution by which you can import and export a variety of common spreadsheet formats, including Excel files, is Google Spreadsheets, part of the Google Apps suite of integrated online tools. What makes Google Spreadsheets even more useful is that it integrates with another app called Google Forms.

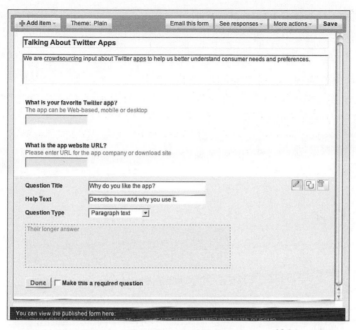

Fill in your form based on the types of questions you'd like to ask.
(Courtesy of Google via screenshot permissions policy)

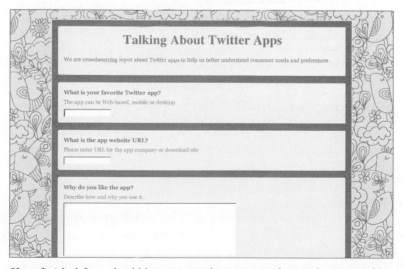

Your finished form should be concise and easy to complete, and you can add a background design using pre-made templates.
(Courtesy of Google via screenshot permissions policy)

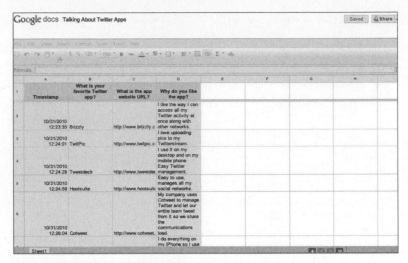

All data is fed into a Google Spreadsheet for your review.

(Courtesy of Google via screenshot permissions policy)

To create a Google Form:

1. Choose **Create**, and then **New Form**, from the menu in your docs area of Google Docs.

2. Click on **Add Item to build your form**. You are given a variety of format options for your questions, including single lines or paragraphs of text, multiple-choice selection options, radio buttons, and checkboxes.

3. Share your form by clicking on **E-mail this form** and adding addresses either manually or using your Gmail contact list.

4. You also receive a direct link to your form, which you can then place as a link on your website or blog or post to your social networks.

5. Your finished form should be concise and easy to complete.

6. All data is fed into a Google Spreadsheet for your review.

The form resides online and feeds directly into a corresponding Google Spreadsheet. The public sees only the form, and you—or whomever else you give access to—will see the spreadsheet on the back end to view results.

Using Surveys and Polls

Although you can use a tool such as Google Forms to create your own surveys, you may want to use a site specifically made for survey building and management that also offers detailed tracking and reporting features. Some of the more popular survey and poll-building sites include Zoomerang, PollDaddy, and SurveyMonkey.

Sample Costs of Poll and Survey Builders

Website	Price Levels
PollDaddy	Free Pro $200/year Corporate $899/year
Zoomerang	Basic Free Pro $199/year Premium $599/year
SurveyMonkey	Basic Free Pro $19.95/month Unlimited $200/year
Survey Gizmo	Free 14-day trial Personal $19/month Pro $49/month Enterprise $159/month Dedicated $599+/month
QuizSnack	Free Premium at $24/month*
TwtSurvey	Free Basic $49/one-time Plus $149/one-time Premium $15/month

QuizSnack uses a point system and pay-as-you-go model, so $24/month gets you the VIP membership with unlimited points per month to use premium services on QuizSnack and other products from the company. You can also purchase points incrementally, such as 10 points for $19, 25 points for $39, and 150 points for $99.

Using surveys or polls for crowdsourcing is a natural fit when your project involves getting input from the crowd. A poll provides a format that is easy for an individual to take, particularly because it gives a limited number of choices to a single question.

Surveys can be much more involved and can take more time than a poll, but they are crafted in a format most people recognize and aren't usually too complicated.

Developing surveys and polls is a skill unto itself. Even if you're a strong copywriter, you won't necessarily know how to craft surveys and polls that result in responses that actually tell you something of value. Make sure you understand the difference between *quantitative* data (relating to quantity) and *qualitative* data (relating to quality) in order to use the right kind of data-gathering tool. When you are doing it yourself, you should probably use a survey or poll builder. These are created utilizing surveying and polling best practices, and they provide instructions and tips for crafting more effective surveys and polls.

DEFINITION

Quantitative data analysis is when one assesses the quantity of something and usually involves amounts and/or percentages. **Qualitative** data analysis is when one assesses the quality of something and usually involves descriptive words or responses.

Using Databases

If you have large amounts of data that you need to gather and manipulate in some way—such as sort, calculate, and generate reports beyond what a spreadsheet can handle—you may need a database. Databases can vary from simple to complex, with relational databases being more complex and involving inter-relations between data within different sections of the database.

There are many desktop database programs, including Microsoft Access and FileMaker Pro, with which you can build your own repository for the data you collect. FileMaker Pro offers iPad and iPhone apps for mobile access. FileMaker also offers a more personal plug-and-play database product called Bento, which can be useful for smaller projects, but which won't scale up for larger ones and cannot be shared among more than five people.

Like any software, if you don't have a way to integrate it with the Internet, you may have some work ahead of you when you want to get the data you collect from your online crowd into the database. Both Access and FileMaker offer web interfaces for your database, which can assist you in data collection.

Inputting the data you gather into the database shouldn't be a constant manual task; you should be able to gather it online, convert it into an importable format such as .CSV or comma delimited, and then import it into your database for further processing.

Leveraging a Crowd

What's a crowdsourcing project without a crowd? It's like an ice cream sundae without the ice cream. If you aren't reaching out to a crowd to get something done in an organized way using Internet- and web-based tools, you're probably not crowdsourcing. Without a crowd—and without the Internet—you are either doing it on your own, engaging in more traditional outsourcing, or hiring someone else directly to do something for you. To crowdsource, you need to have access to a large number of people online and the right technology tools to manage them as a crowd.

How large is large when it comes to a crowd? That often depends on your needs and what you are trying to accomplish. If you are working with a crowdsourcing site, it likely has gathered crowds of hundreds, thousands, even tens or hundreds of thousands of crowdworkers or participants in crowd powered projects.

To give you some perspective, the crowdsourcing site CrowdFlower claims to reach over 500,000 workers from over 70 countries. They do this by tapping into the crowds of sites like Samasource and Mechanical Turk. The site 99designs.com claims over 81,000 designers, and Crowdspring claims nearly 75,000.

You may not need thousands of people in your crowd. Just having dozens of people providing input may be all you need, but you need to make sure you can manage their input. You are the best person to determine what the "magic" number of individuals is.

Crowd Response Rates

As with any crowdsourcing campaign launched via any network, platform, or tool, you need to keep an eye on the responses and measure your results. Consider response rate. What if you aren't getting the number of responses you were expecting? Or what if they aren't happening in a timely manner? You may need to modify some aspect of your campaign, such as increasing promotions. On social networks, this could be as simple as tapping into a wider circle of connections or asking your immediate connections to share your campaign with their friends. You may also have to increase the incentive, if you have one, or add one if you don't. Take into consideration the effects of incentives on crowds discussed in Chapter 2.

Take a look at response quality. Is the quality of the responses you are getting from the crowd less than suitable? You may have to revisit the components of your campaign—from the way you explained what you need, to the mechanics of how the work is being sourced, to the project's complexity—to see if you need to modify something. If the project is too complex, you may need to break it down further or explain what you're looking for in a more detailed fashion.

Watch for response drop-off. Are you seeing that many people visit the site, tool, or page where you're gathering responses, but just a mere fraction are actually doing something? Perhaps you have a survey running and it has been viewed by 500 people but you have received only 80 complete responses. This is another sign that you need to revisit each aspect of your campaign. Your crowd is telling you something by abandoning your campaign midstream.

Although it may be discouraging if your campaign doesn't get enough responses, at some point you should accept the responses you have received and analyze the information you have. Sometimes, there is no single reason why your campaign fell short. Crowdsourcing isn't like throwing spaghetti up on the wall where every piece sticks. It's a much more involved and deliberate process, which is why people turn to established crowdsourcing sites—with built-in systems and crowds—to navigate the process.

Places to Crowdsource

Where can you crowdsource? Just about anywhere you can gather a crowd online is a potential crowdsourcing pool. Every online community, however, isn't necessarily ready to be sourced. Part of the readiness is based on why the community was formed in the first place.

Community members like to know what they are getting into when they join a community. If being sourced for work or opinions isn't on the agenda, your efforts will not only fall flat, but you'll also probably experience a backlash.

Even if the crowd is eager to participate in your crowdsourcing campaign, you still need to integrate some communications tools and data-gathering tools into the community or link the members to tools hosted elsewhere on the web. You need to put some structure around your crowdsourcing activities. Otherwise, you're just asking a community random questions, and you'll get mixed results. You'll also have trouble tracking, analyzing, and archiving the data you gather.

Web-Based Online Communities

People form online communities for many reasons, often based on shared interests or experiences. Many of these communities happen organically, with people finding each other through conversation and then creating a space where others can join them. They invite their friends, they post announcements in public forums, and they actively manage the community to keep the conversation flowing.

In other cases, online communities are formed deliberately and with a purpose. A company might build an online forum where their staff can be more readily accessible to answer questions and provide customer support. At the same time, customers participating in the forum can help each other. This is a form of crowdsourcing by community.

Online communities often form on the web within sites that have tools to facilitate community building. Each of these online community sites offer different community features, but they all start with a message board system—also called a posting board, discussion board, discussion forum—where messages are posted by community members and where other members can respond. Additional features offered by some web-based online community sites include member profiles, private messaging, group or broadcast messaging, and a chatting or instant-messaging function. If you have a popular, highly trafficked blog, you might be able to tap into your blog community as your crowd, offering polls or inviting them to participate in another platform more conducive to crowdsourcing.

Social Networks

If you can gather people together in one place online, chances are you can crowd-source through your interactions and communications with that crowd. Social networks are really newer versions of online communities. They offer more features and more integrated ways to connect with others than most traditional web-based online communities.

Threaded message boards are at the heart of online communities. On social networks, communications can occur in other ways as well, including directly with individual members, broadcast messages that appear in members' news stream, or even via the social network's e-mail (depending on the network).

If you are crowdsourcing input in social networking forums, you may end up with more qualitative than quantitative input, unless you use more formal surveying through polling or survey tools to capture more complex responses. You can use social networks as your gateway to your data capture tools hosted elsewhere. Social networks can be rich environments for dialogue that provides feedback and opinions, and for carrying out idea exchanges.

You can create custom social networks using a myriad of fee-based tools and platforms such as Kick Apps, SocialGo, and Ning. Some fee-based platforms also offer free versions with fewer features or no tech support. A free option is Evly, which lets you create a custom social network specifically for crowdsourcing. See Chapter 10 to find out more about crowdsourcing in popular social networks.

Collaborative Spaces

One popular tool for bringing people together to work on a project is the collaborative workspace. This virtual space exists on websites and contains integrated features to facilitate work and communications between groups of people. Sounds like crowdsourcing, doesn't it?

Both online communities and collaborative workspaces share some features, including discussion forums, person-to-person messaging, and group or broadcast messaging. Some features set collaboration workspaces apart from collaboration tools:

- **Whiteboards:** Areas where multiple people can edit a document or illustrate something together.
- **Wikis:** An instrument to build a website with multiple people.
- **Project tracking:** To enter and manage the aspects of getting a project completed.
- **Task tracking:** To assign tasks and track status of work and time spent.
- **File uploads:** Allows you to upload, share, and—in some cases—edit documents in various formats, including Word documents, Excel spreadsheets, and PDFs, among others.

Some popular virtual workspaces and collaborative workspace tools include Glasscubes, Basecamp, and Zoho. Each offers free levels or free trials, as well as paid levels ranging from $12 per month to $149 per month and higher for more enterprise-level solutions.

Features for Popular Collaborative Online Spaces

Feature	Basecamp	Glasscubes	Zoho
Free trial	30-day	28-day	15-day
Free level	No	Yes	Yes**
Discussion	Yes	Yes	Yes
File sharing	Yes	Yes	Yes
E-mail integration	Yes	Yes	Yes
Projects	Yes	Yes	Yes
Tasks/To-Dos	Yes	Yes	Yes
Time tracking	Yes	Yes	Yes***
Whiteboards	No	Yes	No
Wikis	No	No	Yes
Polls	No	Yes	No
Chat	No*	No	Yes

See the Campfire application that integrates into Basecamp.

**Zoho has a free level, but only for individuals to use.*

***Available in paid levels.*

Not all features of an online collaborative workspace are critical to crowdsourcing, but some are good to have. For example, if the work you are crowdsourcing requires real-time collaboration, being able to co-edit the same document or illustration could prove useful. If each of your projects involves many tasks, incorporating the project and task-tracking aspects of a collaborative workspace could prove useful.

Executing Your Process

Whether you do it yourself or you're using a crowdsourcing site, you need a process to properly set up your campaign. If you are working with a crowdsourcing service provider, they will most likely walk you through similar steps to make sure you know what you are trying to accomplish, can communicate it clearly to crowdworkers, and can receive the best results you can.

Whether you are doing these preliminary steps yourself or are being guided by a site or service provider, you shouldn't embark on crowdsourcing efforts without some kind of prep work, particularly complex projects or projects that potentially have major implications for your business.

Mapping Out Your Steps

Each crowdsourcing site has its own set of steps, depending on their methodology for sourcing their crowds and on the type of crowdsourcing they handle. Here are some steps you can use as a guide to your own crowdsourcing process:

1. Identify your need.
2. Name and define your project.
3. Write out specifications for your project.
4. Articulate the outcome you wish to achieve.
5. Outline special skills or considerations for crowd participants.
6. Specify a timeline.
7. Establish a price.
8. Assemble/upload project assets and supporting documents.
9. Publish your project.
10. Review work submissions.
11. Provide feedback.
12. Review iterations or modifications.
13. Accept work.
14. Pay worker.

Depending on what you are crowdsourcing, these steps can vary. If you are getting feedback from your customers, you wouldn't necessarily be setting a price or paying workers unless you're holding a competition for ideas and setting an award for the best idea.

Setting Up Your Tools

If you're doing the crowdsourcing on your own, chances are you aren't planning on investing large sums of money in programming proprietary tools to manage the entire process. Instead, you are leveraging communications and data-gathering tools that already exist to handle the various aspects of your crowdsourcing efforts.

Before you begin crowdsourcing, you need to download or access and register for the tools you've chosen, configure them properly, and look for ways to integrate them. You need the tools you're going to use to manage your crowdsourcing process and data to work together as much as possible for a smoother workflow. For example, if you are building a private community and are inviting your customers to join you to source ideas for improving your existing product, you might do the following:

- Set up a community platform like Ning that lets you export your community member list into a .CSV format.

- Set up an account with a polling application like PollDaddy. You can export poll results into a .CSV format.

- Set up a spreadsheet or database like Google Spreadsheets or FileMaker Pro to capture data. You can import .CSV files into these tools to manage your data.

- Embed the PollDaddy application into your Ning community so the polls are seamlessly accessible to members.

- Use Ning's broadcast feature to make announcements to your members, their blog feature to provide detailed information, and uploaded or embedded images to illustrate your project.

- Continue discussions in the forums within your Ning community, on both community-wide and private forums.

Ultimately, you must find and use the tools that help you communicate with members, share and archive data, and receive and analyze results.

Gathering a Crowd

If you don't yet have a crowd, you need to build one. Start with who you know and who your contacts know. Look at your current e-mail contact lists, customer relationship management (CRM) databases, and other places where you can reach out to people. Your goal is not only to reach your contacts, but also to encourage them to pass your message along to others. You can also make announcements through more traditional routes, such as sending out a press release.

Here are some resources you can use to invite people to join your crowd community:

- Your e-mail address book.

- Your e-mail lists.

- Your social network contacts.

- Online communities where you are a member. (First get permission from the community host.)

- Online communities or lists specifically created to make announcements.

- An announcement on your website.

- An announcement in your social network status update.

- Send a Social Media Release through sites like PitchEngine.com or PressItt.com.

- Send an electronic press release through free services, such as Free-Press-Release.com and PRLog.com.

- Pay for a wire service release such as PR Newswire or Business Wire.

- Buy ads on websites that reach your target group.

- Approach existing crowds such as university classes, associations, and other groups where you can publicize your project and invite members to join your crowd.

Make sure your invitation or announcement states clearly what you are doing, why you are doing it, and what action you want people reading your message to take. Your best bet is to get them to submit their information to you right away and to confirm their interest in participating so you can contact them with more details. Or you may want to link them to a place where they can join your community straight from the announcement.

Make the calls to action in your announcement simple and obvious. Once someone is compelled enough to click on a link in your announcement, you want to establish a connection with them so you don't lose their interest. Throughout your entire crowdsourcing campaign, make sure you provide clear instructions so your crowd members know what to expect and what to do.

Managing Your Crowd

Once you have a crowd, provide everyone with your project details and instructions on what they need to do. Perhaps you want them to participate in a survey, submit ideas, or provide feedback you can consider for important business decisions. Regardless of what you're asking of them, keep the actions straightforward and consistent with what you first announced.

Remind your crowd members why you've brought them together and what you hope to achieve. Are you looking to improve a service you offer? Emphasize why their input is important to you and what you will do with it. Assure them that their information will be kept private. Explain to them that, while you cannot incorporate every idea, their participation helps to stimulate positive change.

If you are looking for fresh ideas for a new dish your restaurant can serve, provide instructions on how to submit those ideas and an easy-to-use mechanism to retrieve and store their responses. Be careful not to be overly controlling of what your crowd says. Sometimes, the best ideas come from thinking outside the box—that's one of the benefits of sourcing a crowd for ideas, as opposed to tapping into a smaller group of people in a highly controlled environment.

At the end of the day, people who participate in crowdwork want to know what's in it for them. As explained in Chapter 2, what people want out of being a crowdworker or crowdsourcing participant can vary greatly. They need you to articulate the benefits of their participation, whether monetary, in-kind, or simple recognition. Improving your product or service can be a great motivator because your current customers will experience the benefits and new customers will get something better than what currently exists.

Analyzing the Results

If you're looking to get a task completed, you probably already know the right way for that task to be done. In some cases, there are right answers and there are wrong ones. In your process, you need a stage to review and vet responses to weed out the wrong ones. Task completion as a crowdsourcing activity tends to generate more clear-cut results.

If you are sourcing ideas, you will end up choosing the best idea or ideas. The "best" is very subjective, so you should have some concrete criteria that are more objective. Even though the subjective might dominate your final decision, having some framework to the selection process helps you stay on track and helps your crowd understand outcomes. When ideas that are being sourced are meant to solve problems, you are back to selecting the correct result, the most effective solution, or the right answer, which are more black and white results.

You may consider assembling a panel of experts to advise you and help you vet completed work. Picking and managing your expert panel creates extra steps in your overall crowdsourcing process, but it can give you greater clarity when analyzing results. For more sensitive or complex projects, you may want to "expert-source," casting a wide net to identify individuals with the credentials and skills to provide quality work or to help you assess completed work.

DULY NOTED

A handy tool to have in your crowdsourcing toolkit to archive data you are gathering from an online crowd is a web page to PDF converter. Use a site such as Web2PDF (web2pdfconvert.com) by entering the URL of the web page where the data resides and hitting the convert button. Voilà!

In crowdsourcing, you may discover a gray area when it comes to sourcing opinions and feedback. You can put some structure to this kind of data-gathering with polls and surveys. By asking quantitative questions, you receive data in a format that can be sorted, reordered, pulled apart, and used to generate reports. If you have open-ended, qualitative questions or use loose forums such as social networks to carry out a dialogue, you begin creating challenges for both extracting the information and analyzing it.

As long as you can get all the input from your crowd into one place—preferably in a unified format that you can manipulate in some way—you will have an easier time analyzing the results of your project or campaign. Spreadsheets and databases come in handy as do-it-yourself crowdsourcing tools because they become both your data repository and your tool for data analysis. They take disparate information and help you bring some order and control over it. When you have a crowd and a lot of input, having the right tools will make a big difference when it comes time to analyze the results of your crowdsourcing efforts.

The Least You Need to Know

- Start your crowdsourcing process by identifying what your project entails and breaking the project down into smaller pieces.
- Streamline your crowdsourcing activities without skimping on quality controls.
- For a smooth workflow, pick tools to manage your process and data that work together.
- Find and use the tools that help you communicate with members, share and archive data, and receive and analyze results.
- People who participate in crowdwork want to know what's in it for them, so articulate the benefits of their participation—whether it's monetary, in-kind, or recognition.

Outsourcing Your Crowdsourcing

In This Chapter

- Determining when to outsource
- Crowdsourcing service providers (CSPs)
- Costs of outsourcing your crowdsourcing
- Choosing not to outsource
- Partnering with a contractor

Doing your own crowdsourcing works well for basic tasks and simple projects, but more complex tasks and projects may make handling all the steps yourself untenable. In those cases, you can turn to a website created specifically to help facilitate the crowdsourcing process, such as CrowdFlower, which handles task-oriented work, or 99designs, which sources the best design from a crowd of designers.

The very idea of crowdsourcing on your own can be daunting, even given the tools and sites available to streamline the process. If that's the case, consider outsourcing your crowdsourcing efforts, which means hiring someone else to manage the process of crowdsourcing.

When It's Time to Outsource

There are many different ways to crowdsource. You can use many different sites and tools to gather and source a crowd, with more options being developed each month. Given the growing number of self-service resources you can use to crowdsource, why would you outsource your crowdsourcing to someone else? Following are some valid reasons.

- You don't have time to manage your crowdsourcing project.

- You're not looking for the do-it-yourself method.

- You prefer to pay someone else to do what they do best.

- You aren't on a tight budget.

- Your project is more complex and requires more diligent expert guidance.

Just because you can crowdsource yourself doesn't mean you have to. Like anything we need to do, sometimes it is fine for us to take the do-it-yourself approach, and other times it is worth turning the work over to professionals. Don't feel guilty if you want to outsource your crowdsourcing. Many people do it, from individuals to small business owners to corporations.

Who Provides Crowdsourcing Services?

There are companies, such as CrowdFlower and Mechanical Turk, that create sites to help you manage the crowdsourcing process and offer a self-service system where you fill out forms and do most of the management with the help of some automated and mechanized tools. As more and more people consider crowdsourcing, there are now companies that offer crowdsourcing services for a fee, known as crowdsourcing service providers (CSPs). Most of these companies gather their own highly specialized crowds, develop their own proprietary sets of tools to manage the crowds, and help you conceptualize your project and break it down into the most appropriate pieces to be effectively crowdsourced.

CSPs are middlemen, and their job is to manage the crowdsourcing process. Cloudcrowd, for example, takes an assembly-line approach. Whinot provides project managers to shepherd the crowdsourcing process. For any project you need to get done, a CSP can help you look at all the smaller tasks that make up the greater whole. They know how to crowdsource, they have the crowd, and you tap into their expertise. There are also creative agencies that incorporate crowdsourcing into their service offerings but do not consider themselves CSPs.

Say you're a small business owner and you want to have a blog to market your company but don't have the time to maintain that blog. How would you break blogging down into smaller bits? A company like Cloudcrowd might break blogging into the smaller tasks of brainstorming blog post topics, researching those topics and identifying relevant news items on the web, and actually writing the blog posts. Additional tasks could be editing the post, uploading the text to a blog publishing tool, and finding and uploading appropriate stock photography. All you have to do is approve the posts. What started out as blogging turned into at least six tasks.

On a larger scale, big corporations can outsource their crowdsourcing to CSPs such as Chaordix or Spigit that specialize in enterprise solutions. These CSPs offer custom systems for internal as well as external crowdsourcing and provide strategic consulting services to help corporations integrate crowdsourcing processes into their production flow and internal communications.

Not all outsourced crowdsourcing has to be done by a CSP. The work can be done by a consultant who understands crowdsourcing and helps you through the entire process utilizing proprietary or existing crowdsourcing tools. The idea of outsourcing crowdsourcing is that you don't want to do it and are comfortable turning things over to someone else who knows how to do it well.

DULY NOTED

There are the companies that take over your crowdsourcing project and manage it for you. Then there are companies, like blur Group, a full-service, integrated creative agency that leverages crowdsourcing as a way to enhance creative thinking and augment creative output. They gather five specific crowds of their own: designers, writers, marketers, photographers/videographers/artists, and innovators, using Ning as their community crowd platform.

They work closely with a client to develop a creative brief that is put out to the appropriate crowd. The client not only gets the benefits of talent beyond blur's own team, but blur can also pass on cost savings to the client by cutting back on traditional agency overhead. Their crowds are virtual and work independently. Crowd members pitch for jobs, and only crowd members chosen for the project do the work and get paid. Payment is fairly commensurate to market value.

When Not to Outsource

There are reasons not to crowdsource, and there are reasons not to outsource crowd-sourcing. In fact, the reasons are pretty similar.

If the work is highly sensitive or confidential, the very nature of reaching out to and interacting with many people increases the risk to your data's integrity. Some CSPs may assure you of the highest security for your data, but even they can't guarantee there won't be some kind of breach if they don't take the appropriate precautions, such as conducting background checks on their crowdworkers (many do not).

If the stakes are high for the accurate completion of your project, you may be better off paying someone to do the highest-quality work. You can get good quality from crowdsourcing, and a CSP has a lot on the line to ensure the quality of the completed work they oversee, but without many quality assurance procedures in place, quality can sometimes be sketchy.

Only you can determine the cost and overall benefits of using crowdsourcing. If you decide to crowdsource, putting in the extra layer of a CSP can ratchet up the quality of results—but only if the company you're working with puts a major emphasis on quality assurance and controls.

The Cost of Outsourced Crowdsourcing

CSPs have a number of different business models and pricing structures. Most providers use an agency model by which they come up with custom prices based on a client's needs and the scope of the client's project. Some may offer some packages for fixed fees and set parameters.

Packages for discrete crowdsourcing projects, such as a logo redesign or coming up with a new product name, may cost between hundreds and thousands of dollars. Larger and more complex projects may start in the thousands and then move into the tens of thousands. Consider the difference between hiring a single contractor versus hiring an entire agency. Often, you are paying agency overhead in their service fees. Still, an agency can handle more robust projects and larger crowds than a single individual.

There are CSPs of every size to fit any budget. As with agencies, you are often paying for some overhead, but a reputable provider that leverages crowds to create efficiencies within their company will probably pass some of those cost savings on to their clients. Many providers in this space see themselves as pioneers completely reinventing the agency model of work. If you work with a CSP, you are also pioneering a new way of work.

Partnering with a Contractor

Before you hire a CSP, compare companies to identify the professionals and avoid the fly by night. Look at several key indicators:

- **A clearly articulated discovery process:** They should have a process in place to get as much information from you as possible to understand your goals and objectives.

- **A transparent cost structure:** Although some CSPs provide a custom price for major jobs for bigger enterprises, they should be able to provide you with both a range and their pricing model so you can anticipate costs.

- **An established process:** Good providers have their own procedures for working through crowdsourcing with their clients, and some of the more effective processes are hybrids of old and new processes.

- **A technology platform:** Most providers have thought through the technology they need to carry out the crowdsourcing process and many have developed proprietary and complex systems to facilitate it.

- **A built-in crowd:** Your project might require assembling a custom crowd, but you should work with a CSP that has a base of primed crowdworkers ready to perform the kind of work you need.

- **A track record:** Look for providers with a list of satisfied clients, with referrals at the ready, and with proven examples of how crowdsourcing has worked and how they have successfully helped to carry out projects and campaigns for others.

When you hire a CSP to manage your crowdsourcing project, you should be able to rely on them to handle the mechanics of crowdsourcing, starting with the discovery phase, during which they get to know you and what you're trying to achieve. Part of their process may involve breaking your project down into smaller tasks. Then, they'll reach into their crowds to manage inputs and outputs strategically.

PITFALLS

Beware of CSPs that rush you into crowdsourcing without going through steps to vet your project. Not everything should be crowdsourced, and a reputable provider will acknowledge that.

Defining Everyone's Roles

You have a critical role in the crowdsourcing process because only you know exactly what you need to achieve. A good CSP will be clear about your role and their role, and the tasks they will perform. In standard relationships with CSPs, roles break down as follows:

Your job is to ...

- Articulate your need.

- Provide timely and honest feedback at every stage.

- Review the results with your CSP.

- Make a decision on the results received.

The CSP's job is to ...

- Help define the project.

- Provide strategic guidance every step of the way.

- Break the project down into manageable tasks.

- Craft the creative or project brief (with the client).

- Announce the project to their crowd.

- Help vet or refine submissions (that is, provide a layer of quality assurance).

- Provide you with the best submissions.

- Complete the project.

When you hire a CSP, you expect them to do a lot of the heavy lifting and vetting, to streamline the crowdsourcing process, and to minimize your burden. If they don't relieve you of a lot of the minutiae, or at least help you navigate through it, you might as well do the crowdsourcing yourself or find a site with a built-in crowd where you can go the self-service route. You cannot shirk your responsibility, though, as the originator of the crowdsourcing project.

Getting a Clear Process

When you're working with a CSP, they usually have a well-defined process in place and will walk you through it. Most processes that CSPs use may not be immediately recognizable but are grounded in a combination of traditional steps that have been enhanced or have evolved based on the new tools and technologies available.

You can expect to see steps similar to the ones you might take when you crowdsource from scratch. The main difference is that your CSP is handling most of those steps. Here are some of the steps in the outsourced crowdsourcing process:

1. Work together to identify your need and desired outcome. (You and the CSP)

2. Develop the project or creative brief. (CSP)

3. Draw up a list of deliverables and a timeline. (CSP)

4. Assemble/upload project assets and supporting documents. (CSP)

5. Publish the project to the crowd. (CSP)

6. Review work submissions. (You and the CSP)

7. Provide feedback, make selections, or continue the process. (You and the CSP)

8. Review iterations or modifications, and then accept work. (You and the CSP)

9. Pay the worker or work team. (CSP)

10. Apply the results or leverage the outcome. (You and the CSP)

CSPs don't usually identify themselves as crowdsourcing companies. Instead, they use a crowdsourcing work model for some aspect of the services they deliver.

Maintaining a High Level of Oversight

No matter what type of agency you work with on a project—from advertising and marketing to public relations to web development—the key ingredient to a successful relationship is you. Your involvement and your ability to communicate what you expect is the starting point of any successful client/agency relationship.

Working with a CSP should start with open communication to establish a good client/agency relationship. A reputable CSP roots their core offerings in solid business practices to provide you with quality results. Crowdsourcing may be one of the services they offer, or they may have totally changed how they deliver services by using crowdsourcing. Either way, communication comes first.

> **BEST PRACTICES**
>
> Even though you've hired a CSP, don't shirk your responsibility to be involved and engaged. You need to participate in the process and oversee the overall project.

Knowing what to expect from your CSP helps keep everyone on track. Having a clear list of deliverables and a reasonable timeline keeps the process moving forward and gives you a road map that you can follow as you put your work into someone else's hands. If you're unhappy at any time with the process or results you're getting, it is important to speak up.

If you feel the process is getting off track, you have every right to bring this to your agency's attention. Crowdsourcing should not create a situation that is hard for you to understand or handle. When you put an agency between you and the crowd, you are paying for hand holding, education, strategic guidance, and management.

Assessing the Results

You may be wondering, if you are not familiar with crowdsourcing, how you can properly assess the results of a crowdsourced project or campaign. The crowdsourcing portion of getting something done—such as creating a new logo or business card design or 30-second television spot—should be relatively seamless or even practically invisible to you, the client. When you are analyzing the results of a crowdsourced project or campaign, you should be dealing with tangible, recognizable outcomes that reflect what you needed done. Getting to the end of a crowdsourcing project and feeling it is a success is a process that starts at the beginning, when you articulated what you need, developed your project or creative brief, and mapped out a plan. Use the materials you created at the start to determine whether the decision to crowdsource your work paid off.

Did you get what you asked for or do the results miss the mark? If you have been diligent throughout the project, you should have noticed when things seemed to be going in the wrong direction and clearly communicated this to your agency. In turn, they should have taken actions to bring things back on track based on what you set out to do in the first place.

You are part of the equation for a successful outcome, whether you use a crowdsourcing self-service site, do it in-house, or outsource to someone else. Without your clear vision, your crowdsourcing may fall flat. No technical tool, service provider, or crowd can be a substitute for knowing what you want.

The Least You Need to Know

- Outsourcing your crowdsourcing means you are hiring someone else to manage the crowdsourcing process.
- A good CSP is clear about your role, their role, and the tasks they will perform.
- Part of a CSP's process involves breaking your project down into smaller tasks and reaching out to their crowds to manage inputs and outputs strategically.
- When analyzing the results of a crowdsourced project or campaign, you should be dealing with tangible outcomes based on what you wanted done.

Crowdsourcing for Feedback and Input

In Part 2, you'll learn how to source crowds to receive feedback and input. I also outline how to build an online community geared around crowdsourcing activities, particularly various forms of information gathering. You'll learn how to gather and assimilate information you receive from your crowd that can impact your company and the products and services you offer. You'll also find out how to use crowdsourcing for innovation.

I also show you the different types of crowds you can source, from global, to local, to internal to your company. You can also get answers from crowds, and I've reviewed a number of answer sites so you know what's out there.

Building a Private Crowdsourcing Community

In This Chapter

- Building an online community
- Understanding the legal issues of online communities
- Managing an online community
- Developing community policies and guidelines

You can start an online community to bring together a representative sampling of your target market and ask questions of your community members for online market research. Unfortunately, this approach to crowdsourcing is relatively time consuming.

Anyone can build an online community—instead of going to a site or company with an established community—and conduct crowdsourcing. There are many issues to consider when you build your own community, and building and growing the community can be a major undertaking—even before you begin crowdsourcing your community.

Managing Online Communities

Building an online community from scratch isn't an exact science, and there are no formulas you can follow to ensure good results. There are positives and negatives to setting up and putting together your own private community for crowdsourcing. On the positive side, you have more control over the community you host, although "control" is a loose term when it comes to community management.

Here are some good reasons to form a private online community:

- You can create a custom, branded community environment.
- You can have administrative control of community features.
- You can get to know your crowd members better than if they were part of a larger, less structured community.
- You can discuss and get feedback on something that isn't "ready for prime time" (isn't ready for general public consumption).

You can't really control the people who make up an online community, but if you build your own private community forum, you can have more control over its appearance and mechanics. Using an online community for crowdsourcing purposes is only effective when the community members feel comfortable, trust you as the community host, understand your intentions, and implicitly or explicitly agree to participate.

Online Communities as Gardens

A common analogy used to describe an online community is a garden. First, you till the soil or identify and configure the structural aspects of the online community. There are a myriad of tools for constructing the virtual space where your community members will gather. Some of the more popular tools are covered later in this chapter.

After you build the structure of your community and add the branding and features you want it to have, you invite people to your community. You can then begin seeding it with conversations. Just as in a garden, where seeds need an environment with sunshine and fertilizer to sprout and grow, so do conversations. Just posting questions and hoping people in the community will answer them usually won't render very good results.

After you ask a question, pay attention to who responds and comment on their responses. People want to know they are heard. Ask a follow-up question. Get a dialogue going with those who are responding. Create a fertile environment for ongoing dialogue. Sprinkle the conversation with interesting and relevant anecdotes. Ask for further input. Ask individuals questions directly.

Managing a community is actually like a cross between growing a garden and hosting a party. Being a good host includes paying attention to the details, introducing people to one another, not letting the conversations lag, and giving everyone a stake in the community's success. If there is a problem in the community, everyone will look to the host for solutions.

Liabilities and Legal Headaches

Many companies shy away from building, hosting, and managing online communities because of potential legal liability issues. The most common fear is that someone will say something in the forum and a problem will ensue that will be blamed on the host rather than on the individual who created the problem.

Picture this: A company manufactures and sells a line of hair-care products. To get feedback from their customers, the company creates an online forum on their website. A commenter says, "Try this hair care product on your face if you have acne, it really works." Another person tries the commenter's suggestion, has a violent reaction, and is hospitalized. What if that person sues the company that makes the products and hosts the online forum? Is the company actually responsible? Should they have deleted or corrected the false information? What if the company puts disclaimers all over the forum stating they are not responsible for the information posted in the forum unless it comes from an official company rep? Does that reduce the company's liability?

These questions all have some legal precedents, but there are no definitive answers. Such concerns keep companies from embracing online forums in which they don't have full editorial control, even over conversations. With the advent of social networking communities, companies have even less control over what is being said about their company and their products and services.

BEST PRACTICES

Whenever you have any doubt about legal issues surrounding activities you may be considering for yourself or your company, consult a lawyer. Cyber laws and regulations can vary from state to state, depending on where you—and your customers—are based.

Policing Crowds

Anyone who has managed an online community can tell you how challenging it can be to keep everyone in the community happy, and it's even more challenging to keep the peace when emotions get in the way. Communities are made up of many people, and where you have many people, you have a myriad of personalities, attitudes, perceptions, and even agendas.

Good managers know you don't really control online communities. You can guide them, help shape their tone and direction, and set some ground rules so you can police them if there is a problem. But control is limited, and sometimes the more control you exert, the more you can exacerbate a problem and turn it into a bad situation.

Online communities commonly "police themselves," which means the community members take it upon themselves to keep the peace. Knowing when to take a more hands-off approach takes experience, and things don't always go as planned. In a strong community, members who are respected and recognized for their contributions take pride in keeping the community vibrant and trouble-free.

Ultimately, the online community takes on a life of its own, and the best you can do is be visible, vocal, active, and fair. Community managers spend most of their time seeding conversations and moderating discussions to keep participation high and attention focused.

Some companies avoid running online communities because of the time commitment required to do so. If you are crowdsourcing within your private online community, you need to make sure the community stays on track. Online communities rarely function on a set time schedule, and—depending on time zones and people's schedules—the conversations can happen at all hours of the day and night, with or without your involvement. How will you monitor what is happening when you're asleep? What will happen if there's a problem in your community over the weekend? Running an online community doesn't have to translate into a 24/7 job, but you need a way to know when something is wrong or needs attention. When and how you respond is up to you, but your choice can have a major impact on the success of your community.

Planning Your Crowd Community

Community building doesn't happen overnight—it's often a slow and steady process. If time is of the essence, starting a community from nothing may not be the way to go. But if you're looking to build long-term relationships and cultivate an ongoing resource for crowdsourcing, a private online community can be useful.

Starting an online community can be as simple as setting up a community platform on one of the popular community sites or even on social networks. Before you open the virtual doors, make sure you've set up not just the technical structure, but the community structure as well.

Although you can't expect to have full control over your online community, you can set up some ground rules. Before you even build your community, you need to establish both internal and external policies and guidelines to follow. Written guidelines can help you better manage your community. Having something in writing gives a framework for everything that happens, from how others can participate to what happens if someone violates a rule to actually defining the community rules and what constitutes a violation.

Establishing a Community Purpose

Before you build your community, be clear on why you are building it. Start with crafting a written statement of the purpose of your community. Here is an example of a purpose statement:

> *The purpose of this community is to exchange ideas about product improvements for ABC Company's products.*

> *The purpose of this community is to provide personal and peer-to-peer customer service for ABC Company's products.*

> *The purpose of this community is to gain insights from consumers regarding their online purchasing habits.*

Publish a purpose statement like this in your community, and use it when you are inviting others to participate. Include it in important documents, such as community guidelines and terms of service.

Setting Community Guidelines

Try to make your community guidelines as accessible to the layperson as possible. Have a lawyer look over them to make sure the guidelines aren't potentially problematic, should a legal issue arise in your community.

You can find sample guidelines on the web to use as a template for your community. Search for "sample community guidelines" with your preferred search engine, and you'll find a variety of examples. You can also check out the ones for the online communities to which you belong.

Here are some basic guidelines you can use as a starting point for your community rules:

- **Be kind.** The Golden Rule applies here. We are looking to crowdsource comments on content and issues, not on individuals.

- **Be truthful.** We work hard to check our facts and tell you what we believe is true. We ask you to do the same. If something seems suspect, we may be obligated to delete it to avoid creating a negative situation for everyone.

- **Don't spam.** If you come to our crowdsourcing community to promote your company, service, or product, we reserve the right to remove promotional or inappropriate posts, unless it is relevant to the conversation and is posted in a non-commercial fashion.

- **Add value.** While we know value is in the eye of the beholder, we hope you contribute comments in the spirit of elevating this community to higher levels of discourse and to provide information useful to the community at large.

Community guidelines do not constitute a legal document, but they set the tone for your community. Make sure to include your community purpose in your guidelines.

Providing Terms of Use

Most websites have or should have a Terms of Use document—also known as a Terms of Service or Terms and Conditions document—that outlines the responsibilities of both the site host and the user or site member. This document isn't legally binding, but it should get specific about what is considered inappropriate and what actions will be taken for violation of the site's rules. Terms of Use can apply to online communities as well. In some cases, sites post a Terms of Use in their registration process and require that new members click an **I accept** button to gain entrance into the site.

Elements of a Terms of Use document vary, but any lawyer well versed in cyber law should have a template you can follow. It is a good idea to include the following sections in this formal document:

- **Conditions and Restrictions:** This outlines what the conditions of use and community participation entail.

- **Member Conduct:** This specifies what members can and can't do.

- **License to Use:** This states that anything posted in the community forum is automatically owned by the community host.

- **Disclaimer of Warranties:** This states that the community is presented "as is", without any guarantees from the host.

- **Limitation of Liability:** This provides clear statements about the community host's limited liability.

- **Disclaimers:** This statement is intended to limit the community host's liability from actions or statements made by others not under their direct employ.

- **Acceptance:** This requires that new community members agree to the terms.

Include contact information in the Terms of Use, in case a community member has a complaint. Make sure there is someone on the other end of the e-mail address or telephone number who can respond promptly.

Privacy and Security Policies

Your site should have a privacy statement and a security policy, especially if you request any personal or identifying information from community members. A lawyer can guide you in crafting your policies. State them on your site or within your community forum to make sure they cover the main legal issues and laws pertaining to privacy and security.

When crowdsourcing input from your crowd community, you probably won't be asking for highly personal information that needs to be carefully secured, such as a credit card number or Social Security number. You'll likely use semi-anonymous data-gathering tools, such as surveys and polls, for which you'll not even need to collect a person's identifying information. Regardless of the personal and private information you might glean, privacy and security policies are now standard for any online community, and are highly recommended, given the Federal Trade Commission's increased involvement in online activities.

DULY NOTED

In addition to consulting a lawyer, you can find more information about privacy issues for your website through the Federal Trade Commission's website at ftc.gov.

A written privacy policy should include at least these elements:

- Information you might ask your members to provide.

- A declaration of any information that will be automatically collected from community members, such as through cookies. A simple explanation of cookies is helpful.

- A notice of what you will or won't do with the information someone provides to you via your community or site, such as sell or provide that information to a third party.

- A declaration of any information that might be placed into members' web browsers using cookies, and to what end.

- A declaration of how data collected from members is shared, if at all.

- A reference to a security policy, with a link to it, to outline how privacy and security go hand in hand.

Here's an excerpt from a sample privacy policy:

> *For each visitor to our web page, our web server automatically recognizes no information regarding the domain or e-mail address. We collect the e-mail address of only those who subscribe to our e-newsletter. The information we collect is used to improve the content of our web page, to notify consumers about updates to our website, and to contact consumers for marketing purposes. With respect to cookies, we do not set any cookies. We keep private information you provide us secure. Please read our security policy (link).*

Security policies are brief, but are technical. You should outline the security-related software used on the server where you host the community and the type of encryption used to transmit a member's personal data. A brief statement of how data is transmitted, where it goes, how it is stored, and how it is protected usually covers the technical side of the security policy. Addressing cookies in a security policy is also helpful.

Here's an excerpt from a sample security policy:

> *We do not ask for any confidential or physically identifying information except for your name, age, and contact information. This website contains secure areas, including the membership intake form and your personal account information. That information is obtained by secure web-based forms. We use Secured Socket Layer (SSL) encryption in those secure areas. We host our community on _____'s servers. That company's security policy is available here: (link). Please do not reveal any personal, confidential, or identifying information in our community's public forums; those areas are not secure. All information you publish to public areas of this site will be considered non-private and not confidential.*

Make sure the information you include in your policies is true and accurate.

Community-Building Tools

Building an online community takes the soft skills of communication and personal relationships on a large scale, and the technical skills of actually constructing a virtual space to house community activities. There are many pre-fab and custom solutions for building communities on the web. Most involve web-based templates and tools to create a particular look and feel, and to add or subtract interactive features. These templates are easy to use and take you through a step-by-step process in which you answer basic questions, fill out forms, and complete the building process for your community.

Some community-building tools are entirely free, although the companies that make those tools probably get their money from advertising revenues, so your free community might be peppered with online ads. Other community-building tools have a monthly hosting fee and sometimes a one-time set-up fee. You can custom-build an online community; given the extensive plug-and-play tools available, however, you may not need to undertake such a major investment.

Because you will likely be building communities to conduct fairly basic tasks, there is probably little need for a highly customized community tool. If you have very specific needs that involve the creation of intricate tools to facilitate your crowdsourcing process, you may want to do research to make sure another company hasn't already created a suitable tool that you can license or use.

Using Ning

Ning (ning.com) is a fee-based online platform for community building and hosting that lets you build online gathering spaces with familiar social networking features such as profiles, friends, blogs, status updates, photos, videos, and an activity feed. Prices range from $2.95 to $49.95 per month, with the cheapest level limited to 150 members.

To sign up for Ning, start by choosing your plan. Ning then asks you to name your community and complete their easy sign-up process to select basic features, such as a design template. Once you have completed the community creation process, you can modify your community's appearance, upload images, rearrange features, add or take away additional features, and set permissions for group members. If you know how to utilize cascading style sheets (CSS), you can further customize your community's appearance.

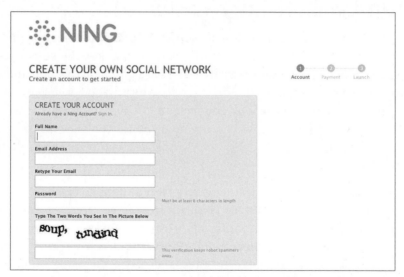

Start the Ning sign-up process by creating your account.
(Courtesy of Ning)

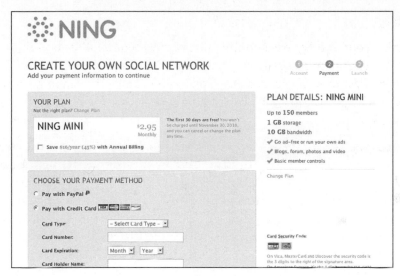

Enter your payment information after you've selected the right plan for you.
(Courtesy of Ning)

Name your network and fill in the rest of the set-up form.
(Courtesy of Ning)

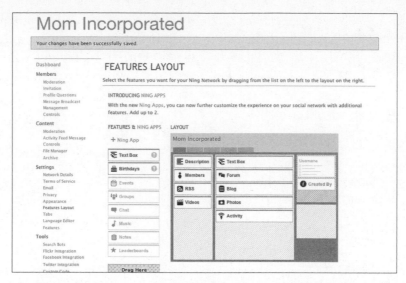

Select the applications you want to add to your network, and rearrange them by dragging and dropping.
(Courtesy of Ning)

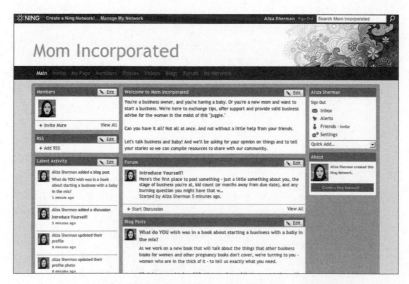

Launch your network, change the design using templates, and add your content.
(Courtesy of Ning)

Ning offers integrated applications that can help with crowdsourcing input from community members, such as the PollDaddy poll builder, which seamlessly embeds quick polls into the community forum. The polls taken on Ning pull data from and feed into a full-featured PollDaddy account for tracking polls and accessing reports with poll results.

Using Google Groups

Creating a free Google Group offers an easier process than Ning, but the features are more basic. When you start a Google Group, you fill out a simple set-up form where you can name your group, select a group e-mail address, select a group web address, fill in a group description, flag the group for mature content (if relevant), and choose an access level (public, announcement-only, or restricted). Google offers instructions for every step of the Google Groups registration process.

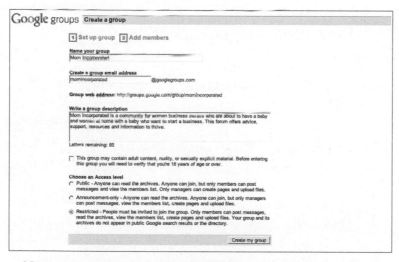

Name your group and provide a description to get started creating your Google Group.

(Courtesy of Google screenshot permissions policy)

You can skip the step of inviting others until you are ready.
(Courtesy of Google screenshot permissions policy)

Launch your Google Group and start adding content.
(Courtesy of Google screenshot permissions policy)

The announcement-only setting works best for an e-mail list or e-mail newsletter format by which you can post messages out to community members while not allowing others to post messages to the group. Set your access level to restricted to be invitation only, which gives you more control. Only make your group private if you are looking to cast a very wide net and you're not concerned with the management of your community. Announcement-only groups are of limited use to your crowdsourcing endeavors because they lack the proper mechanisms to allow you to glean information from your crowd community.

Customizing your group with Google Groups is also basic from a look-and-feel standpoint. To change the design, you have only to select a new template and modify the fonts and font sizes. These groups are straightforward and utilitarian versus the media-rich and custom designed. The feature-management tools for your Google Group are self-explanatory and contain standard moderation and spam controls.

Google Groups may be light on the features, but they do the trick for quick-and-dirty crowdsourcing projects where you just need a place to gather your crowd to exchange information. For anyone familiar with old-school e-mail lists and online forums, Google Groups will feel familiar, and the entry barriers will be low. For anyone looking for more branded and designed solutions, fee-based Ning or a free site called Grouply might fit the bill.

Using Grouply

Grouply (grouply.com) is a free platform for building online community spaces that falls closer to Ning in its features and capabilities than Google Groups. Starting a group on Grouply is as easy as naming your group, describing your group, choosing the type of group (such as a discussion group), choosing a category for your group (such as Technology or Sports), and specifying a physical location for your group (if relevant).

Name your group on Grouply to get started.
(Courtesy of Grouply)

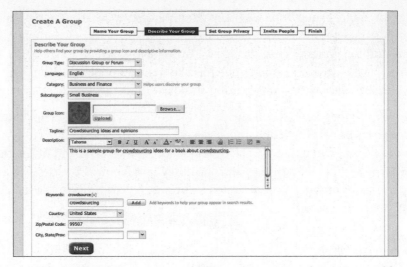

Make selections that best fit your group, including type, category, description, and keywords.
(Courtesy of Grouply)

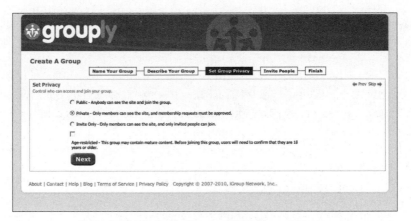

Determine the best privacy settings for your group.
(Courtesy of Grouply)

You can customize your group's appearance, select features, and invite others. Then, you can launch when you're ready.

(Courtesy of Grouply)

Next, you must choose privacy settings. You can select **Public**, which is completely open and visible to anyone, and anyone can join the group. You can also select **Private**, requiring that membership requests be approved by you and allowing only members to see the group site. A third option, **Invite-only**, allows only members to see the group site, and individuals must be directly invited to join. Invite-only also allows for an age restriction, an additional setting that requires a potential member to input their age as part of their acceptance into the group. As with Google Groups, you don't want to limit yourself to an invitation-only format. The rest of the restrictions are up to you, and are based on your need for control over who joins your community membership.

Once you create your Grouply group, you can add applications and features, re-arrange features, and change the design theme in a similar fashion as you would do on Ning. In fact, if you have built a community on Ning and decide you no longer want to pay a monthly fee, Grouply offers an easy import feature to pull data from your Ning community into a new Grouply community.

Other Community-Building Platforms

There are many options for building the framework for an online community that include forums and messaging tools. Some even let you build online spaces that are closer to social networks, with features such as profiles and friending. The options range from free to fee-based.

A free solution similar to Google Groups is Yahoo! Groups. As with Google Groups, you can set up anything from an open community to an announcement-only e-mail list (which may not be helpful to crowdsourcing). Yahoo! Groups has a set-up wizard to help you customize your group. In addition to message boards, you can upload files and photos, create a simple database to manage information, add events to a calendar, and poll your community members.

Wall.fm (wall.fm) is a free tool for community building. It includes photo and video sharing, blogs, forums, friends, groups, commenting and tagging, a rating system for content, wikis for collaboration, and file-sharing tools.

SocialGO (socialgo.com) has a free level and a premium level for $24.99/month. Their features include profiles, messaging, groups, events, chat, forums, blogging, and media uploading.

KickApps (kickapps.com) has robust, flexible features including video, audio, and image uploading and sharing; blogging and tools for idea-sharing and gathering insights; comments and ratings systems; message boards; and even points and levels to motivate members. It offers a free 30-day trial and several levels for small businesses, including Starter at $9.95 per month, Pro for $19.95 per month, Gold for $39.95 per month, Platinum for $99.95 per month, and Titanium for $299.95 per month. Their price structure is based on the number of page views per month and the amount of storage and bandwidth.

There are tools and platforms for carving out a virtual space for community building that can fit any budget and provide the necessary features. Look for a platform that has built-in tools for crowdsourcing—such as rating, voting, and polling—or be prepared to use other tools with these functionalities and link to them from your community.

Leveraging Your Crowd Community

Building a community takes time and effort. Even as people begin to join your community, there can be a long silence when nobody makes the first move to post something. It's always a good idea to seed your community with content before you even open its doors.

To seed your community in preparation of members' arrivals, you can start several discussion topics posing questions to new members. A common ice-breaker is to ask people to tell the group about themselves. You need to ask questions in your own words, and be yourself. Keep the topics as related to your crowdsourcing purpose as possible. Here are some ideas for conversation-starters:

> *Tell us about yourself!*
>
> *How and where did you first hear about our company or our products?*
>
> *What other crowdsourcing projects have you been involved with?*
>
> *What questions do you have for us?*

Not everyone will say hello or post a question or response, but this is your first chance to see who might be active group members. Knowing who is active early on can help you determine how much larger you'll need to grow your community to get the number of responses you need.

Inviting Others to Join

Many online community platforms have mechanisms for inviting people to join your community. Some provide an invitation form where you can manually type or paste in e-mail addresses. Yahoo! Groups limits you to 50 addresses. Google Groups doesn't limit how many e-mail addresses you can enter, but it does caution you against abusing the system to spam people.

Other community platforms, like Grouply, let you invite others through integrations with Yahoo! Webmail, Windows Live Hotmail, Gmail, and AOL mail. They still offer a manual-entry option, and they have the ability to import addresses from your e-mail address book.

You can find potential community members in other places, too:

- Your e-mail lists
- Social networks and microblogs
- Customer relationship management (CRM) system
- Other online communities and forums
- Offline connections and communities

To get people into your community space, you need to make announcements, invite others to invite their friends, and employ all the usual marketing tactics you might use to draw attention to something, including press releases and marketing materials. Here is a sample invitation for a crowdsourcing community:

> *We're looking to brainstorm with our customers for a name for a brand new dog snack we're bringing to market next year. As a dog owner, we know you appreciate quality products for your pet. Please join our community to answer a few surveys and take a few polls over the next two months so we can make sure we make the best dog snacks on the market. With your help, we'll produce a product people will be proud to give their pets.*
>
> *If we choose your name, you will receive a $1,000 reward and free dog snacks for a year. We hope you'll join us in this creative project. Click here to read the rules regarding participating in our project (link). Click here to sign up to be a part of our community (link).*

Make your call to action clear and provide enough details to fully explain what your community will address and what you expect from community members. Potential members will want to know what kind of time commitment they'll need to make and what's in it for them. You may want to use terms other than "crowdsourcing," such as "feedback" or "brainstorming," to reduce confusion.

Spurring Community Participation

Once people start signing up for your community, you need to make them feel welcome. You can do this through private messages to them or by posting to their profile page or announcing to the group. You can say—in your own words—something like this:

> *Welcome to our community! We're glad you've opted to participate in our brainstorming process to come up with a new name for our dog snack. Stop by the discussion forum where we have a few questions for you to answer as we gear up for the surveys and polls that will help us get closer to our goal of finding the perfect dog snack name. We look forward to hearing from you throughout this process. If you need a reminder of the description of our project or the ground rules, click here (link).*

To warm up your crowd, start by asking straightforward questions. Let them test out your polling feature with something basic. An example of wording for a preliminary poll could be:

1. **How often do you feed your dog? (Choose one.)**
   a. Once a day
   b. Twice a day
   c. Three times a day
   d. More than three times a day

2. **How often do you feed your dog snacks? (Choose one.)**
   a. Once a day
   b. Twice a day
   c. Three times a day
   d. More than three times a day

3. **What kind of snacks do you feed your dog? (Choose all that are applicable.)**
   a. Store-bought, processed
   b. Store-bought, all-natural
   c. Homemade pet snacks
   d. Table scraps or people food

4. **How important to you are the ingredients in your dog's snacks? (Choose the one that best reflects your opinion.)**
   a. Very important
   b. Important
   c. Neutral
   d. Not important

When you're ready to begin discussions with your group, the results from a previous poll can spur conversation. Keeping your community informed every step of the way gives them a sense of being an integral part of a process and gives them a chance to express their opinions and feel like they are being heard. Make sure you're listening.

Crowdsourcing Conversations

As you move further into your information-gathering process, open up the questions to invite more input and creativity. Try to avoid using open-ended questions in the beginning; closed-ended questions will allow you to more easily calculate and evaluate results. Ask open-ended questions when you are ready to receive creative input.

In the dog-snack example, you could use a private submission form to receive actual name suggestions. If you are offering a prize for the best name, you won't gain anything from having brainstorming discussions in your forums because people want to compete for the prize, not share their creative ideas with others. If you've set up your community as a brainstorming forum, you should be the first to put out ideas to gauge people's opinions.

After reviewing submissions and narrowing down the names, the next step could be to put the top names to a community vote. Using a poll format, you could simply ask community members to choose their favorite name or—if you are using a ranking survey—to rank the names. You can even ask an open-ended question after each name, such as "What do you think of when you see this name?" You can ask questions such as "How likely would you be to buy a product with this name?" or "What would convince you to buy this product for your pet?"

Every step of the way, you need to demonstrate that you are interested in hearing what your customers have to say.

Crowdsourcing Etiquette

Throughout your crowdsourcing project, be careful not to spam your members. Most communities let members change the way they receive notices from an online community they join, including turning off e-mail notifications. Your best tool for reaching your members is through e-mail, so keep the volume of notices down enough to avoid annoying anyone.

When you're ready to dive deeper into a crowdsourcing campaign, allow your members time to read through the instructions or assignment and to opt in or out of the project. Determine how many people you need to participate in a campaign and remind members where you're at and how many more people you need to complete a campaign. This can create awareness of the importance of member participation.

Remind your members periodically why they are part of the community; thank them for what they've done to date and again invite feedback about your crowdsourcing process and projects. Don't forget to ask for feedback every step of the way. Was the poll easy to access? Are there any technical issues you need to know about? You can improve your crowdsourcing process constantly by engaging your crowd members in dialogue and making them feel their input is valued.

When the Size Isn't Right

Your community may not grow to the size you need, or it may be large but still isn't delivering the kind of results you are hoping for. In some cases, your online community may grow at an exponential rate and become too large for you to manage. There is no magic number for how many community members you should have to be just the right size for crowdsourcing. You'll begin to get a sense of your particular community's critical mass when you start receiving good results from your crowd.

Keep in mind that, if you want 200 responses to each survey or poll, that doesn't mean you need 200 members. Even if you have 500 members, you may not always get 200 responses. If a common response rate for things like direct mail and online advertising is 1 to 3 percent, then a crowd of 500 would return 5 to 15 responses. Luckily, most active online communities see a 10 to 25 percent response rate to questions posed through a variety of mechanisms—usually higher for short polls than for long surveys or questionnaires. In that case, you can expect between 50 and 125 responses.

If you need at least 200 responses, you should gather a minimum of 2,000 people, and that is counting on 10 percent of your members to respond to any given survey. If you are less interested in the number of responses than the quality, 2,000 members could create a lot of noise that you'll have to sift through to get to the useful content.

If your private crowd community is not the right size or isn't rendering suitable results, it may be time to turn your crowdsourcing efforts over to a resource that has a built-in crowd with a proven track record. Your main options for crowdsourcing are a self-service site or a service provider. Use the option that renders the best results for you and fits your budget.

The Least You Need to Know

- You can't control the people who make up an online community, but you can control the appearance and mechanics of your community if you build it yourself.

- A Terms of Use document isn't legally binding, but it is specific about inappropriate activity on a site and what actions would be taken for violations of the site's rules.

- Building an online community takes the softer skills of large-scale communications and personal relationships and the more technical skills of actually constructing a virtual space for community activities.

- It is always a good idea to seed your community with content and questions before you even open its doors.

- Remind your members periodically why they are part of the community, thank them for what they've done to date, and invite feedback about your crowdsourcing process and projects.

New Product Development

In This Chapter

- Sourcing product feedback
- Improving existing products with crowds
- Crowdsourcing new product ideas
- Crowdsourcing services
- Developing idea generation sites

Whether you're crowdsourcing on your own or using a self-service crowdsourcing application, getting feedback on your company, products, and services or general input on a myriad of topics relevant to your business from a crowd is a good place to start. Involving your customers, potential customers, or the general public in discussions that can better guide your company's marketing, communications, sales, and customer relations can be invaluable.

Typically, formal market research can cost thousands or even tens of thousands of dollars. Crowdsourcing can be a more cost-effective way to get many people—especially your target market or existing customers—to give you specific product feedback.

The more highly targeted your crowd, the more relevant the responses will be as you go through your product development cycle. Keep in mind that what you ask and how you ask it can have a major impact on the results.

Crowdsource Product Input

If you are crowdsourcing for product input, as with any crowdsourcing project, you need to first identify what you want to achieve. What information do you want from the crowd, and what will you do with that information? You must then break down what you are trying to do into smaller parts. Even though you are looking for input instead of getting tasks done, distilling larger projects or concepts into smaller pieces makes them easier to manage and easier for your crowd to digest.

In terms of product input, you're likely either looking to modify an existing product or to develop a new one. In the first case, you already have a tangible product. You need to determine how to use crowdsourcing to affect some aspect of that product. You could do one or several of the following:

- Get feedback about product features and functions.

- Get new insights about your product.

- Get specific ideas for product improvements.

- Get input comparing your product to your competitors' products.

- Get ongoing feedback as you make modifications.

If you're using more traditional focus groups for product feedback—or cannot afford to implement a formal focus group—crowdsourcing feedback and input can be easier and more affordable at various points of your product cycle, from early product innovation to later research and development. Crowdsourcing is done exclusively online, so it involves fewer logistics than bringing people together in a physical space. You may also get more candid and revealing answers from an online crowd. Using the right tools and set-up, these answers would also be in a format that can be easier to review and analyze. If you've been using focus groups to date, consider adding some crowdsourcing campaigns online to complement and supplement your focus group findings.

What could crowdsourcing product input look like in action? Say you manufacture dog toys. You can pose specific questions to your crowd about features and functions, such as, "What does your pet seem to like about our Woof Ball?" and "What do you like about Woof Ball as a dog owner?" You might learn that customers are concerned that their dog might swallow the ball or that its slick exterior makes it hard to grip and throw when wet.

You might receive suggestions such as a recommendation to make medium- and large-sized balls to accommodate different-sized dogs, or to add soft bumps to the surface to make the ball easier to hold on to. You could then provide these ideas for your crowd to rank to learn which changes are most desirable. You might even find out that customers who also have cats wish they had a similar toy. Now you have the opportunity to create a new product line. You could ask your crowd if they like the name "Meow Ball," take pre-orders for the new product, and encourage your crowd to share the news of the upcoming Meow Ball with their friends.

All of these steps are crowdsourcing activities. You can move crowdsourcing for product input into more long-term product testing using the same crowd that provided the initial feedback. You could send out product samples and get real-life testing. You could also turn to a professional testing crowd through self-service crowdsourcing sites or companies.

When to Ask for Input

If you are already developing products and bringing them to market, you are probably familiar with a product development cycle. At the start of the cycle are the activities you do in pre-development. Some steps in this early stage include looking into the technical aspects of manufacturing your product and checking out the supply chain landscape to figure out where you'll get your product made and how you'll get it to market. Most of the technical side of product development requires research that shouldn't necessarily be crowdsourced.

Simultaneous to the behind-the-scenes steps to getting a product to market, you need to conduct market research to evaluate the size of your potential market and clearly identify your target customers. You can implement crowdsourcing techniques during the market assessment stage, bringing together or reaching out to people who represent your potential customers to gain insights into their needs and interests, and to determine the likelihood that they will buy your product. All the testing of your product concept is done before you go into production.

Once you develop a product prototype or sample, you can continue to use your crowd—or other specialized crowds—to evaluate your product. You could send them samples and get their feedback in an organized fashion, usually by requesting they fill out web-based forms or participate in online discussion forums. It's up to you whether you consider the feedback you get from the crowd at each step of the product development cycle. You can revise your product concept, revise a prototype, and if necessary, make additional revisions after the first run of your actual product.

Involving an organized and receptive crowd in your product development cycle can bring information to bear that may never come out of more formal focus groups or more limited data gathering from your own organization. Through crowdsourcing, you can reduce time to market and improve outcomes, as well as have a pool of potential customers ready to purchase your product as soon as it hits the shelves. Involve your internal supply chain experts or bring in external experts if you are crowdsourcing product-cycle input to help vet and process crowd feedback.

Improving Existing Products

In the same way you can tap into a crowd for input on product concepts and prototypes, you can bring a crowd together or reach out to a crowd to get feedback on an existing product. This type of interaction is often referred to as a *feedback loop*, a term taken from the plant sciences to refer to how negative feedback can counterbalance positive feedback to maintain homeostasis (balance and stability).

> **DEFINITION**
>
> A customer **feedback loop** is a mechanism set up to get feedback—both positive and negative—from customers so that you can make modifications to a product or service, particularly in response to negative feedback, to improve that product or service.

Crowdsourcing can drive the engine for your customer feedback loop. You need to build the mechanisms to solicit, assess, and use feedback from customers who are already using your product. This mechanism can be as basic as a feedback form on your site that inputs the data received into a repository, such as a database or spreadsheet, where you can sort through the feedback and then put that information to use. The mechanism can also be a more organized crowd effort to obtain specific and ongoing feedback that informs changes and improvements to your product before your next product run.

Changing a product post-production can be very expensive, which is why leveraging crowd input earlier in the process can help you avoid major changes needed later.

Sourcing New Product Ideas

Many companies use crowdsourcing to test concepts for new products they've already conceptualized or to improve existing products. Some companies have research and development divisions that identify opportunities for new products, analyze those opportunities, assess the product concepts, and then select and refine the best ideas. You can turn this process over to crowds to source ideas from broader and wider groups.

Crowd members can contribute ideas that are then assessed by a company or by a middleman—a crowdsourcing services provider (CSP)—or even voted on by their peers. The best ideas rise to the top, and the company can select the idea or ideas they want to use. With the right process and tools in place, you can put out a call for ideas to crowds who enjoy coming up with ideas. In some cases, monetary awards are offered to the "winning" idea.

Once an idea for a new product is selected, the new product development cycle kicks in with market testing and prototyping until the product is ready for market. In some cases, a new product idea is scrapped as it moves through the assessment cycle but before it goes into production, saving wasted money in the long run.

Examples of Crowdsourced Products

Putting systems into place to capture a crowd's critical feedback is important to building a better product or offering a better service than your competitors. Market research and focus groups aside, crowdsourcing offers flexibility, immediate and varied responses, and the ability to get ongoing input throughout the development cycle.

Companies from startups to mega-corporations are finding ways to cull and analyze input from crowds—consisting of both their own customers and other relevant crowds—to obtain feedback on their product or service offerings. Their feedback loop systems can be as simple as feedback forms or as complex as crowd gatherings and interactions.

Crowdsourcing Goods

Many manufacturers of hard goods use crowdsourcing techniques to integrate customer feedback into their product development and sales cycles. Furniture company Furniture4Home lets customers vote on new products directly on their website before they manufacture them. The most popular items based on crowd input are produced in an amount commensurate with actual demand. Another furniture company, Made.com, presents a similar voting process on its site and adds the most popular products—including sofas, chairs, tables, and cabinets—to their collection.

Some crowdsourcing product development is conducted through more organized crowds and a third-party CSP. When high-end footwear company RYZ first started out, they turned directly to their customers for sneaker design ideas for their website. They let other customers vote on the ideas and then produced the winning designs, awarding the winning designers $1,000 each. Later, RYZ turned to the Keystone Design Union (KDU), a design and communications agency with a crowd of over 1,000 creatives spanning 80 countries who are members of the "union." RYZ was looking for fresh designs for their footwear, and chose 20 designs from submissions that came via KDU artists in the United Kingdom, Europe, Australia, South America, Central America, Asia, Canada, and the United States. They called the subsequent product line the World Paradigm Collection.

DULY NOTED

From the start, wine brand development company Canopy Management wanted their core market—women who drink or purchase wine—to become an integral part of their brand and product development cycle. After bringing a number of new wine brands to market, the company launched the Wine Sisterhood, consisting of a Facebook Page and a Twitter account where they invited women to join discussions about wine.

On their Facebook page, they regularly survey their fans using the survey builder site Zoomerang, asking questions specific to new wine brands they are developing. In one survey, they asked for feedback on the font size on an existing wine label, PromisQous. The crowd picked the largest version at 120 percent of the original font size. The company made the change.

In another survey, Canopy asked their Wine Sisterhood community to pick the name they liked the most out of four names: Goodie Two Shoes, Divalicious, Fashionista, and Super Star. Forty-six percent of the crowd chose Goodie Two Shoes. The company debuted the Goodie Two Shoes Pinot Noir within months of the final vote.

Crowdsourcing Services

Crowdsourcing techniques for input and feedback don't have to be limited to real products. Services companies can modify the services they offer and how they deliver their services, add features to existing services, or even come up with new services based on customer input and demand. Services can be offered in person offline, entirely online, or both. Any service company can benefit from going straight to the crowd before, during, and after they develop and deliver services.

Chargify, a billing-systems company, lets customers vote on new features listed in their customer service forums. Some of the ideas generated in the forum include a way to calculate simple sales tax and a way to easily convert invoices into a PDF format. Customers click on a **Vote** button, and the most popular feature suggestions rise to the top of the list for the company's developers to review, consider, and potentially implement.

> **DULY NOTED**
>
> Before you open up your project to a crowd, pay close attention to privacy issues of crowd members and any legal issues that might arise regarding the data you use or distribute to the crowd. When in doubt, check with a lawyer.

Not all crowdsourcing efforts happen quickly. If you're not careful, some could land you in hot water. In 2006, the online movie rental company Netflix challenged the general public to build a better recommendation algorithm for their service. They offered a $1 million prize. To get to a solution, Netflix provided over 40,000 groups from nearly 200 countries with over 100 million movie recommendations culled from Netflix members to evaluate.

Three years later, the Netflix competition was considered a success, when a team of mathematicians and computer engineers calling themselves BellKor's Pragmatic Chaos improved Netflix's own Cinematch recommendation system by 10 percent. This seemingly incremental improvement made the company's service offerings significantly better. But despite the original competition's success, Netflix decided not to pursue a similar competition the following year due to concerns from the Federal Trade Commission (FTC) regarding the privacy of Netflix member data. The FTC objected to the personal information that may have been revealed in the data culled from Netflix members and provided to teams participating in the first contest.

Trying an Idea Generation Site

Ideas are the sparks that allow things to happen, the basis of almost everything one does in business. Every product or service a company offers starts with an idea. Every aspect of marketing consists of ideas. Moving forward on any project involves coming up with good ideas.

What happens if you feel like you've run out of ideas or your team is stuck in a creative rut? Some companies embark on inspiration activities to get their creative juices flowing, such as going on innovation retreats. Others bring in consultants to facilitate internal brainstorming sessions. At times like these, putting a project out to a crowd and letting many minds work on generating new ideas may be a useful step.

Idea sourcing can range from problem solving to new product ideation, or from naming a company to coming up with its tagline. Self-service crowdsourcing sites or CSPs can bring together crowds to supply ideas. These sites and companies often use an awards system or some kind of monetary incentive to motivate and compensate participants—or at least those who come up with winning ideas.

Social Product Development

There are companies that gather crowds specifically to help source great product ideas they then put into production. The ideas can be voted on by crowd members to not only identify the best ideas, but also to foster a built-in customer base for the products. Some of these companies work with other companies and individuals to make their product ideas a reality by offering not just the idea gathering and vetting but also the manufacturing process to bring the product to market.

If you have an idea for a product you want to bring to market but don't have the manufacturing infrastructure in place, you could submit your idea to a site like Quirky. Quirky is backed by a creative team partnered with an online community to develop and sell products worldwide. As the product inventor, you provide the idea, and the eventual revenue from the product that goes to market is split between you, Quirky, and community members, also known as "influencers."

You can post your idea to Quirky for $10, and the company picks one idea per week as a winning idea. Then, the Quirky community weighs in on everything from the product name, tagline, and logo to the actual product specifications and design. Next, the Quirky engineers and designers render 2D and 3D illustrations of your product.

Along the way, Quirky and their community determine the product price point and how many pre-sales are needed to break even. The community members can even pre-order products to provide a sense of interest and demand. Additional sales and marketing efforts take place even before the product has gone into production. Quirky community members promote the products via social tools. You can see your idea become a tangible product and track your earnings through the Quirky site.

Social Idea Generation

There are sites where you can seek out ideas. IdeaOffer is a basic site for idea generation to help you on a variety of projects. On IdeaOffer, pose your project, situation, dilemma, or question to the crowd. Then, decide on a reward amount you will pay to someone whose idea you select. You can also opt to pay several people. Rewards range from under a dollar to about $100, although the prize sizes continue to grow and there is no upper limit. Reward amounts can affect both the number of ideas you receive and the quality of those ideas. You also need to set the duration of your project.

Next, transfer money into your IdeaOffer account to pay crowd members when you pick an idea to use. You can pay via PayPal or credit card. IdeaOffer adds a small percentage on top of your reward for an administration fee. Once you publish your project, crowd members are notified by e-mail of new offers that may be of interest to them. They can view your project and, if they have ideas, submit their responses easily. You're then notified that you have responses to review. You can log in to the IdeaOffer site to see ideas submitted.

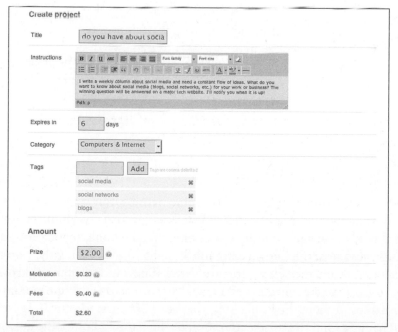

To crowdsource ideas for a project, give it a title and description, and then set the duration, a category, tags, and a prize amount for the winning idea.

(Courtesy of IdeaOffer)

Manage your projects on your IdeaOffer dashboard, where you can access idea submissions and select the winning response.
(Courtesy of IdeaOffer)

You can pick an idea at any time prior to the project's expiration, or you can let the project expire and then pick from the submissions within seven days. IdeaOffer not only pays the responder you've selected, but also gives small motivation amounts split amongst all legitimate responders. You can disqualify responses by flagging them for review.

Appropriate projects for a site like IdeaOffer include ideas for articles you are writing, feedback on your website, ideas for how to make your site more effective from a user standpoint, marketing and public relationships queries, and even requests for business contacts and connections. IdeaOffer provides a crowd who will address your questions. Responses vary in quality, but the site is a useful tool for a small monetary commitment. There is also survey functionality that makes feedback from the crowd quantifiable and exportable as a CSV file.

An idea generation site specifically for sourcing ideas for names—for products, websites, companies, and more—is NamingForce. Create a naming assignment—also referred to by the company as a crowdsource naming contest—fund the competition award, and then monitor submissions. Namers may also send a query for a better description of the assignment or pose additional questions to you. You can purchase a naming package at the budget level for $150—$50 of which is the non-refundable processing fee—and expect to receive around 100 or more submissions. The Standard Level costs $250 and generates 150 names or more, and the Premium level costs $575 for 300 names or more. For the latter, the fee is $75 instead of $50. If you can't find a suitable name within the 30-day duration of the naming competition, you can apply for a refund of the award amount, but not of any additional fees.

Putting Customer Input to Use

Companies use crowdsourcing in different ways and at different stages of their product development cycle. Similar techniques can be used to source ideas and feedback on actual goods, tangible products that are then manufactured and sold online or at retail establishments, or both.

Bringing a crowd in at any stage of the development cycle can prove valuable, but make sure the feedback is aggregated and assessed at points when you can implement actual suggestions. Crowdsourcing challenges companies to be more receptive to feedback—not only to hearing it, but also to actually using it. A commitment to crowdsourcing means a company needs to be more nimble and flexible to implement change.

Legal Issues of Ownership

Many idea-generation sites include legal language that informs crowd participants that they relinquish all claims to rights or ownership of what they submit when they submit an idea, name, or other content.

A sample disclaimer could contain the following message:

> *By posting an idea as content to this site, you are agreeing to transfer intellectual property rights for any and all content submitted. Posting content that violates, misappropriates, or in any way infringes on the intellectual property rights of others is prohibited. To ensure compliance, please review our Terms of Use before posting content to this site. By posting to the site, you are confirming you have read the Terms of Use (link) in its entirety.*

Confer with a lawyer to ensure your disclaimers and Terms of Use are appropriate, effective, and compliant with laws and regulations pertaining to what you are doing and putting online.

Creators as Customers

Sites that source crowd input prior to manufacturing a product not only get a sense of the demand for the product, but also cultivate a customer base even before anything has gone to market. Many sites bring people together to generate ideas or designs that the crowd can then purchase when the product is finalized—for example, Quirky, the t-shirt company Threadless, and the furniture sites Furniture4Home and Made.com.

The website ModCloth lets customers pre-order and fund the collections of up-and-coming designers, putting them in the role of the fashion buyer. Anyone can help determine what fashions get produced and sold on the site by clicking the buttons **Pick It!** or **Skip It!**. Those who vote can then buy their picks and see upcoming products that made the cut. Involving site visitors and actual customers in the fashion buying process reinforces the designs most likely to sell well on the site. Being involved in the selection process is a stimulus for someone to then purchase the designs they've voted on and liked.

Creators as Marketers

A possible byproduct of bringing together a crowd of people as a source for ideas and input is that your crowd could become a built-in marketing force for you and your company. Consider the Quirky model of product development: the members of the Quirky crowd not only provide input during the development cycle of a product, but they also become de facto product marketers. Quirky builds in social tools so their crowd members can spread the word about a product idea before it even becomes a tangible product.

Using Facebook, Twitter, and other social tools, community members can point more attention to your product, including driving traffic directly to an order-taking mechanism. You could get pre-orders by spurring your crowds into letting their contacts know about your product.

With your crowd serving as a built-in customer base, you can encourage members to spread the word by involving them in product development and input, producing a great product, and providing good customer service. Crowdsourcing for input can help you with everything but the hard manufacturing tasks.

Customers as Creators

When you crowdsource product input, it usually means you are taking input from many people at once, using the crowd as a vehicle to obtain answers or solutions. What if you take the suggestions and ideas of individuals—many individuals over time—and gain important insights about customer preferences from their choices and actions?

Co-creation is sometimes mentioned along with crowdsourcing, but it doesn't quite fit the model. Co-creation is a form of product customization wherein companies give consumers the tools, supplies, or resources to create a more customized product or service on the fly. Tech companies like Cisco and Dell have been co-creating custom electronic and computer solutions for years, letting customers pick and choose the features of their hardware purchases and then custom-building to order.

Some examples of co-creation in less technical arenas include:

- **Blank Label (blank-label.com):** Lets customers design their own dress shirts for men from a blank slate.

- **FashionPlaytes (fashionplaytes.com):** Lets girls select from different design elements to customize clothing that they—or their parents—can buy.

- **Design a Tea (designatea.com):** Lets customers pick a base tea and add their favorite flavors to create a custom blend.

- **Chocri (createmychocolate.com):** Lets customers select ingredients to add to chocolate bars—from dried strawberries to bacon bits to gold flakes—that they can then purchase.

This kind of hyper-customization doesn't seem to fit the conventional definition of crowdsourcing, but the process puts more power into the hands of consumers—the crowd—and they can pick and choose elements of a product before the company produces the product. Companies can then take this data in aggregate and predict what new product will find a market based on individual customers' creations and purchases.

Accessing the input of many individual customers can lead you to creating a product that addresses real consumer needs and tastes. That kind of data mining can take you beyond the ideas and input generated through internal brainstorming, external market research, and focus groups.

The Least You Need to Know

- What you ask and how you ask it can have a major impact on the results of your crowdsourcing efforts.

- Involving an organized and receptive crowd in your product development cycle can provide you with information that you might never get out of formal focus groups or more limited data gathering within your organization.

- You need to build the mechanisms to solicit, assess, and use feedback from customers who are already using your product.

- Bringing a crowd in at any stage of the product development cycle can prove valuable, but make sure you aggregate the feedback and assess it when you can actually implement the suggestions.

Employee Crowdsourcing Communities

In This Chapter

- Sourcing your internal company or virtual team
- Understanding privacy and security issues
- Creating a safe space for internal crowdsourcing
- Using tools to crowdsource with your team

You can find a crowd in many places, both online and off. The trick to crowdsourcing is to utilize online tools and communities to access or gather the crowd, and then manage communications and interactions with them. Ultimately, you must use Internet and web-based tools to crowdsource.

Your Employees as Your Crowd

A crowd you're probably tapping into on a regular if ad-hoc basis is your on-site employees or virtual team members. Wikipedia's definition of crowdsourcing suggests you can't do it with your internal team. It makes sense that sitting in a boardroom with staff or participating on a conference call and having a discussion or brainstorming session isn't sourcing a crowd. But what if you put online mechanisms in place, in either an open or private forum, to garner input from everyone in your company—not just a specific subset of your team? Certainly sounds like crowdsourcing.

You can probably point to many situations in which internal crowdsourcing has taken place within your company—you just didn't call it that. Like the time you didn't have an answer to a business question, so you sent out an e-mail to everyone in the company and posed the question to them. Then, you manually sifted through the answers to find the best one. Chances are, you gleaned information from almost every answer you reviewed, gaining new insights into how your team members work and think.

Input, feedback, and problem-solving are all viable uses of crowdsourcing, even with your work team as your crowd. By using an open-source method, you open up the process to everyone, regardless of their role in the company or their location. As long as everyone has access to the same online tools and can gather and participate in a shared space on equal footing, they are your crowd.

Reaching Out Securely

The Internet is an essential business tool for almost every company these days, but how are you using it to crowdsource your team? If your team is physically in one location, you could use a combination of your company's Intranet or internal communications systems for crowdsourcing efforts. If you plan to use anything on the Internet at large, you need to make sure the crowdsourcing tools you choose are compatible with your company's firewall.

Here are some top-level things you need to consider before you crowdsource your team:

- **Security:** Consider how secure your internal communications need to be and choose the tools and their locations accordingly.

- **Redundancy:** Make sure the software applications you use and the data they contain are backed up, and be sure to have failsafes in place so you don't lose data if any system goes down.

- **Access:** The easier it is for your team members to access the crowdsourcing tools and campaigns you initiate, the more likely your campaigns will succeed.

- **Compatibility:** Choose crowdsourcing tools that integrate well with one another, or that at least do not present a conflict with other software applications and server environments already in use.

- **Policies:** Put policies in place that team members must read and sign off on to ensure they understand proper use and engagement and the consequences of abusing the tools or forums.

- **Training:** Provide team members with in-house training or provide online training tools to get them up to speed on any new application you use for crowdsourcing, to reduce entry barriers.

In some cases, companies put their internal interactive and collaborative spaces on the Internet outside of their firewall, a process referred to as *cloudworking, cloud computing*, or *working in the cloud*. Team members can upload content onto secure servers on the Internet so the work and communications archived there can be accessed by the team via usernames and passwords from anywhere at any time.

> **DEFINITION**
>
> **Cloudworking,** or **working in the cloud,** refers to utilizing online-based systems and applications on secure servers to share resources, software, and information. The more technical term for this type of arrangement is **cloud computing.**

You can host collaborative tools in a private cloud, a more secure server environment outside of your company's on-site servers. Private cloudwork spaces can't be seen or accessed by anyone outside your company. An even more secure option is to have crowdsourcing applications installed on a server within your firewall that integrate with the rest of the on-site applications on your Intranet.

Reaching Virtual Workers

The Internet is at the heart of assembling a virtual workforce. Without the Internet, we wouldn't have the prevalence of telecommuting, cloudworking, and virtual companies we have today. Because the Internet has completely transformed communications across borders and time zones, the idea of a company needing a physical location, with its workers traveling to a single office, is starting to seem almost quaint.

If you have a virtual office consisting of a virtual team, and everyone works from their own locations, you're already connecting and using the Internet to communicate online. Depending on the sites and applications you're using to interact with your virtual team, you may already have the basic tools you need to crowdsource. You need to put them together to source your crowd—in this case your virtual team members—in a more organized way.

Pay close attention to security issues to ensure information is safe; redundancy issues, so information doesn't get lost; access issues, to make sure everyone on the team can get in; compatibility issues, to better integrate your crowdsourcing tools into the tools you're already using; and policies and training for your virtual team.

What to Crowdsource Internally

Before you research the tools you'll use for crowdsourcing your team, consider what you can accomplish by sourcing your internal crowd. There are many situations in which crowdsourcing makes sense. Here are some scenarios.

You're looking to augment your sales pipeline. This is the sales department's territory, but what if you opened up lead generation to the team and offered incentives? You could create a leads submission form that team members could fill out when they have an idea about a new prospect for the company. You never know where your next lead will come from, but if you don't ask, you could be overlooking a potential wealth of ideas from outside of sales. Offer to pay a finder's fee to each lead that turns into a contract.

Let's say you want to improve workflow. You can gain insights to better understand the barriers to efficiency and discover ways to improve work processes from the very people who are doing the work. You can post an anonymous questionnaire that feeds input into a spreadsheet for your review. Pose tough questions, and assure everyone that their identities will be hidden to prompt more candid responses. Ask for solutions. Apply what you learn to develop a more appropriate model for change.

You're considering rebranding your company, including a new name and logo. Why not turn the assignment over to your employees for their feedback and input? Explain the rationale behind the change. Allow the team to submit questions to further clarify the direction. Provide mechanisms for employees to submit name ideas. Include a voting platform so team members can vote for their favorites. Even if you don't choose an employee idea for the final name or logo, clearly explain the final decision and give recognition to the most popular suggestions. Being part of the creative process—even if they're not on the creative team—can give employees a sense of ownership, and that can increase loyalty.

Crowdsourcing your team doesn't mean you're obligated to put their ideas and input to use if they aren't suitable. Chances are you'll get valuable insights you never anticipated, regardless of the final outcome. Keep the lines of communication and information exchange open even when you're not running an active internal crowd-sourcing campaign, and make sure participants feel appreciated and heard.

Company-Wide Crowdsourcing Toolkit

In organizations, adopting new software takes consideration and planning. Not every type of crowdsourcing with your internal team or employee crowd requires specialized tools. Looking at the do-it-yourself approach to crowdsourcing, your internal team can probably be most useful with projects that are easy to track and measure.

Using e-mail to ask questions can work for ad-hoc crowdsourcing, but there are limitations to e-mail that could hamper your internal crowdsourcing efforts. Consider the following:

- **Privacy:** When you send an e-mail and carbon copy or "cc" recipients, everyone copied on the e-mail sees everyone else's name. This can create confusion and unintended communications. This is not an optimal way to gather responses. You can blind carbon copy or "bcc" people to avoid confusion, but then you still face the task of managing responses.

- **Tracking:** After a certain point, e-mail is less than ideal for keeping track of responses. A spreadsheet could make tracking easier, but you still have to extract the data from the e-mails. Usually, this is done by copying and pasting responses into a spreadsheet from each separate e-mail.

- **Archiving:** Keeping e-mails in your e-mail program isn't the ideal way to archive data you're collecting, even if you organize the e-mails in folders or use labels or tags. If you're using e-mail for crowdsourcing, you could save each e-mail as a text file, or copy and paste e-mail contents into a single document, to preserve an archive. Again, you're forced to use a lot of manual measures to manage crowdsourced data.

- **Anonymity:** Something you may not have considered when you've asked for input from your team in the past is the issue of anonymity. Do you want to allow team members to respond anonymously, so they feel more comfortable being open with their input? Unfortunately, e-mail doesn't preserve a respondent's anonymity from you, the recipient.

When crowdsourcing your internal team, be sure to efficiently capture and preserve the data you gather and organize it in a format that is easy to sort and analyze.

Collaborative Workspaces

If you engage in crowdsourcing with your internal team, you could use one of the popular virtual workspaces or workplace collaborative tools, such as Glasscubes, Basecamp, and Zoho. See Chapter 4 for a breakdown of some of the features included in popular collaborative workspace products.

A more enterprise-level collaborative application for organizations is Socialtext, which offers internal social-network features, blogs, microblog-like announcements, groups, collaborative spreadsheets, wiki workspaces, and document integration. Socialtext offers a free version of its software and services for up to 50 people, along with a 30-day trial for paid levels. Pricing starts at $5,000 per year for larger groups, or you can call the company for a quote if you require additional customization. Instead of using e-mail, you can pose questions using the microblogging tool on the Socialtext platform and tag each question with a unique tag to track responses.

Being able to reach out to your team and communicate as a group can produce fertile ground for crowdsourcing. A collaborative workspace may not always work for internal crowdsourcing, particularly if you need to preserve individual anonymity or if you have strict security needs.

Real-Time Communications Tools

Some collaborative workspace tools include a real-time communications mechanism such as instant messaging (IM) or web-based chat. You can also find free-standing IM solutions such as Skype and Windows Live Messenger. In most crowdsourcing activities, real-time response isn't needed or would be hard to manage, especially if you're seeking participation from hundreds or thousands of people. But when you're crowdsourcing your own team, or a small division within your larger company, the ability to ask a question in real time and get responses back almost instantly can be handy. If you're dealing with dozens of employees or team members, you may be better off using the *asynchronous* communications of collaborative workspaces.

DEFINITION

Asynchronous means not happening at the same time. Most crowdsourcing happens asynchronously, meaning your activities and the activities of the crowd are not happening simultaneously.

You can install many free-to-use IM tools behind your firewall in an enterprise situation. Some of them can also be used securely on the web. IM applications include the following:

- **Google Talk:** Also known as Gtalk, this feature is built right into Gmail and Google Apps. It also has call and video features, although these aren't necessarily needed when crowdsourcing.

- **Windows Live Messenger:** Formerly known as MSN Messenger, this IM client comes with the Windows operating system, and includes audio and video. There is also a Mac version.

- **iChat:** This IM client is built into the Macintosh operating system and works with AIM. iChat offers video chat in addition to text IM.

- **AIM:** A product of AOL, this IM client works on Windows, Mac, iPhone, Android, iPad, Blackberry, and Windows Mobile.

- **Skype*:** This free voice-over Internet protocol (VOIP) application lets you make long-distance audio and video phone calls, but it also has an IMing system and desktop-sharing feature.

- **Campfire**:** This product is designed for groups and offers team collaboration with real-time chat. You can share text and files within the group. You can get a 30-day free trial, but this is a paid service. They also have an iPhone app.

- **Socialcast:** You can start using this system for free, and then ramp up to an enterprise solution to access a microblogging-style communications tool that includes groups, private messages, polls, employee profiles, and desktop clients.

- **Jabber:** An enterprise-level collaborative communications and IM system offered by Cisco.

Skype is also a free solution for long-distance calls over the Internet.
**Campfire integrates with the collaborative tool Basecamp.*

Even though some of the IM solutions also offer voice, crowdsourcing for input should facilitate gathering many responses with the least amount of manual effort to accumulate the data into a format that is easy to assess and analyze. If you have voice conversations, you need to record those conversations and most likely transcribe them, too. Crowdsourced data in text is easier to analyze than audio and video content. If you need transcription services, see Chapter 19.

In-House Surveys and Polls

Some collaboration and communications tools have polling features built into them. Both Glasscubes and Socialcast contain built-in poll builders. There are also numerous poll and survey builders, including PollDaddy, Zoomerang, QuickSnack, SurveyMonkey, and Survey Gizmo. See Chapter 4 for a breakdown of costs.

You can use Google Forms to generate simple surveys or input forms that connect to Google Spreadsheets, all for free. You can then export the data from the online spreadsheet into a number of different formats, including Microsoft Excel and comma-delimited text files.

Whether you want to use a free-standing poll or survey-building tool, one that plugs into other communications tools you're using, or a polling system already integrated into your communications platform, there are a variety of solutions to suit your needs.

Creating a Safe Space

Any organization that bases its internal and external communications on honesty with positive feedback and support can cultivate an environment that is perceived as safe for employees. Hostile environments occur when employees speak their mind and are then ridiculed, chastised, reprimanded, or made to feel threatened in some way.

When team leaders are honest and open, it gives everyone else permission to follow suit. When you as a leader accept feedback in a positive way—even if the feedback is negative—you become a role model for the positive behavior and attitudes you expect your team to adopt.

Creating a safe space depends on clearly communicating expectations. You can't expect your team to read your mind and know your expectations just by watching your behavior. Clearly state your communications philosophy and your ideas about collaboration amongst team members, especially across departmental lines. Lay the ground rules for participation and engagement in crowdsourcing activities, including rules regarding confidentiality or nondisclosure of information and ideas generated in internal group forums.

Here are some other things to keep in mind to help foster a culture of openness and inclusion:

- Use "we" instead of "I," but "I" instead of "you" to minimize blaming.

- Accept criticism calmly and consider it thoughtfully, rather than responding in a knee-jerk way that may seem defensive.

- Thank everyone who provides feedback, either personally if submitted in private or publicly if submitted in an open forum.

- Provide a mechanism by which team members can submit input anonymously. If needed, explain how this can be used.

- Take important or sensitive issues offline, rather than carrying out the mediation in the public forum.

- Be sensitive to the personalities and politics that can dominate group interactions, but don't enable them.

- Focus on the idea, issue, or problem—not on an individual.

- Allow for a healthy dose of competition to energize and motivate team members, but keep an eye on dialogue to make sure there are no personal attacks or undermining behavior.

Regardless of how open, honest, and positive you are, you may still be faced with the dynamic of the employees as a group. Not everyone responds well to the same openness you might be trying to foster. Negative competition and attitudes could stem from insecurities of a few individuals. You need to identify where the negativity is coming from and address it head-on to demonstrate your commitment to open communications.

Avoiding Groupthink

When groups come together to collaborate, a phenomenon that organizational analysts and psychologists refer to as *groupthink* can occur. Wikipedia describes groupthink as "a type of thought within a deeply cohesive in-group whose members try to minimize conflict and reach consensus without critically testing, analyzing, and evaluating ideas."

DEFINITION

The term **groupthink** was coined by organizational analyst William H. Whyte in a 1952 *Fortune* magazine article. He defined it as "a rationalized conformity—an open, articulate philosophy which holds that group values are not only expedient but right and good as well." Irving Janis, a Yale University psychologist, studied and published extensively about groupthink.

Groupthink causes a group member's independent thinking to weaken in favor of either the opinions of others or of a dominant leader. In the case of employees, expressing ideas or opinions that differ from the rest of the group may be intimidating for some on your team. Some employees may also agree with you or echo your ideas, rather than challenge a leader.

There are several ways to avoid groupthink or to recognize and minimize it. First, check yourself and the way you lead your company or department. Do employees readily come to you for input or advice? If a situation is high pressure, are you able to respond to requests from employees with a calm and nonthreatening demeanor? If you've bred a culture of fear in your organization, chances are others may be unwilling to express ideas that contradict yours.

Next, check the environment. Functional and collaborative groups support their members. In a healthy group, members provide improvements on ideas submitted for group consideration, and the group doesn't diminish the contributors of those ideas. Encourage and reward diverse and out-of-the-box thinking. Also, put group-developed ideas into action so everyone can see the fruits of their collective labor. All these steps are the foundation of an effective crowdsourcing model.

Here are some additional suggestions for avoiding groupthink:

- Provide a clear and organized process for group participation.
- Include diverse contributors and accept diverse contributions.
- Hold off on sharing input from company heads until the team has had a chance to participate.
- Let several independent groups work separately on the same project.
- Incorporate outside experts to keep group participation fresh and dynamic.

The problem of groupthink may seem like a group's shortcoming, but more than likely the problem stems from the leadership and environment exacerbating underlying issues. Take a personal and environmental inventory before you write off the potential benefits of team crowdsourcing.

Fostering Crowd Collaboration

Surveys and polls are individual exercises, but collaboration requires interaction. Even though employees should work as a team, this isn't always the case. Your company's culture may not be conducive to collaborative crowdsourcing or brainstorming. If that's the case, you need to first begin to nurture an environment in which you and others encourage, support, and even reward open communications and idea exchange.

In addition to a supportive culture, team collaboration works best when you have a ...

* **Shared vision:** This should be guidance from the top, but it shouldn't be dictated by the leadership in your company.

* **Shared workspace:** This can be real or virtual space where collaboration can happen.

* **Shared forum:** This is a place or time for live or asynchronous discussions.

* **Shared knowledge base:** This is an archive of information that involves technology behind the scenes, where any data exchanged can also be stored, accessed, and searched.

Provide an environment and platform where team members can submit their input; give candid—and in some cases anonymous—feedback; and even review, comment, and vote on peer submissions. The culture you lead can greatly affect your team crowdsourcing efforts.

BEST PRACTICES

The best collaboration and brainstorming takes place in an open environment with diverse participation. Your team should have access to outside information sources—namely the Internet—without the company firewall restricting their access.

Sharing Outcomes

Every person is motivated by his or her own set of conditions, but for most people, seeing the fruits of one's labor can be a strong motivator. When you're crowdsourcing with your employees or virtual team as your crowd, remember to present the results of what you've crowdsourced in an appropriate way so everyone can feel a sense of contribution and ownership of the outcome.

What constitutes an appropriate way to share outcomes? There are many ways to present and discuss the results of your crowdsourcing efforts. Because you are sourcing your team online, posting results online in the crowdsourcing forums you're using makes sense. Depending on the type of project you crowdsourced, sometimes presenting only the facts in writing isn't enough—you might miss some of the nuances that could prove valuable information for your team. Consider presenting the results in person or, if you're working with your virtual team, by phone or video conference.

Empowering Your Team

Team members can be empowered through crowdsourcing, but only if the projects or campaigns are clear. With an anonymous crowd, you have to be clear when explaining what you want. With your internal crowd, you have to be even clearer. Make sure you clearly articulate your internal crowdsourcing process, describing exactly how you will approve, accept, or determine the final outcome. Without a clear path to the finish line, your employees or team members could get lost along the way and misunderstand how you will approve the final outcome, which could breed frustration or impact outcomes negatively.

Even when your crowdsourcing campaign has come to a close, don't miss opportunities for continued discussion and ideation about the outcome. This doesn't mean enabling a never-ending collaborative process that doesn't yield definitive results, but it does mean keeping an open mind for future improvements or additional input. Crowdsourcing can be utilized through an iterative process.

Groups function best with leaders who are open, accepting, encouraging, and nonthreatening. Every collaborative situation and system benefits from continued modification and improvement. Look for ways to improve your own crowdsourcing methods by requesting and incorporating suggestions from your internal team so that your outcomes get better and better over time.

The Least You Need to Know

- Foster a culture of openness to ensure your internal company crowdsourcing efforts bear fruit.

- Be sensitive to how others in your company respond to you to gauge if crowdsourcing can work.

- Consider setting up an anonymous feedback mechanism to create an alternative communication form that employees or team members may find comfortable.

- Avoid the pitfalls of crowdsourcing in closed groups by modeling acceptance of both positive and negative input.

- Empower your team by including them in group collaboration and decision-making, and by sharing the results of their participation.

Going to Crowds for Answers

In This Chapter

- Crafting questions to get the "right" answers
- Recognizing limitations of free general answer sites
- Using fee-based answer sites
- Working with problem-solving crowds
- Understanding answers from the crowd

The concept of going to crowds for answers isn't new. In fact, reaching out to groups to find answers to questions or to solve problems went on long before we had Internet-based communities. Today, there are open and managed crowdsourced answer sites, and you can find either free or fee-based services. These answer sites offer a service referred to as informational crowdsourcing.

When Crowd Answers Count

Since the 1990s, there have been websites that attempt to bring people together to answer questions. In most early cases, the answer communities were made up of researchers and responders who were contract workers or who were paid nominal fees for their time or per question.

One site that brought a crowd together to answer questions was Google Answers, formed in 2002 by Internet giant Google. The site was referred to as an "online knowledge market" where the general public could offer bounties, usually ranging between $2 and $200, to get answers to their questions. Questions ran the gamut from business topics such as where to print company holiday cards to industry research and statistics to more personal queries about household appliances or family issues. Askers could offer a reward to the responder. Google kept a percentage of each reward, plus a small per-question fee. Google closed their answering system at the end of 2006; maintaining a question and answer site with paid research contractors was a challenge.

Most current general-topic crowd answer sites don't involve contracting researchers, mainly because that model is hard to sustain. The flip side to using a free answer site where responders are not compensated is you may get less-reliable answers.

Crowdsourcing answers may not always generate consistent results, but more often than not, you will receive some kind of value in return for a fair price. The simpler your question, the less of an expert or qualified crowd you need to get acceptable answers. Some sites have a system in which you offer a *bounty* for the best answer. More complex questions may require a larger bounty, or you might be better off going to a more targeted, organized, and vetted crowd.

> **DEFINITION**
>
> A **bounty** is a payment made by one party to another. In the case of crowd-sourcing, a bounty is also referred to as a prize, award, reward, tip, fee, payment, or compensation.

Crafting the Right Question

The type of questions you ask and the way you ask them can guide the success of your campaign. Using a crowd to answer questions works best when you have several factors in place:

- **The right type of crowd:** What is the right crowd? The answer to this question is subjective, but you can cast a wide and broad net or reach a more targeted crowd for answers depending on the site you use.

- **The right size of crowd:** This question also is subjective; it's hard to predict the "magic number" that will generate enough quality responses.

- **An appropriate bounty:** Some sites provide a mechanism to get answers to your questions from the public at no cost. Others may specify a minimum payment for the best answers, or leave the amount entirely up to you.

- **A well-crafted question:** The wording of your question can dictate the type of answers you receive. To achieve optimal results, utilize clarity, brevity, simplicity, and specificity.

Crowdsourcing answers work well for questions that seek factual, specific, and finite information, as well as for more general questions in which the answer is based on individual opinion or experience. So you can crowdsource to reach a lot of people to try to get at one answer or to get many answers, depending on your needs. You can use crowdsourcing specifically for market research, but general answer sites aren't the best place to go because you can't vet or manage the crowd.

Sample Question Formats

There is no single or definitive right or wrong way to word a question. Over time, you will see what works and what doesn't. Here are some examples of poorly formed questions and the rewritten versions where needed:

What are the best coffee beans?

Rewritten: *What are the best coffee beans I can order for my one-touch Jura coffee and Saeco espresso machines? I prefer a slightly acidic aftertaste.*

The first draft of the question lacks specificity, so the answers will likely be broad and entirely subjective. The rewrite is longer, but the specificity eliminates broader, less relevant answers.

What is the best way to filter news?

Rewritten: *What is the best way to filter business news so I receive a summary of posts via e-mail every day?*

The rewritten question specifies the type of news, the amount of content wanted, and the format for receiving the content. With detail, someone can recommend a particular tool or filtering method that fills the need.

What is your favorite e-mail software?

Possible rewrite: *What is your favorite free, web-based e-mail software?*

This question is asking for opinions, so answers will likely be subjective. You can narrow responses by being more specific, mentioning the platform (such as web-based e-mail software), or asking about software just for Macintosh computers.

What is the law that provides restrictions on how you market to minors online?

This question is clear, but to get the best answer, you should turn to the expertise of a lawyer familiar with cyber law. You can get a quick answer from a variety of sources and general-topic answer sites.

Try to avoid putting your explanatory text before you ask your question. Instead of saying, "I'm looking for a solution that can help me remember and manage tasks. What is a good app for the iPhone that I can use?" Start with your question: "What is a good iPhone app for managing tasks? I need help remembering them and prefer notifications by e-mail and SMS." Provide your question first, and include the supportive content after you've posed the question. Some sites may not give you room to ask longer questions with descriptive text.

Caveats to Crowdsourcing Answers

Getting quality answers to your questions starts with you: how you ask the question, how and when you ask any follow-up questions (if the site permits interaction), and your own expectations for the types of answers you will receive. Depending on the answer site you use, your ability to manage the questioning process may be limited to simply asking questions and getting answers. Other sites may provide mechanisms or forums for a more back-and-forth dialogue to get you closer to the answers you seek.

Many of the questions you ask that have concrete answers could also be answered with the results of a search on Google or another search engine. It is better to use crowdsourcing when you can benefit from receiving a lot of different responses—where activating a crowd to provide multiple responses helps you accomplish something you can't do with a simple Google search, such as getting a variety of recommendations for a laser printer.

You can pose questions that have concrete, accepted, and verifiable answers to crowds, but doing so might not necessarily save you time or money. A challenge of crowdsourcing answers is not knowing the person who responded to your question or whether they're qualified to give a reliable response. Even after crowdsourcing answers, you may still need to run the answers through another vetting process. If you have a technical or highly specialized question, you're better off going straight to experts with established knowledge on the topic.

Certain people are probably not answering questions on information crowdsourcing sites. Anyone working in highly regulated industries—such as lawyers, medical practitioners, and financial advisors—could risk their licenses or jobs by providing information in public forums without an eye to compliance issues, privacy issues, and regulations.

Be careful about relying on the answers you receive from general-topic answer sites for critical issues. Many of these sites have disclaimers that warn against accepting legal, financial, or health information via their forums. Do so at your own risk.

Tools for Sourcing Answers

A variety of answer sites have forums and tools where you can ask your questions using various communications methods. Some sites provide custom tools for posting your question, offering a bounty, reviewing questions, engaging in dialogue with the responders, sorting and rating questions, promoting the best questions to the top of the list, and making a payment to the person with the best answer. Other sites incorporate posting boards, e-mail, instant messaging (IM), phone options, texting, and even mobile applications.

Free General Topic Answer Sites

The more random and general topic answer sites that don't charge a fee for answers rely on the general public's willingness to respond to posted questions. Sites with active answer communities can provide a reasonable number of responses to your questions. Most responses on these sites are of fair to average quality.

Answers.com (answers.com) is a highly trafficked site that gives you the option of getting answers from web-based reference sites, from its WikiAnswers community (wiki.answers.com), or from all the sources at its disposal. When you post a question on Answers.com, you are asked to register on the site to receive your answers via e-mail. Asking a question on their main site generates a combination of encyclopedia and Wikipedia entries, links to related products (such as books on Amazon), video pertaining to the topic, and matching questions posed to the wiki community (if there are any). Answers from the WikiAnswers community that have already been provided tend to be short and simple.

Yahoo! Answers (answers.yahoo.com) shows you questions that the system thinks may be a match to your question so you can review any relevant answers contributors have already given. This can save you some time, but the answers vary in quality. You can also share your question on Yahoo! Updates, if you use those. You can also share your question on your Facebook profile, if you have one. Site users can rate answers and the question asker can choose the best one.

Answerbag (answerbag.com) is another general topic answer site. The site lets you specify whether you're looking for advice, looking for facts or instructions, looking to encourage discussion, or just asking for fun. You need to log in to Answerbag using your Facebook account or create an Answerbag account before your question is submitted through the site. You can also share your question on your Facebook profile.

If you're looking for detailed or high-quality responses, free answer sites are probably not your best bet. These sites are also not known for speedy response rates.

Fee-Based General Answer Sites

Sometimes you can enhance response speed and quality through payments, even small ones. Mahalo Answers (mahalo.com/answers) increases the quality of responses by building in a tip feature with which you can set a price for the best answer before you pose your question. After you pick the best answer, the person who provided the winning answer gets paid in Mahalo dollars, a virtual currency that can be converted into actual currency after the responder accumulates 150 Mahalo dollars. You can buy Mahalo dollars to offer tips using a credit card or PayPal. Or if you choose to answer questions on the site, you can accumulate points to use for tips.

> **PITFALLS**
>
> Pay attention to how fee-based answer sites handle payments for answers. Some sites require you to pick and pay for a single "winning" answer. Others let you distribute a bounty across all acceptable answers.

ChaCha (chacha.com) has trained guides who are paid to answer questions. You can get answers via phone or text message. You can text your question to 242242 (that spells "ChaCha") or call 1-800-2ChaCha (800-224-2242). There is no charge for questions answered except when you request that you receive your answer via text message (the charge depends on your texting plan with your mobile phone company).

Even with a payment model, general answer sites that use open or mildly vetted crowds still may not provide you with the kind of responses or feedback you need. Pay doesn't always translate into speed and quality. Responses may trickle in days after you've submitted a question, and they may still fall short despite the monetary incentive.

Using crowds for sourcing answers works better when you know or can identify your crowd to some degree. You'll increase the quality of answers using a site or service where you can manage the question-and-answer process and have follow-up dialogue.

Niche and Vetted Answer Sites

Some answer sites bring together more niche or vetted crowds. Aardvark (vark.com), a social search site Google acquired in 2010, is one example of a slightly more vetted answer crowd. The crowd that sees your question can include your own actual connections in social networks. Your question doesn't go out to general Aardvark users until after your personal networks aren't able to respond.

The Aardvark system lets you ask your questions using IM or e-mail and masks your personal contact information. When you ask a question, you are matched to an appropriate responder in several ways: First, your question is sent to people in your social circles on social networks (friends or friends of friends) or people you've invited to and connected with on Aardvark. Then, if needed, the Aardvark system finds relevant experts for you by sending your question to people with "tags" or keywords that match your question, meaning they've identified their expertise in a related area. Finally, if you still don't get a match for an answer, your question is sent to the site's entire user base. The Aardvark site hosts the back-and-forth dialogue that occurs between askers and responders.

By combining your actual network and social networking contacts into a crowd that can provide you with answers, Aardvark becomes a much more valuable system than one that is open to anyone and everyone. Another system that uses your actual connections to help answer your questions is LinkedIn Answers. See Chapter 13 for more details on that service.

Problem-Solving Crowds

You can crowdsource for answers at high-end, self-service, ideas-and-innovations sites as well as at crowdsourcing service providers (CSPs) that offer problem-solving leveraging crowds. Most general answer sites are best suited for answering simple questions. Problem-solving crowds can often tackle complex questions because the sites and companies that gather and manage these specialized crowds look for participants with high-level skills and qualifications. With proper vetting, a problem-solving crowd can combine the intelligence of its members to help you get to a better answer or to solve a problem you couldn't solve on your own.

Another way to get answers is through a process called *open innovation*, which is the coming together of intellectual minds to solve problems or generate new ideas addressing specific situations and needs. Open innovation took place for centuries but became less common around the last century when companies became more secretive about their information as they created and protected their proprietary intellectual property.

DEFINITION

According to Henry Chesbrough in his book *Open Innovation: The New Imperative for Creating and Profiting from Technology,* **open innovation** is a process where companies use ideas from outside and inside their enterprises as they seek to "advance their technology." Chesbrough encouraged companies to build internal and external paths to help bring new technology to market.

In more recent years, corporate leaders began realizing they couldn't find all the answers to their research and development quandaries solely by tapping into their internal teams. Instead, they began reaching beyond their corporate walls, sourcing ideas and solutions from a greater base of experts. Open innovation is experiencing a renaissance, especially because of efficient and global communications and connectivity via the Internet. By engaging in open innovation, companies can increase their capacity multiple times over. Open innovation can also allow companies to get products to market more quickly.

Today, there are a variety of open-innovation and problem-solving sites that range from self-service tools to hands-on consulting services. Open-innovation sites and service providers get varyingly successful innovations and answers through their systems. Using open innovation does not guarantee results, but it does offer another way to get input from a potentially global crowd of experts or interested participants.

Open-Innovation Service Providers

Open innovation happens when companies, organizations, or government entities look for solutions outside their own research and development department or internal infrastructure. NineSigma is an open-innovation service provider connecting clients with their global network. Their community consists of over two million solution providers around the world who receive notices of problems that need solved. Because of their highly targeted methodology, they are really "expert-sourcing" versus using broader crowdsourcing.

If you contract to work with NineSigma, they can help you find capable problem-solvers using their patented search platform to globally identify experts who might be able to develop solutions for you. The company adds a human layer to their search—a team of cross-disciplinary, Ph.D.-level scientists and engineers to vet and identify the individuals who are a potential fit to respond to your query.

After potential candidates are identified, NineSigma sends out a request for proposal (RFP) to approximately 8,000 potential solution providers per project. Some of those will submit a proposal; others may pass on it. Then, NineSigma aggregates the proposals and presents you with a technology roadmap, working closely with you on each step of the process, from reviewing proposals to facilitating deal negotiations. To date, the company has completed over 1,800 open-innovation projects.

Another open-innovations site that works with large and small corporations, non-profits, and governments is InnoCentive, with access to over 200,000 solvers in 200 countries. The company has posted over 1,000 challenges and claims a 50 percent success rate. An example of a successful challenge handled through InnoCentive was a company looking to develop a dual-purpose solar light that could be used as both a lamp and a flashlight in African villages and other areas of the world that don't have electricity. The solver was an electrical engineer in New Zealand who was awarded $20,000 two months after the challenge was posted on InnoCentive's site.

Steps for Working with IdeaConnection

IdeaConnection brings together seekers and solvers for open-innovation challenges and is hands-on with clients. The company assembles teams and assigns facilitators to projects, handling client relationships and related intellectual property transfers. All challenge data remains confidential between the company, the client, and the team members selected to work on the problem. Seekers are usually Fortune 500 and Global 1000 companies trying to tackle research-and-development challenges. Awards on the site range between $20,000 and $100,000, with the average award being around $50,000. Steps for working with IdeaConnection include the following:

1. **Confidentiality:** Both parties are asked to sign a confidentiality agreement. All challenges remain private.

2. **Client Agreement:** Both parties sign a Client Agreement.

3. **Challenge Detail Document:** The client submits the site's proprietary Challenge Detail Document. This is IdeaConnection's term for a creative or design brief specifically outlining their idea challenge.

4. **Receive solutions:** After submitting the Challenge Detail Document, the client receives at least one solution within 12 weeks of the start of the project. (The project begins with the receipt of the Client Agreement.)

5. **IP transfer:** If the client accepts a solution, he or she will receive documentation to transfer the intellectual property from the solver to the client.

6. **Payment:** If the client rejects all the submitted solutions, he or she isn't required to pay an award. If the client does pick a winning solution, the award specified in the Challenge Detail Document is due for payment within 30 days.

IdeaConnection teams are comprised of individuals from different disciplines. While they produce fewer results than an open crowdsourcing solution, they are able to address problems in depth.

Self-Service Open Innovation

Some service providers take a less hands-on approach, offering tools that automate some or all of the process of crowdsourcing ideas and solutions from a global network of skilled individuals. Hypios is a company that facilitates open problem solving, a classification of open innovation by which something entirely new is not being innovated; instead, contributors solve specific research-and-development problems using new or existing solutions.

Hypios isn't a consulting company. You can sign up for a Hypios account and gain access to the search system to go through the crowdsourcing process yourself using the automated expert identification tools. Individuals can join the Hypios custom-built solver community platform to receive notices of new problems. All participants must sign nondisclosure agreements.

Hypios takes a crowdsourcing approach to problem solving by broadcasting your research-and-development problem to their community of over 150,000, while also launching their automated Solver Surfer technology. Their search tool helps find people on the Internet outside of their own crowd community to invite them to join the competition to solve your problem. For better results, the Hypios system seeks individuals with specific expertise in areas best related to your problem. Each problem is given a corresponding price tag. If you want to use one of the solutions you receive through the Hypios system, you need to pay that amount to receive rights to the winning solution.

Evaluating the Outcomes

The type of questions you ask greatly affects the type of responses you will receive. As you can imagine, fact-based questions one can answer concretely will solicit answers you can more readily evaluate and confirm. Questions that allow for subjective responses are more nuanced and require you to use your own subjective judgment to determine whether the answers are right for you.

How do you evaluate the answers you receive? In some cases, you might get responses, but you may need to verify them by doing additional research, by asking a reliable source, or by performing Google searches. When you get an answer from a stranger in a crowd, you don't always know if the responder has the appropriate credentials, particularly if the crowd members aren't vetted, rated, or otherwise identified.

An example of a verifiable response is in answer to the question "How much should I expect to pay for a website redesign?" You'd likely receive a range of prices, but you can find actual prices on website developers' sites or you can call website developers to find out what they charge. Crowdsourcing the answer could save you time or it might just add another layer to getting to the best answer.

Plausible responses are more subjective. To find out if an answer that sounds plausible is good or not, you may have to try it out to see the results. A plausible response might be given to a question such as "How does one remove juice from a laptop keyboard without damaging the computer?" Even if you receive a variety of answers—each sounding better than the last—you still have to choose the best answer or try one of the suggested methods. If you successfully clean the juice out of your keyboard without ruining your computer's motherboard, then you've found a good answer. Of course, if your computer is at risk, how likely are you to try what a total stranger suggests versus bringing your laptop to a computer repair shop? Not every question can be safely or appropriately answered by a crowd.

You may deem some answers you receive acceptable and useful. If you ask crowd members to provide their opinions, you are more likely to accept the answers you get because you aren't looking for a right or wrong one. If you ask, "What small business tech topic should I blog about on my company blog?" you will likely get a variety of responses based on each crowd member's interests and needs. You can use your own judgment to pick the best answer or answers.

Sourcing opinions is one case where multiple responses are more useful than a single "right" answer. However, you need a process for gathering answers, sorting them, reviewing them, and—if you have the right tools—rating them or letting crowd members rate them. Ultimately, it is up to you to determine the quality of the answers you receive through crowdsourcing.

The Least You Need to Know

- Crowdsourcing answers may not always generate consistent results.
- The type of questions you ask and the way you ask them can guide the success of your crowdsourcing campaign.
- With proper vetting, a problem-solving crowd can combine the intelligence of its members to help you find an answer or solution to a problem.
- Use open innovation for high-level crowdsourced problem solving or idea innovation, but make sure solvers or responders are vetted and qualified.

Crowdsourcing on Social Networks

In Part 3, I lay out how social networks like Facebook and LinkedIn can be leveraged for crowdsourcing. I also explore the microblog Twitter for crowdsourcing activities. You'll get some practical information about tapping into your social-media friends, fans, and followers as your crowd.

To get the most out of popular social networks for crowdsourcing purposes, I've broken down the best crowdsourcing features of each, including surveys, polls, voting or rating, and feedback mechanisms. You'll also see the limitations of social networks as crowdsourcing platforms, so you'll have realistic expectations.

Accessing Crowds in Social Networks

Chapter

10

In This Chapter

- Getting to know the basics of social networking
- Identifying crowdsourcing best suited to social networks
- Using social networks features for crowdsourcing
- Gathering and organizing input from your networks

You're engaged in social networking, aren't you? Everybody's doing it, or so it seems. These days, the question is not, "Are you on Facebook or Twitter?" but, "How many ways are you using social networks?" Crowdsourcing is just one way you can use social networks to interact with an audience consisting of people who have chosen to connect with you.

Social networks were not created specifically for crowdsourcing—or even marketing or sales, for that matter. Social networks began as platforms where people could connect easily with friends, family, and colleagues, or make new friends by meeting or connecting with people connected to their immediate contacts. Simply put, networks facilitated meeting people online and networking with them in a social way.

In this chapter, I'll show you why and how you can use social networks as communications platforms for your crowdsourcing campaigns. I'll also show you how to organize the input you receive from your social network crowds.

Social Networking Dynamics

All social networks connect you with others. Each network tends to use its own specific terms to identify those contacts, although there are some consistent terms used amongst the networks. On Facebook, you can have "friends," "members," or "fans" of your page. On Twitter, you are a "follower," but if someone follows you back, they become a "friend." On LinkedIn, you have "contacts"; on MySpace, you have "friends." People don't usually connect with you on a social network to be crowdsourced, but handled appropriately, a crowdsourcing campaign can tap into your connections on your favorite social networks.

Understanding the intimacy and personal nature of social networking can help you approach crowdsourcing in social networks with sensitivity for better results. Even if someone is using a professional social network such as LinkedIn, they probably regard their account as a personal space where they are wary of unsolicited messages and requests.

Most people use social networks to connect with others either personally or professionally, and they choose to use a particular social network based on a myriad of reasons, including:

- People they know use it.

- They like the features of a particular network.

- The social network is for people with interests similar to their own.

- They joined it and continue using it out of habit.

- They have an agenda and are using it for a strategic reason.

- They heard about it and are just trying it out.

People participate in social networks for different reasons, so not everyone in your network will respond to your request for input or participation in your crowdsourcing campaign. You cannot expect 100 percent response from any online crowd community; if you are using one of your social networking channels, you may experience even less participation than with other avenues. Don't be discouraged. There are still solid reasons to use social networks.

PITFALLS

If you are not clear about your intentions with your social networking crowd, you might turn people off, which could result in losing their connection. People may show their displeasure by "unfollowing" or "unfriending" you.

Some upsides to crowdsourcing in social networks include the immediate responses you can get and the excitement you can generate. One of the most compelling aspects of social networks is how quickly and easily people in your network can share your campaign with others. The reach of your campaign can multiply exponentially and quickly.

Crowdsourcing in Social Networks

Considering the many types of crowdsourcing campaigns you can run, probably the least effective would be using your social network as a labor pool to complete tasks. Micro-labor often requires a set of specific tools to streamline workflow. Luckily, savvy programmers have developed robust micro-labor websites that help you manage all the steps of getting work done by a crowd. The features of such sites include forms so you can outline your project and discrete tasks, mechanisms to calculate fees for labor, built-in quality-assurance systems, and detailed reporting to itemize tasks completed along with the results. Micro-labor sites also provide crowds of workers who are primed and ready to do micro tasks.

Popular social networks like Facebook, Twitter, and LinkedIn are not usually equipped with the technical tools that work well for crowdsourcing. They're more socially oriented, so it stands to reason that you can tap into your networks for input and participation that involves conversations, providing information, and sharing. Therefore, social networks can work well for the following:

- Idea generation
- Feedback
- Opinion
- Polling
- Collaboration

Social networks have been used for fundraising, but not every network has a built-in way to collect funds. Social networks are more often used for gathering crowds to lead them to a fundraising campaign on another site or platform.

Some social networks may allow or provide "add-ons," or *third-party applications*, to enhance the tools and features available on their site. An example of an add-on feature is Polls on Facebook: you can create short polls to share with your friends or fans and add them to your Facebook profile as a new tab.

The simplest campaign usually generates the best response. Look for ways to pare down what you are asking of your social networking crowd, or break a larger campaign into smaller elements that are carried out over time. When it comes to successful crowdsourcing, you need more than a lot of people. Social networks are about relationships. Building trust takes time and a concerted effort. Being upfront, open, honest, and responsive sets the stage for a more successful campaign.

What Social Networks Do You Need?

Not all social networks function the same way. Knowing how each social network differs in features and functionality can help you pinpoint the best network for your crowdsourcing campaigns. Make sure the network has a variety of communication features, including a public communication space, such as the Wall feature on Facebook or a publicly viewable Twitter page; a private communications mechanism, such as Direct Messages on Twitter or Facebook Messages; and ways to easily and prominently embed or link to additional tools, to help you gather, track, and manage data or responses.

All social networks are not created equal. Consider MySpace and the ways you can communicate with your MySpace friends. MySpace does have private message boxes, but they don't provide a suitable public posting area for ongoing dialogue. MySpace pages do have a Comments section, but it's not effective for discussions because most people just leave a comment and don't return for ongoing conversation. Although MySpace has a status update feature like Facebook, it feeds into a stream that's not published on your public page, so it is hard to revisit responses. Overall, the communications features on MySpace—like many social networks—are too fragmented for continuous, managed conversations.

Communicating with Your Crowd

Every social network offers public communications spaces where you can create publicly viewable profiles. Some networks, such as Facebook, keep profiles accessible only to other members of the network. Most provide a space where you can publish messages that others can access and comment on. On Facebook, that space is called the "Wall." On Twitter, your Twitter page is publicly viewable by default, unless you change the settings to make it private.

Determine how many people you need to participate in your crowdsourcing campaign to better assess which social networks can get you to that critical mass. Even though most social networks make it easy for you to invite others to connect with you through features such as integrating with your Gmail, Hotmail, or Outlook address books, not all networks have fast and easy ways to invite others to connect with you and join your crowd.

Building a following on Facebook, for example, can happen more quickly than on Twitter because there are so many ways others can become aware of your Facebook presence. If you have a page on Facebook, you can encourage your existing friends to suggest your page to their friends. You can suggest your page to potential Facebook friends. Once someone likes your page, that action is posted on their Facebook profile feed with a link to your page so their friends can potentially see your Facebook page name and click on a link to go there. It isn't enough to get others to "like" your page. You must be diligent about posting updates, posing questions, and otherwise presenting a rich stream of content and encouraging interaction to keep your page on the top of people's minds and their news feeds.

Twitter, on the other hand, requires a lot more effort to get people to follow you; even if they choose to follow you, they might not always see what you post to your Twitterstream. If someone follows you, their followers do not see that action as a notification in their stream. Following someone on Twitter is an invisible action to everyone but you and the person you're following. Unless someone actively mentions you in their tweets, their followers probably won't even know you exist—unless they are following you, too!

Picking Your Social Network

There are several factors to consider when picking the social network—or networks—where you'll crowdsource, including who you are trying to reach and where your audience interacts. If you are trying to reach Baby Boomers, chances are you won't often find them interacting on social networks like MySpace or Bebo, but you may find them on Facebook, Twitter, and—even more likely—LinkedIn.

Another consideration is what you want your audience—or crowd community—to do. Not every social network has the right features to carry out specific types of crowdsourcing steps, because most social networks aren't set up for crowdsourcing in the first place. The reason you might use one is because it lets you build a following or gather and communicate with a crowd in one place. You can also do more unstructured and informal crowdsourcing simply by "listening" to what is being said about your company in social media channels, and aggregating and analyzing what you find. Use monitoring tools such as free ones like TweetDeck and Seesmic, or fee-based tools like SproutSocial and Radian6. Web-based solution HootSuite offers both a free and paid version.

After you know what you want to crowdsource, check to see which networks provide the right features to handle your project. Do you want your crowd to provide their feedback by taking frequent polls? Choose a social network that lets you easily integrate polls that can be an element of your overall crowdsourcing efforts. Facebook and Twitter have polling applications created by third parties, while LinkedIn has a built-in polling feature. Even once you settle on a social network, you may find it doesn't have every feature you need. For example, if you want your crowd to vote on something or rate something, you may end up having to link to yet another site to use a voting or ratings tool.

If time is of the essence, pick a social network with the best tools for marketing and growing your crowd community. Look for multiple ways to not only reach those with whom you are directly connected, but also reach—or at least be visible to—their connections. Facebook is the master social network for offering these kinds of internal connections, but other networks keep trying to emulate Facebook and are always adding new features that may make building your crowd faster and easier. Growing a crowd community on LinkedIn may be faster than on Twitter because you are linking with people you already know and most likely already have in your contact database, or inviting people you know to join LinkedIn. Unless you have a contact database that includes your contacts' Twitter accounts, building a Twitter following tends to require a more long-term investment.

Useful Social Network Features

Social networks are popular for good reason: they allow people to connect easily with others and to expand their networks. Most are free, so there's not really much of an entry barrier. Other social networks, particularly those geared toward business professionals, offer a free trial to test them out even if they have a premium paid subscription, or a free version in addition to the paid one (like LinkedIn).

Because every social network offers different tools for communicating with your friends, fans, and followers, familiarize yourself with a number of networks to find the one with the right features to help you crowdsource. To learn more about potential networks, join them personally if you don't already have your own accounts.

Let's take a quick look at three popular social networks—Facebook, Twitter, and LinkedIn—and some tools within those networks that can serve as platforms for crowdsourcing activities. You'll find more detailed information about these networks in Chapters 11 through 13.

Facebook

When you sign up for a Facebook account, you create a Facebook profile. You can also create a Facebook page for companies, organizations, or individuals that is viewable by the public. Individuals who might want a page in addition to or instead of a profile include authors, artists, celebrities, and consultants. You can connect with friends through your Facebook profile, but on a page, people connect with you as fans or people who like your page (sometimes referred to as "likers").

When you create a Facebook page, your name and the names of all page administrators aren't visible to anyone. Once someone becomes a fan of your Facebook page, you can communicate with them publicly on your page's Wall, which is like a posting board with messages running down a single web page. You can also use the discussions feature to carry on multiple conversations. The discussions area—or application, as it is referred to on Facebook—is available as a tab across the top of your page.

When you post a message or status update to your Facebook page, it appears in your fans' news feeds on their Facebook page by default. Some people might turn off this feature so they won't see your public status updates.

You can directly message your fans by posting an announcement, called a "Status Update." You can access this via a tab adjacent to their Facebook Messages inbox. Updates to fans are the closest you can get to sending a private message to all your fans at once. Facebook strongly discourages sending a private e-mail to each of your fans, which could result in the freezing or loss of your Facebook account.

BEST PRACTICES

Status Updates are meant to be brief messages, but don't simply broadcast announcements through them. Use them to engage your followers in conversations by asking questions. Reference others to get their attention.

Facebook Groups

In addition to profiles and pages, Facebook offers groups. To invite people into your group on Facebook, you must be connected to them as Facebook friends, which limits who you can gather into a crowd. If you aren't friends with someone, you first need to extend a friend invitation to include them in your group. This can pose problems because it forces you to friend anyone you want to be in your group, but you may not actually want them as a Facebook friend.

Groups are for ongoing and active conversations amongst people who know each other. The conversations can be accessed through regular e-mail, similar to an e-mail list. Participants can continue conversations with a group chat on Facebook, or with messages they post on the group's main page. You can get quick feedback through groups, engage in ongoing dialogue, post photos, share links, and add events. Facebook has also provided a document feature called "Docs," which is a shared notepad where you can edit with group members. Note: you can't add applications to groups to enhance functionality.

If you are looking for control over crowd membership, Facebook groups are not the best solution. Any member of the group can add friends regardless of whether it is set as open, secret, or closed. Still, Facebook groups provide a more direct way of contacting its members than with pages. Groups are best suited to conversations and casual crowdsourcing of your Facebook friends—those people with whom you are already connected.

Twitter Accounts

Twitter differs from Facebook in many ways, but a feature they share are status updates, called "tweets" on Twitter, which are the brief messages you share with your connections.

Twitter communications tend to move quickly and disappear soon after the tweets are posted. Because of this, using Twitter for crowdsourcing may have less consistent results than with Facebook. If you have a strong and attentive Twitter following, you can run successful crowdsourcing campaigns, or you can use Twitter to help drive traffic to another network or forum where your crowdsourcing activities actually take place.

There are third-party applications you can use to add more features and functionality to your Twitter communications; for example, applications such as PollDaddy for Twitter, TwtPoll, and Zoomerangs Twitter surveys can be helpful for crowdsourcing.

See Chapter 12 for more details on using Twitter to get the attention of and to interact with specific groups of people.

LinkedIn Groups

LinkedIn is the place to reach professionals or business-minded crowds. Because LinkedIn was one of the first social networks, it has gone through many changes over the years. LinkedIn has learned from its competitors, particularly Facebook, so you may see some similarities between the two networks, including status updates—called simply "Updates" on LinkedIn—and network activity, which is like Facebook's news feed.

LinkedIn provides a community-building feature also called groups, which has more traditional online community features than Facebook groups. Because of that, you may find LinkedIn groups useful as a destination for some crowdsourcing initiatives. We'll look more closely at groups on LinkedIn in Chapter 13.

Building a Smarter Presence

Once you join a social network and determine it is suitable for reaching your target audience to crowdsource, you need to build a presence specific to gathering and communicating with your crowd. You can go the do-it-yourself route and set up a presence entirely on your own or you can engage a consultant, designer, or developer to do it for you.

If you do your own crowdsourcing through social networks, each network will walk you through the basics of set-up, some with more explanation and recommendations than others. For example, Facebook leads you through the main steps for creating a page or group, but leaves out a lot of customization options and only presents you with a few default tabs to get you started. Setting up a Twitter account is quick and easy, but Twitter doesn't walk you through any design options during your initial set-up. Setting up a LinkedIn account is a lengthier process because it requires more information, and setting up a group requires understanding what features are available.

There are pros and cons to doing it yourself. It may be cheaper, but if you don't have the necessary skills or any familiarity with the service, setting it up on your own could cost you more in the long run. It's pretty easy to set up your own social network accounts, but it takes time, and each service is different. Doing it yourself means you may miss out on leveraging all the features and add-ons available and possibly struggle with customization options. Keeping up with the latest feature changes and developments can be a full-time job.

Most social networks offer minimal custom design features or templates to enhance the design, but these provide little flexibility. Facebook, for example, uses proprietary code called Facebook Markup Language (FBML) to enhance your Facebook pages with content and design drawn from files hosted on an outside server. Using FBML involves some knowledge of programming, or you can hire an FBML developer. In some cases, there are workarounds and tutorials on the web to help you create custom features, but only where the network allows it. For crowdsourcing, you need to optimize these networks' interactive communications and community-building features.

Attracting Friends, Fans, Followers

Each network allows you to connect in similar ways using different terms such as "friends," "followers," "contacts," and "connections." How you reach out to people to join your network and become part of your crowd differs from service to service.

To attract the right people to join your crowd, first identify the social network(s) where your target audience is "hanging out." If you use Twitter, start by following them and then engage them in conversation. Make sure you post information to your network that is relevant to your audience and informative about your upcoming crowdsourcing campaign. If you're looking for input on a new gardening tool you've brought to market, emphasize topics related to gardening to attract the right people and engage in the right conversations. If you are brainstorming a local community project, your messages should be related to your local community and to community-specific issues.

PITFALLS

Don't get duped by the countless offers to help you get followers fast. These offers are almost always scams and won't provide targeted connections. Look for quality, not quantity.

Social networks are platforms for broad interactions, so you need to either choose networks that are relevant to your target and goals, or choose niche, topic-specific forums within those networks. Using the gardening tool example, you could gather a group on a social network specifically for gardeners, or create a forum on a general interest network and draw attention to it in other gardening-specific communities. Gathering a crowd takes time, but gathering the right one will get faster, better results.

Coaxing Input from Social Crowds

Your friends, fans, and followers have willingly connected with you on social networks. They've given you permission to communicate with them in appropriate and non-invasive ways, but before you invite any of them to participate in your crowdsourcing campaign, you need to lay some groundwork for success.

First, clearly state your intentions. From establishing your presence to sending messages to attract your crowd to initiating your campaign, be sure to always state your intentions clearly and concisely. Start with, "Thank you for joining my group (or page or community, and so on)," and explain in simple terms what you want from your crowd: "We are seeking feedback on our new product. Your input will help us make product improvements to better serve your needs." Or you might say, "We would like you to take our weekly polls for the next six weeks so we can gather your input to help us plan our upcoming event."

Post steps, rules, and guidelines to your online forum. Draft and publish all the behind-the-scenes information about your campaign to answer any questions in advance. You can do this in the form of a frequently-asked-questions (FAQ) document. FAQs are posted online and can be written in advance, anticipating common questions, or compiled over time as questions are asked and answered. You can even crowdsource your FAQ by asking your crowd for their questions and answering them in a document.

Post a privacy policy. People online are often concerned about their privacy. You may want to contact a lawyer to obtain the appropriate wording for a privacy policy after you determine how you will protect the privacy of your campaign participants.

Provide a realistic time frame. You may be in a hurry for results, but the rest of the world is not necessarily working on your time line. If you need quick results, let your crowd know. Forthright communications can move your crowdsourcing campaign forward and put it on the right track.

Extracting Data from Social Networks

You have a presence on a social network, and you have a growing and engaged crowd. Before you launch your first crowdsourcing campaign, you should already have in place the tools you'll need to gather data and responses, in addition to what the social network you use provides. These tools include the following:

- **Communications mechanisms:** Private messaging, public messaging, and ways to broadcast messages to the group.

- **Data-gathering tools:** Polls, surveys, questionnaires, rating tools, voting tools, and basic spreadsheets.

- **Monitoring tools:** You can use an array of social network monitoring tools to manage conversations, such as HootSuite, Seesmic, and TweetDeck, and the more enterprise-level solution offered by Radian6. You can even use applications to conveniently monitor your crowd's conversations on your mobile device.

- **Calculating tools:** Spreadsheets are a tried-and-true tool to manually deposit and analyze responses, and other sites and applications that calculate, collate, and analyze responses include PollDaddy, Zoomerang, and SurveyMonkey, just to name a few.

See Chapter 4 for more details on a do-it-yourself crowdsourcing toolkit that can support your efforts in social networks.

You can ask, nudge, prompt, and cajole your crowd to respond, but make sure you always give them good incentives to do so. What's in it for them? Just letting others know that participating in your campaign will show them tangible results can work wonders in motivating them to participate.

Crowdsourcing is not an exact science, and doing it in social networks can affect accuracy and effectiveness. You can set up your campaigns in a formal manner, incorporating proper survey practices to produce better results. You may need a consultant to help you format your campaign and tools or to integrate more sophisticated polling and surveying processes.

Sourcing a social networking crowd adds many variables that can make a formal campaign challenging, starting with their tendency toward more casual, free-wheeling, and inconsistent communications. Sourcing the crowd in social networks can also be fruitful, especially as your crowd becomes more engaged and more trusting.

The Least You Need to Know

- Social networks are best suited for getting input, such as feedback and opinions from a crowd, rather than for getting work done.

- Gathering a crowd in social networks takes time, so you may not be able to use them effectively for crowdsourcing until you have a big enough crowd to provide sufficient input.

- You need to supply your crowd with the same kind of campaign rules, guidelines, and policies you'd supply to more traditional online communities.

- You can build trust in your social networks by being upfront, open, honest, and responsive to your audience.

Fostering Crowds on Facebook

Chapter

11

In This Chapter

- Using Facebook pages
- Adding applications to pages
- Crowdsourcing through Facebook
- Understanding Facebook's terms of service
- Accessing Facebook on your mobile device

Facebook is the largest social network in the United States with over 500 million active members worldwide. Using Facebook for marketing or communications efforts makes sense not only because of its sheer size and reach, but also because of some of Facebook's integrated tools for reaching individuals, groups, and the public at large.

Crowdsourcing on Facebook can be easier than on most other social networks because of the available third-party applications and its limited customization options. The greatest thing Facebook allows you to do is accumulate a crowd through the various interconnected communications mechanisms, which makes it easy for people to show their friends what they're doing, and for any member to communicate easily with others within the Facebook system.

Facebook Pages or Groups?

Facebook offers three ways for members to create a presence on the network: profiles, pages, and groups. Profiles are what individuals get when they sign up for Facebook and are intended to be personal rather than commercial accounts. Pages are

Facebook's only fully publicly accessible feature, meaning people who aren't Facebook members can access information on a Facebook page. Groups are mechanisms by which people can invite their friends into a conversation with some structure to the gathering.

Decide whether to use a profile, page, group, or some combination of these features to crowdsource. Most people start out with a personal profile on Facebook, but you may not want to use one for crowdsourcing, depending on how business-related your project is and the image you'd like to put forward. If you are looking for a large group and your crowdsourcing activities don't have to be private, a page is appropriate. If you are looking for an active and ongoing dialogue, a group will likely work for you.

Most companies opt for Facebook pages as their public presence on Facebook. You can interact with customers and potential customers and use the page for marketing and sales purposes. Remember that crowdsourcing on a Facebook page means everything you do is viewable by the public at large.

DULY NOTED

If you don't want a personal Facebook profile but you do want a Facebook page, Facebook offers business accounts. From the Facebook.com home page, create a page and go through the steps, without opting to create a profile.

To build a private space on Facebook, you can start a Facebook group and set the level to "secret" instead of "open" or "closed." This removes the group from public view, but it doesn't prevent group members from inviting their friends into the group. For crowdsourcing, this means your campaigns are not confidential, but your crowd can grow easily if you encourage group members to invite others.

With either Facebook pages or groups, you can gather a crowd, interact with them in several ways, and share links to additional tools to conduct your crowdsourcing if those tools aren't available within Facebook. Facebook can be useful for gathering a crowd, conducting open discussions, and acting as a gateway to other sites and resources.

Creating Your Facebook Page

If you already have a Facebook account, you can create a Facebook page for crowdsourcing purposes by going to facebook.com/pages to create a page. If you're already on someone else's page, scroll down and click on the **Create a Page** link on the lower-left side of the page. If you don't want a personal Facebook profile, you can create a business account by going to facebook.com and clicking on **Create a Page**.

Once there, you need to choose a category and subcategory for your page. Your choices are Local business; Brand, product, or organization; or Artists, band, or public figure. If you select Local business, you can choose from a drop-down menu of types of business ranging from Automotive to Travel Services. If you select Brand, product, or organization, you can choose from Airline and Consumer Product, Retail and Website, and more. Choosing Artist, band, or public figure gives options such as Actor, Musician, Sports Team, and Writer.

Choose your page name and page type carefully because you will not be able to change either once you've created your page.
(Courtesy of Facebook via screenshot permissions policy)

Next, enter a name for your page. If the page is for your company, it should be your company name. If it is for you as a public figure, then submit your name. If the page is for your company's product, use the product name. The idea is to use the page to represent something or someone. You shouldn't create a page solely for crowdsourcing; the page should create a public presence on Facebook for your overall marketing and communications purposes.

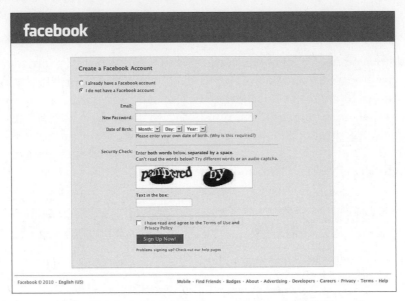

*If you don't have or want a personal Facebook account, click **I do not have a
Facebook account** and fill out the form to create a business account.*
(Courtesy of Facebook via screenshot permissions policy)

In the next screen, you have the option to create a Facebook account. If you want
only a business account, select **I do not have a business account** and then provide
your e-mail address, password, and date of birth, enter the security words in the text
box, check that you've read the privacy policy, and then sign up.

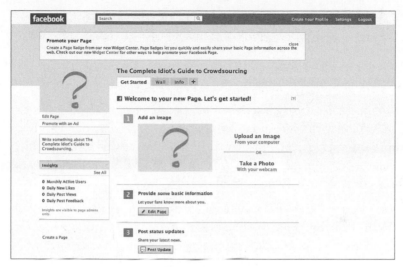

At first, your page contains default content with step-by-step instructions for setting up your page.

(Courtesy of Facebook via screenshot permissions policy)

Facebook will send you an e-mail to activate your account. When you click on the activation link, you'll be logged in to your page automatically. Facebook then walks you through steps to build up your page before publishing it, including optional steps such as adding an image, inserting basic content for the Info tab, posting a status update, promoting your page, setting up for mobile device access to your page, and linking your Facebook page status updates to Twitter.

DULY NOTED

Consider buying a Facebook social ad to attract people to your page. Access the Facebook ad tool at facebook.com/advertising. Facebook walks you through the steps of purchasing an ad, including ways to target the ad to a specific audience.

Enhancing Your Facebook Page

Pages give you a more flexible presence on Facebook than groups; you can integrate more features and have some ability to customize. Facebook groups don't let you add on features such as new tabs using third-party applications or custom programming.

A Facebook page is actually a series of pages users can reach via tabs at the top. You can add new tabs with corresponding content to enhance your Facebook page and insert more interactive features that work well for crowdsourcing. Only six tabs are displayed at once, so make sure you plan how you will use those tabs because as you create new ones, some may be pushed out of view.

When you set up a Facebook page, you are usually presented with a few tabs by default: Wall, Info, and Photos. The tabs that are visible initially are often determined when you create your page based on the category you choose, such as Non-Profit or Business/Retail. With pages, you are not limited to the tabs Facebook gives you; you can add Facebook-created tabs, tabs created with third-party applications outside of Facebook, and custom tabs you created from scratch. You can feature a Poll tab and a Discussions tab—both useful features for crowdsourcing—to give members easy access to that kind of content. Note: the Wall and Info tabs aren't moveable.

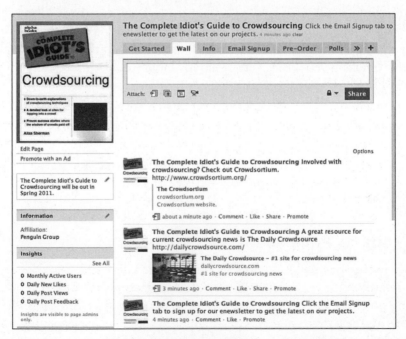

A few images, some content, and some custom tabs can make your page more inviting and interactive.

(Courtesy of Facebook via screenshot permissions policy)

Adding New Tabs to Pages

Adding a new tab to your Facebook page involves either adding a new Facebook application to your page or creating a custom tab. The former is easier and requires little if any programming skills.

To add a new tab to your page, go to the Facebook Applications directory (facebook. com/applications) and search for the type of application you'd like to add to your page. You can search by category, keyword, or application name. Categories include Business, Education, and Utilities.

When you find an application that looks interesting, visit the page to see if it can be added to your page; many applications only work with personal profiles. If you see a **Go to Application** button on the upper-left side of the application page, this means the application is compatible with your personal profile. If you see an **Add to My page** link under the button, that indicates you can add the application to your page as a new tab.

If you are an administrator for more than one Facebook page, you'll be presented with a list of pages you manage so you can select the page to which you would like to add the application. Click on **Add to page** for the appropriate page. You can access behind-the-scenes administrative features for your page by clicking on **Edit this page**, which appears under your Facebook page logo or image on the upper-left side of your page content. To activate or edit your new page application, enter the admin area. Once there, scroll down to the bottom to view your applications. You should see the new application you just added.

To configure the application, click **Edit** under the application's name. When you're ready, go back to your page, click on the + tab to add a new tab or the arrow symbols (>>) next to the page's tabs to view the tab if it is hidden. Select the new application from the drop-down menu under the + sign or arrows. Move the new tab to the left of the last tab so it remains visible to the public; otherwise, it will remain hidden if you have more than six tabs. You can rearrange all tabs except Wall and Info.

Adding Polls to Pages

Polls are useful for crowdsourcing because they're quick and easy for people to take, and standard online polling tools have a data-collections feature to generate reports. Creating polls can be quick and easy for you, but only after you carefully plan your questions and response choices. Crafting polls that effectively compel others to respond while providing you with useful input is a skill you can hone over time, or can turn that work over to a professional well versed in polling.

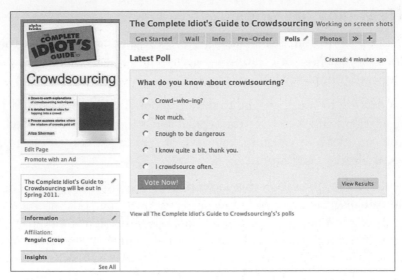

Poll tab added using a third-party Facebook application created by PollDaddy.
(Courtesy of Facebook via screenshot permissions policy and PollDaddy)

You can use several third-party applications to add polls to your Facebook page as a new tab. Going to facebook.com/applications and searching for "polls" yields about 80 results. If you're already using a web-based poll builder such as PollDaddy, you may want to check to see if there's a corresponding application on Facebook for the tool you're already using. Searching for PollDaddy within Facebook Applications brings up an application you can insert into your Facebook page and link with your web-based account.

If you aren't using a web-based poll builder, you can search for "polls" in Facebook Applications using several criteria. Look to see the number of active monthly users; this can help you determine how popular an application is with other Facebook users. An application called "Poll," created by a company called Kremsa, Inc., has over 1.8 million active users. When you click on that application's name in your search results, you can view discussions about the application and even see which of your Facebook friends are also using the application in case you want to ask for opinions on it before you install it.

You can also informally crowdsource ideas for applications by asking your friends, fans, or followers for their opinions. Once you've chosen the polling application you want to use, add it to your Facebook page the same way you'd add any third-party application.

Adding Custom Tabs to Pages

Facebook allows developers to add custom tabs that include embedded images, video, and interactive applications. The main content of these custom pages resides on a server outside of Facebook's system and uses code called Facebook Markup Language (FBML) and hypertext markup language (HTML) to pull the content into the custom Facebook page.

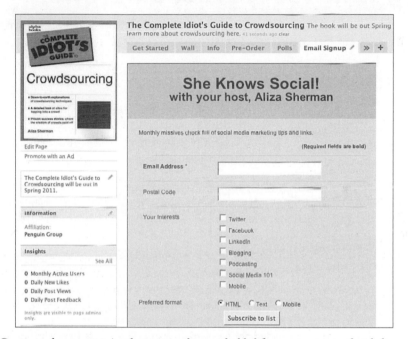

Custom tabs can contain elements such as embedded forms or surveys that help you gather your crowd and communicate with them.

(Courtesy of Facebook)

You can use a third-party application called Static FBML as an interim to a custom page tab. The application works like a template where you can insert text and HTML into a form and publish a custom tab. The content and code you insert into the application's form is stored offsite and is pulled into your Facebook page when someone clicks on the corresponding tab. You can use this application to create a branded landing page or to create a page explaining your crowdsourcing projects in a more readable format than Facebook provides.

You can opt to set your landing tab on a custom tab instead of the Wall, which is the default setting. With a custom landing tab, people who haven't yet "liked" your page can learn more about you. Some companies include a message on their custom landing tab encouraging new visitors to like their page. In order to interact with a crowd on Facebook, people first have to like your page.

Talking with Your Facebook Crowds

Using a social network for crowdsourcing is a little like using a shoehorn. Social networks weren't designed with crowdsourcing in mind, but they give you access to crowds and tools to gather crowds.

An advantage to using Facebook for crowdsourcing is the ability to gather a crowd using Facebook's messaging tools. Communicating with your crowd once you've assembled it can be a little challenging because each Facebook feature allows you to communicate in varying ways, so you may struggle at first to get consistency in your conversations.

First, you need to know what communications features exist on Facebook. Then, you need to learn how to leverage them for crowdsourcing and properly communicate with a Facebook crowd.

> **BEST PRACTICES**
>
> Toppers Pizza, a small Wisconsin-based franchise, tapped into their Facebook crowd of over 17,000. They created a tournament-style challenge they called "Spank Your Pizza." The company gave consumers the chance to alter the actual Toppers menu. The challenge? To invent a brand-new menu item—using any ingredients on their menu—to become a permanent part of the menu at Toppers' franchises nationwide. The winning menu item would then be named after the winning creator.
>
> The company received over 125 entries and the contest helped increase their Facebook fan base by 3,000 new fans. The company estimates a sales increase related to this promotion of over $150,000.

Using the Wall

The main place for initial conversations on your Facebook page is the Wall. The Wall is the default tab where people land when they visit your page, although you can change the landing page to any other tab you've add to your page. Your choice affects only people who are not already fans of your page—those who haven't yet "liked" your page. Once they do, they'll always land on the Wall. Most people familiar with Facebook recognize the Wall feature because it looks like everyone's Facebook Wall. If you change your landing page, make sure you have a good strategic reason to do so, such as directing people first to a custom tab that explains what your page is all about.

PITFALLS

If you specify restricted access to your page, such as a wine company restricting the page to Facebook members 21 years of age and older, your page will no longer be visible to the general public.

To modify where you want people to land when they access your page, go to the administrative section of your page by clicking on **Edit page**. Next, choose **Edit** under **Wall Settings**, and you'll see a pull-down menu that lets you select the default landing tab for **Everyone Else**, meaning people who are not yet fans of your page.

Under **Wall Settings**, you also have the option to set the default view of your page to either **All Posts** or **Only Posts by page**. If you are looking to engage your fans in dialogue, choose **All Posts**, so everyone can see your status updates along with the related Comments made by others. Choosing **Only Posts by page** creates a one-sided broadcast of your messages and doesn't encourage interaction or build your community.

Using the Discussions Tab

If you've determined the Discussions tab on your page is a suitable forum for your crowdsourcing project, then make sure it appears as a visible tab on your Facebook page. If it's not visible, you can add it to your tabs bar. Take a look at your current tabs, and you'll see two small tabs to the right of your last visible tab: two arrows (>>) and a plus sign (+). As a reminder, the two arrows show hidden tabs that aren't showing on your page because you've exceeded Facebook's default limit of six visible tabs. The plus sign lets you add new tabs to your page, but they, too, may be hidden from view.

Pressing and holding the >> tab reveals the hidden tabs you can add to your page. (This is where you'll find the Discussions tab, if it's not already visible.) Select **Discussions**, and the tab will appear as the last visible tab. To ensure that the tab remains visible, drag it to the left so it's no longer the last tab. Facebook will show only six tabs at a time, so adding Discussions could remove another tab from the tabs bar.

The Discussions tab might look familiar to you if you've participated in online communities with forums or message boards. You can start and reply to a topic. Replies appear one after the other. Unlike other Discussions forums, replies on the Discussions tab aren't threaded, which means you can't reply to a specific reply within a topic; that is, your Comment is not directly connected to what you are commenting on.

Threading makes online conversations between many people easier to understand because posts and related replies are grouped together. Without message threading, using the Discussions tab for crowdsourcing can be a mixed bag. On the one hand, the familiar message-board format may encourage input. On the other hand, you already have conversations taking place on the Wall. Most people who visit Facebook pages are used to commenting on the Wall.

Bringing the conversation over to the Discussions tab can prove challenging. Having conversations in both places also creates additional work for you—from monitoring and aggregating to archiving and analyzing content from multiple areas.

Crowdsourcing on Facebook

When you're planning your crowdsourcing campaigns on Facebook, start with setting up data-capturing tools such as polls and surveys. Make sure your back-end processes are in place so you're ready when you announce a campaign to your crowd.

Deciding how much crowdsourcing activity will take place on Facebook will help you determine where and what you'll post. Here are some steps for turning your Facebook page crowd into a crowd for input and feedback:

1. Set up a topic in Discussions for questions related to your crowdsourcing campaign, such as "Have questions about our questionnaire? Post them here."

2. Post detailed information about your campaign in Facebook notes. Once you post a note, it will automatically appear as a status update on your page's Wall.

3. Add a comment to the status update in the form of a quick call to action, encouraging people to participate and letting them know they can ask questions under the Discussions tab. Say something like, "We're looking for your feedback on our latest product. Click here to find out how you can participate."

4. Integrate a poll or survey into your page, or upload images people can review and provide feedback on.

Don't send people away from your page to utilize tools if you can help it. Try to incorporate interactive tools directly into your page. If Facebook's limitations prevent you from incorporating essential crowdsourcing tools, use Facebook as a gateway to the tools you're using to gather data.

Leveraging Likes and Comments

To connect with your Facebook page, Facebook members "like" your page by clicking on the Facebook **Like** button. Some people call those who connect with your page via the Like button "likers," but it's still acceptable to call them "Fans." Once they've liked your page, fans will see your status updates via their News Feed when they access their Facebook account.

Broadcasting messages to your Facebook fans isn't the best way to engage them in conversations or to encourage more people to like your page. To leverage your Facebook page for crowdsourcing, you need to have a dialogue with your fans and post content that compels them to respond in some way.

On Facebook, there are three main ways for people to respond to your status update: they can comment on your status update or others' comments; they can share it by posting your status update on their own profile, perhaps with a note, so it shows up on their friends' news feeds; and they can like it, showing that they like what you posted or the comments from others.

When you use Facebook to crowdsource, you can use the Comment and Like links as ways to glean information from your fans. For example, you can post three different versions of a new company logo and ask your fans to provide their feedback by clicking **Like** under the image they like the most and by providing additional input through Comments.

Processing Data from Facebook

Facebook—like most general interest social networks—wasn't set up for crowdsourcing, so using it can be a bit ad hoc. If you are used to Facebook and have built up a fan following on your page, there's no reason you can't tap into your fan base for smaller or more immediate input and get positive results.

Gathering crowds on Facebook and engaging them in dialogue is less challenging than extracting data from Facebook to analyze it. Facebook doesn't give you an easy way to tally the likes and comments for each status update, photo, or other element that you post. Facebook does provide measurements in the Insights section of your administrative area to view the number of likes and comments your page received on any given day, but this doesn't give you a granular, per-item breakdown.

You may find it challenging to extract conversations taking place on your Wall and look at each image or item you post for likes and comments. If your conversations are happening in the Discussions area of your page, you can more easily copy and paste the replies because of the more simple way these are formatted.

If you're using a Facebook group to get crowd input, you have even fewer measurement tools at your disposal. Facebook doesn't offer Insights for groups as they do for pages, so you have to rely on manually counting every like and comment and manually copying the comments your posts receive.

BEST PRACTICES

The most common ways people gather and archive comments on a Facebook page or group is by manually highlighting them and then copying and pasting the text into a document. Another way is by taking screenshots and pasting them into a document for easier review.

You can use a spreadsheet to deposit comments and likes related to your crowdsourcing campaigns to make it easier to read and analyze them in a systematic way. Although you can count likes and extrapolate more concrete results from numbers, comments and discussion replies will provide you with the more qualitative content you'll need to read over to assess the feedback from your Facebook crowd.

Don't Violate Facebook's Rules

Facebook has a published document on their site they call Terms (facebook.com/terms.php), which outlines what they allow and don't allow on their network. These rules are also known as Terms of Use or Terms of Service, and most reputable sites—particularly ones where visitors or members interact—should have them.

In general, crowdsourcing is not a violation of Facebook's rules if you're sourcing input, feedback, and opinion. If money begins to exchange hands, however, you can get yourself into hot water, so read the Facebook Terms text closely and consult a lawyer. A common violation that takes place is people set up a profile for their company instead of a page, or they use their personal Facebook profile for commercial gain.

Here are some clauses from Facebook's Terms that may have a bearing on how you set up and use your Facebook account:

- Section 4. Item 1. You will not provide any false personal information on Facebook, or create an account for anyone other than yourself without permission.

- Section 4. Item 2. You will not create more than one personal profile.

- Section 4. Item 3. If we disable your account, you will not create another one without our permission.

- Section 4. Item 4. You will not use your personal profile for your own commercial gain (such as selling your status update to an advertiser).

You should review "Facebook Pages Terms" (facebook.com/terms_pages.php) if you're using a page as your crowdsourcing platform. Note Item 9, which states, "You may not establish terms beyond those set forth in this Statement to govern the posting of content by users on a page you administer, except you may disclose the types of content you will remove from your page and grounds for which you may ban a user from accessing the page."

The results of violating Facebook's Terms are clear: "If you violate the letter or spirit of this Statement, or otherwise create risk or possible legal exposure for us, we can stop providing all or part of Facebook to you. We will notify you by e-mail or at the next time you attempt to access your account." You may lose your account and the connections to all your Facebook friends or Facebook page fans if you violate Facebook's Terms.

Managing Facebook via Your Mobile Device

You can access your Facebook account with your phone or mobile device to varying degrees. You can access Facebook via mobile on the go through the mobile version of the Facebook site at m.facebook.com using a web-enabled smart phone. You can also use Facebook's mobile devices applications; they're available for the iPhone, Blackberry, Android-based phones, Palm, Sony Ericsson, Nokia, Windows Mobile, INQ, and Sidekick.

Via your phone, you can add status updates; comment on status updates on your profile or page Wall; browse your News Feed or your page's Wall; and upload photos.

Mobile access can be convenient for checking the status of your crowdsourcing campaigns, but don't rely too much on your mobile phone. Keep in mind that comments on your Facebook page won't be sent to you by text message or e-mail like comments to your personal profile, so you need to check your page regularly. Facebook offers mobile services for free, but you still may be charged by your mobile service provider for text messaging and data transfer.

The Least You Need to Know

- Crowdsourcing on Facebook can be easier than on most other social networks thanks to third-party applications and customization options.
- On a Facebook page, you can interact with customers and potential customers, and it is appropriate to use a page for marketing and sales activity.
- Adding a new tab to your Facebook page involves either adding a new Facebook application to your page or creating a custom tab.
- Facebook—like most other general interest social networks—was not set up specifically for crowdsourcing, so using it can be a bit ad hoc.
- Read Facebook's Terms (facebook.com/terms.php) and Facebook Pages Terms (facebook.com/terms_pages.php), which outline what Facebook does and doesn't allow on their network.

Tapping into the Twitter Crowd

In This Chapter

- Deciding when to Twitter for crowdsourcing
- Interpreting the Twitterstream
- Tweeting etiquette and techniques
- Sourcing the crowd via Twitter

If you've seen one social network, you've seen them all, right? Wrong. All social networks may have some similar features, but each one contains proprietary features and uses its own terminology. In many cases, newer social networks focus on specific or niche topics, from business to knitting and everything in between.

Twitter is not considered a social network, at least not by its creators. Twitter was developed to be a publishing tool similar to a blog, but more abbreviated, only allowing a maximum message length of 140 characters—hence the term used to describe it: microblog. The social networking aspects of Twitter have mostly grown organically from its users, who don't simply broadcast messages to their followers; rather, they have created ways to interact with them. One user-created feature that Twitter has since adopted is putting an @ ("at") symbol before a person's Twitter name when referencing them to help facilitate conversations.

Twitter Is Not Like Facebook

So how does Twitter compare to Facebook? Both Twitter and Facebook allow you to post an update. On Facebook, an update is called a "status update"; on Twitter, it's called a "Tweet." Communicating on Twitter is based on a continuous stream of updates referred to as a "Twitterstream," which combines updates from others and your "Tweetstream," a continuous list of your own Twitter updates. In the Twittersteam, your Tweets are combined with the Tweets from the people you follow. Likewise, if someone is following you, your messages are mixed in with messages from other people they are following on Twitter.

Twitter's "rhythm" and speed is different from Facebook's. If Facebook is like a pool, Twitter is like a rushing river. Getting used to the immediacy and speed of the Twitterstream can be challenging. Given the fast-moving flow of the Twitterstream, and the fact that most people follow anywhere from dozens to hundreds to thousands of people, you may find it challenging to be heard on Twitter. You have to be strategic and diligent about how you reach out to your followers.

The similarities between Twitter and Facebook—at least in terms of their features and functionality—pretty much end at status updates and Tweets. By design, Twitter does not have Facebook's bells and whistles. You don't have multiple ways to build a presence on Twitter like you do with Facebook's profiles, pages, and groups. Although Twitter doesn't offer add-ons for your Twitter account as with Facebook's third-party applications, there are many third-party, Twitter-specific applications developed with Twitter's permission available. These applications are available for free or for a fee.

DULY NOTED

A site that helps you find the best Twitter applications for your needs is OneForty.com. Members rate and review applications, and can search the site by category.

Twitter offers you another way to develop an interactive online presence and build a following. Once you have a following, you can post questions to your followers and gather responses fairly quickly. Sorting the responses you get can be tricky, but there are tools to help you aggregate Twitter content.

When to Crowdsource on Twitter

You can certainly use Twitter to source a crowd, and the crowd you reach via Twitter isn't limited to your own Twitter followers; it can also include their followers. Getting in front of your followers involves being "Retweeted," meaning your post is reposted by someone who is following you for their followers to see.

Crowdsourcing in social networks is less structured than using a self-service crowd-sourcing site because the tools and features built into the networks were not created with crowdsourcing in mind. There are few built-in features on Twitter to aid in your crowdsourcing endeavors. You'll need to use third-party applications to get more functionality out of your Twitter crowdsourcing campaigns, such as tools to monitor Tweets, to search Twitter to extract data, and to generate reports.

There's no single way to get your message out to a lot of people on Twitter, even if you have a lot of followers. There's also no guarantee that most of your followers will see all or most of your Tweets at any given time. You'll likely find that getting the crowd's attention can be challenging.

Twitter, like most social networks, is best used to get quick opinions, ideas, answers, and feedback from the crowd for projects that don't have hard-and-fast deadlines or complex deliverables. Relying on a free-flowing tool like Twitter for in-depth or mission-critical input is risky. Using Twitter to get input can also be time-consuming because success relies on the greatest number of people seeing your request, and you might be hampered by the 140-character limit of your tweets.

Crowdsourcing the Twitterstream

Twitter is less effective for private crowdsourcing, but you can use it as a traffic driver to other web-based data-gathering tools, including polls and surveys. If you're looking for an answer to a question that isn't pressing, you can post it to your followers and even ask them to repost your query to their followers.

Say you're looking for a printer for your business. You can Tweet a query regarding the make and model of the printer and ask your followers for feedback. If only a few people see your Tweet, you may not get a good cross-section of opinions, but some-times just a few responses is all you need.

You can augment the feedback you get from your followers by combining it with a Twitter search for the make and model of the printer you're considering. This is really traditional research and not crowdsourcing, but you can still cull a lot of wis-dom and input straight from the Twitterstream, which may help you with your query.

Of course, Twitter has inherent feature limitations. If you find it challenging to put enough information into the short Tweet format, use Twitter as a gateway. Supply a link to another web destination where you can provide more details, such as your website, Facebook page, or even a self-service crowdsourcing site that you're using for your campaign.

Interpreting the Twitterstream

If you're new to Twitter and you look at a stream of Tweets, chances are they'll be hard to follow at first. Here's a handy breakdown of the elements of Tweets in a Twitterstream, to help you better sort through the cacophony.

- **The @ symbol:** When you see the @ ("at") symbol in a Tweet, it usually comes before a Twitter name such as @alizasherman. This indicates that it's a reference to the Twitter account of a particular person, company, or organization. Twitter automatically makes the @ reference a clickable link. You can click on the name with the @ symbol in front of it to get to the related Twitter page.

- **The # symbol:** The # (hashtag or pound sign) symbol placed immediately in front of a keyword or phrase is referred to in social-media parlance as a "hashtag." When it appears before a keyword or phrase, without spaces, the hashtag helps group together related posts. Hashtags are particularly useful when conducting a search for a particular word or name, but only if people have tagged their Tweet using the hashtag. For example, a search for the hashtag #wine should bring up a myriad of Tweets related to wine; you also can be more specific with #merlot.

- **The RT:** RT stands for "Retweet," which is when someone quotes or repeats someone else's Tweet and gives them credit. Twitter also has a Retweet button, so people can post someone's Tweet directly into their own Tweetstream for their followers to see. Certain Twitter clients—mobile or desktop applications you can use to post to Twitter—present a Retweet by tagging it with "via @janedoe" to cite who posted the original Tweet.

- **The condensed URL:** Because Twitter gives you only 140 characters to post your Tweet content, character spaces are at a premium. Therefore, it's best to use shortened URLs created through services such as bit.ly, dlvr.it, and tinyurl.com.

These are just a few examples of Tweet-specific elements that help create conversations and connections within a free-flowing Twitterstream.

RT, @, #, and condensed URLs are common features in Tweets and messages on Twitter, and each has its own use.

(Courtesy of Twitter via screenshot permissions policy)

Using Twitter for Fifteen Minutes

The best way to use Twitter for any type of communications, including crowdsourcing, is to be organized and strategic. It is easy to get distracted from the work at hand by reading through so many Tweets. Here are a few steps you can take to get the most out of Twitter in the least amount of time.

To get started, post about your crowdsourcing efforts. The short format on Twitter may not be conducive to providing adequate details. You can post more detailed information on a web page or in a blog post, and then provide a link to it in a Tweet inviting people to learn more and participate. You can also post a link directly to a data-gathering tool like a survey or poll. Don't cluster Tweets too closely together, but you can repeat your message a few more times during the day.

Spend five minutes looking for additional interesting and relevant Tweets you can also post, so your Twitterstream is not comprised solely of announcements about your crowdsourcing campaign. You want to keep people interested! If you find Tweets that you'd like to share, use the Retweet button or copy and paste them with an attribution. Retweeting others is a not only a good way to share information, but it is also a great way to give kudos to those whose Tweets you share and it gets you noticed by those whom you Retweet. When crowdsourcing, use tools or Twitter search to track Retweets of your queries and pull responses out of Twitter into a format you can analyze, such as a spreadsheet.

Next, spend five minutes looking for either Tweets addressed to you using the @ symbol and your Twitter name, or for other Tweets of interest. Participate in a conversation by adding a relevant comment or by responding to someone else's Tweeted question. This is a good way to present your viewpoint or expertise and to be more visible to the people who are following you and with whom you interact. When crowdsourcing, conversations are key to engaging your crowd and strengthening relationships. You also want to respond quickly to any questions your Twitter followers ask about your crowdsourcing campaigns.

Spend the last five minutes for crowdsourcing on extracting data that you must analyze. You can use a variety of tools to aggregate Tweets based on keywords or the hashtag, compile them into a more readable format, and then save them as a variety of documents. You can also conduct a search using Twitter's search tool (search. twitter.com), which will constantly refresh and update to track the latest conversations.

After you've posted your crowdsourcing query, engage in conversations to be visible, Retweet others to give kudos, and post additional valuable or interesting information to your Twitterstream. Then step away from Twitter for a while to give the crowd time to respond. Return to Twitter within a few hours to start the process again or use a Twitter management tool with a scheduled Tweet feature to post your crowdsourcing query a few more times, spaced out throughout the day. Return to Twitter just to search the stream for Tweets related to your crowdsourcing campaign and extract the data.

Building Your Twitter Following

Building a following on Twitter can be challenging. People use Twitter for different reasons and follow people for multiple reasons: they know them, they've heard or read about them, someone they know Retweeted them, their Twitterstream looks interesting—you name it. Because who one follows on Twitter is a personal choice, you need to get on other people's radar and post compelling content to compel total strangers to follow you.

One way to get on someone's radar is to follow them. You can find specific types of people to follow by searching Twitter for keywords. For example, if you have a pet food company and are looking for other pet owners, search for "pet," "dog," "cat," and so on. To stay focused and on target, take time to read people's Twitter bios to see how they identify themselves before following them.

If you find a person who loves cats and you want to find more cat lovers, you can look at who that person is following and who follows them to identify new people to follow. Following the people who follow you can be considered "trolling" on services like Facebook, where the friend connections are considered more personal. On Twitter, however, following someone is not intrusive, and a person doesn't have to follow you back. There's never any guarantee someone will follow you back, but having a compelling Twitter stream can help. Building a following on Twitter can be a slow and arduous process.

Proper Tweeting Techniques

Effective Tweets clearly articulate ideas or pose questions. They pack a lot of meaning into one to three sentences. The writer uses active and clear language. When you Tweet, you're not writing a novel, but you can make dramatic word choices to catch people's eyes. Just changing the question "What do you think of our dog food?" to "When you think of our dog food, what comes to mind?" can mean the difference between a few polite answers and a lot more expressive ones.

You can get creative with how you format your Tweet. Instead of typing "What do you love about our product?" you can add emphasis by selectively using capital letters; for example, "What do you LOVE about our dog food?" Add a salutation and a hashtag, and your Tweet is even more effective: "Hey, dog lovers! What do you LOVE about our dog food? #doglovers"

Ultimately, effective Tweets are the ones that get the most response and activity. Ineffective Tweets generate silence.

How to Craft Effective Tweets

Reaching out to your followers can be as easy as posting a message, but how your followers respond is the measure of an effective versus ineffective Tweet.

Certainly, you want people to see your Tweet. To be more visible, post regularly and frequently, but make sure the content you post is valuable or interesting. What is considered "frequently" is subjective, so don't be offended if some people think your usual 5 to 10 Tweets a day is too frequent and decide to "unfollow" you.

With a strong following, you can post a question to your Twitter crowd and receive near-instant responses.

(Courtesy of Twitter via screenshot permissions policy)

You want people to respond to your Tweet. The best way to get people to respond is to pose compelling questions. Respond to anyone who answers your questions, even if you response is just to thank them.

Make your Tweet interesting enough to share because you want to inspire your followers to do so. If you're crowdsourcing on Twitter, make your Tweet succinct and interesting, and include a short URL to drive traffic to your data-capture tool if you're using one in conjunction with Twitter.

How to Get Retweeted

To cast a wider net for crowdsourcing, your followers need to Retweet your posts. A simple way to encourage this is to ask people to Retweet your query or call to action. Be sure to phrase this request politely, and don't do this every time you Tweet or it will seem gratuitous. An easy and compact way to ask for a Retweet is to use the following: "Pls RT." For example, "I'm seeking input from moms about baby food. Interested? @ me. Pls RT." Make sure to limit the length of your Tweet, including the Retweet request, to ensure that it is easy for your followers to Retweet.

Tweets that consist of one part compelling content and one part optimal formatting are best for Retweets. One way to make it easier for people to Retweet your post is to make your Tweet even shorter than the 140 characters Twitter allows. If someone prefers to manually copy and paste Tweets and use RT, or are using Twitter clients that tag Tweets with "via @johndoe" to cite you as the Tweet's originator, you want to leave the other person space for the attribution.

The best formula for calculating a reasonable length is to add up the number of letters in your Twitter name, add 5, and subtract that number from 140. So if your Twitter name is johndoe, that name has 7 letters. 7 + 5 = 12, and 140 – 12 = 128. The ideal length for your Tweets to be easily Retweeted would be 128 or less.

As you type out your Tweet on most Twitter clients and on Twitter.com, you will see the number 140 reducing as you type. When the number gets down to 12, stop typing and see where you can trim your Tweet so it remains at the best length.

Twitter-Related Tools

Many other Twitter-specific tools and applications tie into your Twitter account to add functionality and features that Twitter lacks. Like Facebook, Twitter has allowed software developers to leverage their code to create applications that integrate specifically with and enhance Twitter for the user.

DULY NOTED

If you want to easily export Twitter search results, try using a tool like Searchtastic.com to export search results into Excel spreadsheets, or use Tweetdoc.com to export search results into a PDF file.

Many of these Twitter-enhancing tools are based on the web; others are desktop applications that you download to your computer—some just for Macs, some just for PCs, and others compatible with both. Still others are mobile applications that you can use on popular mobile devices such as an iPhone, a Blackberry, or an Android-powered phone.

Gathering Data via Twitter

Because Twitter is best used to get quick opinions, ideas, answers, and feedback from the crowd, tools such as polls and surveys can be useful to your Twitter crowdsourcing campaigns.

Popular poll and survey tools that are specifically integrated into Twitter include Twtpoll and Twtsurvey, with which you create online polls and surveys that link directly to your Twitter account. For a small fee, you can purchase an annual subscription to place your own custom background behind your polls and surveys to maintain consistent and prominent branding.

Invite people to take your poll by simply asking the following:

> *Please take this poll about our product. We value your input. http://tinyurl.com/ ourpoll*

> *We are looking for feedback on our site redesign. Learn more: http://tinyurl.com/ forfeedback*

> *Got a second? Take our 3-question survey to help us make a better widget. http://tinyurl.com/widget*

PollDaddy also offers an easy and free Twitter poll function at twitter.polldaddy.com. Zoomerang offers a function to Tweet your survey from their site (zoomerang.com/ twitter-surveys), which is also free.

Monitoring and Managing Tweets

Some of the more popular tools for monitoring the Twitterstream and managing your Tweets include HootSuite, TweetDeck, and Seesmic, all of which have web, desktop, and mobile versions, as well as Brizzly, which has web and mobile versions. All three give you different dashboard views of your Twitter account and other social media accounts.

For Twitter, you can view multiple streams, including the Twitterstream of the people you follow, your @ responses, any hashtags you want to follow, saved searches on specific keywords, and any other stream that is useful for monitoring and aggregating Tweets.

Additionally, there are web-based tools that give you a variety of ways to view Twitterstreams; one example is TweetChat, which helps you follow conversations using a particular hashtag, especially while that conversation is happening live as part of a Tweet-based chat. TweetGrid lets you configure a single web screen view of multiple streams in a grid pattern of your choice.

Tracking Your Hashtags

Certain communication techniques are especially helpful when crowdsourcing on Twitter, especially hashtags. Hashtags are used on Twitter in conjunction with keywords to tag Tweets and group them together to make them easier to find in a search. You should create a hashtag specific to each crowdsourcing campaign you conduct.

Using a hashtag tells people who respond to your Tweet or Retweet you that you are tracking responses. Chances are they'll leave the hashtag in. Not everyone, however, will know how to use hashtag properly, so monitor the Twitterstream closely in the hours after you've Tweeted something to make sure you see all responses.

One hashtag-specific tool is WTHashtag, where you can search Twitter for a particular hashtag and add in hashtags you've created. You can then create a page on the WTHashtag site to define the hashtag, add a description, and list external links and any related hashtags. The page automatically pulls in statistics on the hashtag's usage for the last seven days, the top contributors to that hashtag, and the Tweet conversation. You can search related Tweets by date range and output the resulting data as HTML. You can even subscribe to the RSS feed to keep up with the conversation. You can turn a real-time mode feature on and off, which can be handy if you're tracking a popular hashtag.

You can use a site like TwapperKeeper to create hashtag archives, as well as keyword archives and @ person archives.

Managing Twitter on Mobile

Like Facebook, Twitter has both a mobile version of its website at mobile.twitter.com and a mobile application—aptly named Twitter—that you can get for any major smartphone platform. There are also myriad applications you can use to post to your Twitter account, including mobile versions of HootSuite, TweetDeck, Brizzly, and Seesmic, not to mention Twitter-specific applications like Twitteriffic and Tweetberry.

Analyzing Twitter Data

There's not one single way to extract and organize the answers you retrieve from a search, and most often the fastest solution is to use a third-party application or tool. Most search tools for Twitter go through only about 10 to 20 percent of all the data on Twitter. The better tools that cull the entire database of Tweets are enterprise-level solutions that cost hundreds and even thousands of dollars to use.

TweetReports offers a free version of their otherwise fee-based Tweet searching and analytics tool. You can search for keywords or hashtags to see a real-time feed of the results. You can then export results as an HTML file, a PDF, an Excel spreadsheet, or an RSS file. You can also save your search. The site also parses out the sentiment of the Tweets, breaking the data down into positive, negative, or neutral categories.

	A	B	C
1	Twitter name	Tweet	Twitter App
2	DanielleSmithTV	I'm a Tweetdeck girl – feel panicky if I can't use it :)	Tweetdeck
3	DoktaDivah	<3 @Tweetdeck for desktop, easy to use+organizes all accts in one window. @Twidroyd (paid) for my phone, for the same reason.	Tweetdeck
4	rlux	TweetDeck. Does everything I need, saved searches are awesome, plus it works very well across multiple screens / devices.	Tweetdeck
5	RogerSanchez	I'm Torn. I prefer the new twitter. It is equal or better than most other mobile/desktop solutions. Except for Cotweet. Cotweet's solutions for biz are simple and effective.	Cotweet
6	ThinkingFox	Birdbrain. It's great at checking stats and details on followers/following etc	Birdbrain
7	LinkedMedia	Tweetdeck: Great Interface, Runs on Adobe Air, Good Product Functionality, Continuous Upgrades, Reliable.	Tweetdeck
8			
9			
10			

For easy viewing, keep track of Tweet data in a simple and organized spreadsheet.

A lot of the other reporting features aren't related to crowdsourcing but do provide data for analyzing your brand—from Retweet statistics to follower analysis to other indications of your brand's strength on Twitter. Pick Twitter-analyzing tools that give you both a data breakdown and an aggregation of related tweets. There are free analyzing tools, such as Twitter Analyzer and Twitter Counter, that you can use for a quick snapshot of your Twitter stats, but they won't provide more in-depth analysis with actual tweet content.

The Least You Need to Know

- To stand out, you must be strategic and diligent about how you reach out to your followers.
- Getting in front of your followers involves being "Retweeted," meaning your post is reposted by someone to expose it to their followers.
- Because Twitter is best used to get quick opinions, ideas, answers, and feedback from the crowd, tools such as polls and surveys can be useful in your Twitter crowdsourcing campaigns.
- There isn't one single way to extract and organize the answers you retrieve from a search; most often the fastest solution is to use a third-party application or tool.

LinkedIn for the Professional Crowd

In This Chapter

- Setting up a professional presence on LinkedIn
- Using LinkedIn Answers to pose questions
- Polling professionals with LinkedIn Polls
- Gathering a crowd with LinkedIn Groups

Most social networks are geared toward the general population or are focused on broad interests. However, some social networks concentrate on reaching a business-minded community, including BizNik, Sprouter, and the granddaddy of them all, LinkedIn.

LinkedIn launched in 2003 and remains one of the top five social networks in the United States, with over 75 million registered users (compare this to Facebook's 500 million and Twitter's 100 million). When you register for a free LinkedIn profile, you're presented with a form to fill out that allows you to build a narrative of both your professional and educational history, which augments a more traditional online resume.

LinkedIn operates on the notion that we're all separated from anyone we want to meet by less than six degrees of separation. LinkedIn focuses on first-degree contacts who are your immediate contacts; second-degree contacts who are connected to your contacts; and third-degree contacts who are connected to their contacts and thus are three people away from you. LinkedIn encourages you to make contacts for business purposes such as networking, seeking or filling a job, and partnering on a project.

Benefits of Business-Minded Crowds

Why would you want to reach out to just professionals instead of casting a wide net and gathering a crowd without a specific business focus? There are many circumstances in which a business-oriented crowd can prove valuable to your crowdsourcing campaign, including:

- When you need input from people within a specific industry

- When you are seeking input requiring a high level of knowledge, skills, or experience

- When your project is business oriented, such as an executive search

If someone has joined LinkedIn, you can safely assume they did so for career or business reasons. If they were looking to socialize, Facebook would be much more conducive to social networking activities. If they were interested in arts and entertainment, they could join Bebo or Last.fm. They could join a myriad of social networks that aren't focused on professional networking, but they chose LinkedIn and filled out their profile, highlighting their professional background.

On LinkedIn, you can connect with others as "contacts" rather than as friends, fans, or followers. Your contacts are organized within a Contacts database feature where you can also access their list of contacts (on each contact's permissions settings). You have to invite others to connect with you, and they must accept your invitation before they become one of your contacts.

A benefit of gathering and tapping into business-minded crowds is that they tend to be focused and behave in a professional manner because they are interacting with other professionals, often in their own industries. Reputations are at stake. A negative of looking to business-minded crowds is that they are often very busy and may be less inclined to participate in time-intensive crowdsourcing projects. Luckily, LinkedIn offers several tools to reach out to your professional contacts quickly and easily and provides your contacts with the ability to respond just as quickly and easily—namely LinkedIn Answers and Polls.

Setting Up a Professional Presence

Using LinkedIn for crowdsourcing requires that you have a way to reach a group of people with whom you are connected. Setting up a profile on LinkedIn consists of filling out their form and following their step-by-step process for getting your profile to 100 percent completion. After you fill out the details of your work and educational history, you can and should start sending out requests to connect with people you know. LinkedIn works best with a foundation of actual contacts, such as current and former co-workers, current and former clients, and even your current and former bosses.

BEST PRACTICES

Upload a photograph to your LinkedIn profile to create a personal impression. Choose one that's either a professional headshot or one that conveys the professional image you would like to project, particularly to people who don't know you.

You can ask others to submit recommendations about your work. Choose people whom you are confident have positive things to say about you and for whom you feel comfortable doing the same. Don't be careless about who you add as professional contacts on LinkedIn or about making recommendations, because on a business network, your professional reputation is on the line.

To get to 100 percent completion on your profile, make sure to fill out the summary of your professional profile, where you can be creative in describing what you do. Take care to fill out the specialties section where you can use strategic keywords to best describe what you do to make it easier to find you with keyword searches.

You can add multimedia to your profile through applications on LinkedIn, including Slideshare, which imports your slide presentations you've uploaded to Slideshare.net into LinkedIn. You can also display relevant books through the Amazon.com Reading List application. Both features can enhance your profile with relevant images and links.

Completing your LinkedIn profile and managing a growing list of contacts can be the foundation for your future interactions on the network, including crowdsourcing. If people arrive at your profile and see something half-baked, chances are they'll be wary of responding to any outreach you do to crowdsource a project.

LinkedIn Premium Levels

LinkedIn is one of the few major social networks that has a premium level. Usually fee-based social networks are more niche-oriented (focused on highly targeted audiences), but because of LinkedIn's business focus, it charges for extra features that benefit professionals.

The network offers three levels of membership above and beyond their free level: Business, Business Plus, and Business Pro. All premium levels include LinkedIn Polls at no additional cost.

Highlight of Features for LinkedIn Paid Accounts

Business	Business Plus	Pro
$24.95/month* $249.50/year	$49.95/month* $499.50/year	$499.95/month* $4,999.50/year
Access to 75 million members	Access to 75 million members	Access to 75 million members
Reference searches	Reference searches	Reference searches
Priority customer service	Priority customer service	Priority customer service
3 InMails**/month	10 InMails/month	50 InMails/month
5 Profile Organizer*** folders	25 Profile Organizer folders	25 Profile Organizer folders

All premium accounts include two free months.

**InMails is LinkedIn's proprietary internal priority messaging system.*

***Profile Organizer allows you to save and manage profiles of LinkedIn members with whom you'd like to network.*

You can get a lot out of the free version of LinkedIn, but you do get some cost savings out of the LinkedIn Polls feature with a premium account. If you plan to send out a lot of polls, check whether the long-term savings are worth upgrading your account.

Getting Answers on LinkedIn

Like Facebook, Twitter, and most other social networks, LinkedIn is best used to source opinions, ideas, answers, and feedback from the crowd. LinkedIn has a built-in feature for getting answers from others, aptly called LinkedIn Answers. This feature lets you pose questions to your contacts and receive their response messages in your LinkedIn inbox. A copy of the responses goes to your e-mail address as well.

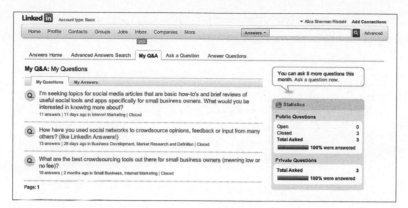

LinkedIn provides an application to pose questions to your contacts and rate the answers you receive.

(Courtesy of LinkedIn via screenshot permissions policy)

When logged into your LinkedIn account, you can click on **More** on the navigation bar and choose **Answers,** or go to linkedin.com/answers.

Once there, you will see a box titled **Ask a Question**; this box is a blank field in which you can type your question. Next to it, there is a field titled **Answer Questions** where you or anyone else can see what questions are still awaiting answers. Click on the **Next** button to progress through the **Answers** tool.

The next step in the Answers tool is the option to include more details about your question for background and context. You can opt to share your question with only connections you specify; choosing this option narrows down your crowd, but also limits the number of responses you'll receive.

Targeting Your Question

Next, you're directed to choose one or more categories with appropriate sub-categories (if relevant) to give further context to your question. The categories in the **Answers** tool are highly business-process oriented, such as "Business Operations: Inventory Management" or "Technology: Blogging," so finding the right categories for your question may take some thought and a bit of creative license.

You can relate your question to a particular geographic area—again narrowing your reach and potential responses. You can also specify whether your question is related to recruiting, promoting your services, or job seeking. If they are related to any of these categories, you are then directed to other services on LinkedIn—namely their job posting area, their recommendations feature, and their job search database.

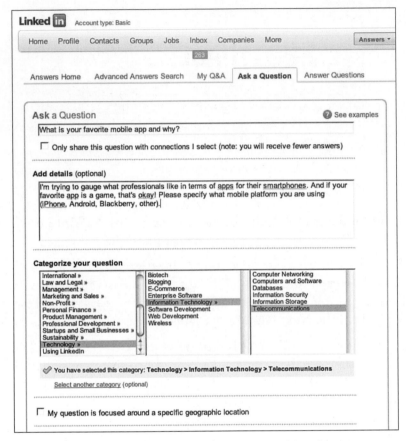

Ask a question and then add details to explain your question, select a category, and specify whether your question is geographically focused.
(Courtesy of LinkedIn via screenshot permissions policy)

Distributing Your Question

When you are ready to send your question out to the crowd, you can choose up to 200 of your own contacts. LinkedIn gives you a seven-day window to gather answers, or you can close your open questions at any time. You can also rate answers once you receive them, which translates to each individual's expertise ranking on LinkedIn for the quality of answers they are giving.

After you rank answers and choose the best, LinkedIn rearranges the answers based on your input; the most useful answers rise to the top. LinkedIn doesn't provide an export tool to extract the answers you've received from their system, so copying and pasting or printing are your best bets.

Publishing LinkedIn Polls

Another useful LinkedIn tool is their polling feature, LinkedIn Polls. You can get to Polls when you are logged in to LinkedIn by choosing **More** and then **Polls** from the navigation menu. You can also access **Create a Poll** when you see a poll on the right side of your LinkedIn screen or when viewing any existing poll.

You can send a basic poll to your contacts for free, but only to your immediate or first-degree contacts (not further out to your peripheral network). LinkedIn does offer a way to send your poll out more widely through their service, including using tools to target who sees the poll beyond your own contacts. For a fee (minimum $50), you can strategically target your poll to a segment of the 75 million LinkedIn members. If you are already a premium LinkedIn member, that poll-distribution fee is waived.

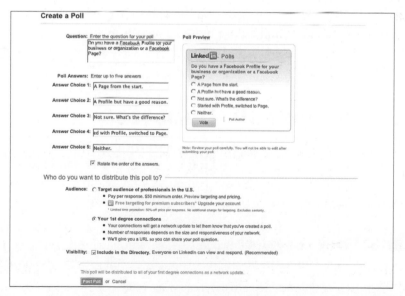

After you fill out the question and answer options for your poll, you can specify how you'd like to distribute it.

(Courtesy of LinkedIn via screenshot permissions policy)

How to Start a Poll

To create a poll, you're given a blank field where you can enter your poll question (up to 125 characters) and five empty fields where you can insert answers (up to 40 characters each). The character limitation of these fields helps your poll stay within a compact box to fit neatly on the side of people's LinkedIn screens. You can choose to rotate answers if the randomness of the responses is important to the input you're seeking.

After you create your poll, you can link to it from your LinkedIn profile using LinkedIn's poll application. Keep track of your polls in the polling section under **My Polls**.

How to Distribute a Poll

LinkedIn lets you notify your first-degree connections of your new poll—at no charge. You also receive a URL to share your poll beyond your LinkedIn network. That means you can e-mail a link to your poll or post it to other places where you have gathered a crowd, including your Twitter account and Facebook page, but only LinkedIn members can participate.

To up the visibility of your free poll, you can choose to be listed in the LinkedIn Directory. This puts your poll before more LinkedIn members in an untargeted fashion. For greater reach, LinkedIn recommends this option when you are not choosing to pay for premium distribution services.

Leveraging LinkedIn Updates

LinkedIn Answers and LinkedIn Polls both start with options to reach out to your own contacts and then have additional ways to contact larger and larger numbers of people. You can also reach out to your contacts by messaging them directly (up to 50 contacts at a time) or by broadcasting to your contacts through updates.

Messaging contacts individually can be time-consuming, between picking 50 contacts at a time and having an organized process so you know whom you've contacted and who has responded. LinkedIn doesn't provide any specialized tools to manage bulk messaging.

Interacting with people using updates can present a challenge because you aren't really gathering a crowd. Instead, the updates you post to your profile page appear on your contacts' LinkedIn news and updates, which is similar to what you find on Facebook or to a Twitterstream.

Using LinkedIn Groups

LinkedIn provides tools to gather crowds on their network through LinkedIn Groups. LinkedIn Groups are more conducive to crowdsourcing than updates because you can gather people into one "place" on LinkedIn where communications and interactions can be concentrated.

LinkedIn Groups are similar to Facebook's, but it has a few different features, such as ...

- **Members:** You and your group members can access a list of all group members with links to their profiles. Facebook doesn't provide an easy way to view all members.

- **Updates:** You can view messages from everyone in the group or just from those members who you also follow on LinkedIn. You can broadcast messages widely or narrow the list of recipients. You can target your Facebook group messages by individual, but it's clunky.

- **Search:** You and your group members can find specific discussions within the group. Facebook doesn't provide a search tool for the content in your own group.

Using LinkedIn Groups to crowdsource gives you a controlled space for your campaigns. You can tap into an existing group, but you will have less control than if you create your own group. If you want to reach out to someone else's group, you should first get permission and guidance from the group owner. Group owners are listed on the Group Profile page on LinkedIn.

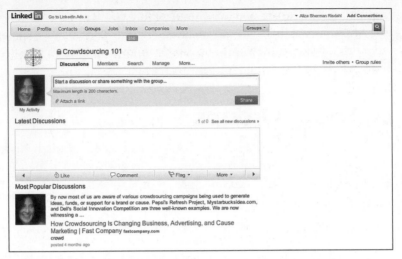

Discussions are the crux of LinkedIn Groups, with the most popular and most recent discussions highlighted on the group homepage.

(Courtesy of LinkedIn via screenshot permissions policy)

Setting Up a Group

While logged in to LinkedIn, go to **Groups** on the navigation menu and select **Create a Group**. From there, you will arrive at a web-based form where you are requested to supply the following:

- Logo
- Group name*
- Group type* (such as corporate, networking, nonprofit, or professional)
- Summary* (to appear in the Groups Directory)
- Description* (to appear on the group page)
- Website
- Group owner e-mail address*
- Access limitation* (open or request to join)
- Language
- Location
- Agreement* (agreeing to LinkedIn's Terms of Service)

Required fields

When you are deciding on the access limitation for your group, You may think you'll gather a crowd faster by keeping your group open. Think less about speed and numbers and more about the quality of the people joining your group. Limiting group access and moderating requests to join seems tedious, but in the long run, you'll be better able to manage your crowd and keep the interactions on track.

Publicizing Your Group

Creating a group on LinkedIn takes only minutes, but it takes time to build momentum and get people to join your group. As soon as you've created your group, you're brought to a page where you can send invitations to your contacts. Your invitation should be brief. You could say …

> *I'm looking for feedback on a new application my company has produced. Please join my LinkedIn Group to learn more and to answer a few questions to help me improve the application. Click here to learn more and to participate (link).*

You are limited to inviting 50 of your own contacts at a time. To speed up your group's growth, you can turn on **Member Invitations** to allow your members to invite others to a group. Doing this will probably speed up your group's growth without compromising too much on quality because you are getting referrals from your own trusted contacts.

LinkedIn also lets you pre-approve people so they don't have to send a request to be added. If you invite others, they are automatically added to the group without the extra step of approving them.

Mobilizing Your Group

LinkedIn lets you broadcast a message by clicking on **Send an Announcement** under the **Manage** area of your group.

An announcement goes out as an e-mail, so your LinkedIn group members are much more likely to see your message than if you were to post an update on your LinkedIn profile. The announcement also appears as a discussion within the group. You can use announcements as a way to ask questions of your group members, but member responses to your announcement appear as comments. All members can view these comments; this may be useful in some cases, but not in others.

You are limited to one announcement per week, so plan out what you want to ask your group. Use announcements to draw attention to a crowdsourcing campaign and then use the appropriate tools to manage crowd input. On LinkedIn, setting up a poll or asking a question is the more structured tool, with some management features built in; the group announcement is another way to drive attention and get more responses.

You can check a box before you send out your announcement to receive e-mail notification each time a comment comes in. If you have a large number of group members, you may want to forego getting e-mail notices and just check the announcement posting in your group periodically.

To crowdsource using a LinkedIn Group, you need to attract people to your group and then engage them in ongoing dialogue. Be clear with them on how you intend to crowdsource and why.

Managing LinkedIn Data

Depending on the type of crowdsourcing you're doing, using LinkedIn will determine the kind of data you'll accumulate and the tools you'll need to extract, sort, and analyze the data. LinkedIn doesn't have easy, built-in tools for data extraction, but because it has several data-gathering tools, it does a good job of accumulating some data for you.

For LinkedIn Answers, you get a list of all the responses and, after you rate them, you can select the good answers and a best answer. LinkedIn reorders the responses so the best is at the top, followed by the good ones, and then the rest. You can easily print, copy, and paste this list, or convert it into a PDF. Questions you've posed are archived under **My Questions** on the LinkedIn Answer page.

When using LinkedIn Polls, you can view poll results on a page where you can view the percentage of responses for each question as a bar graph. You can also view responses according to "Job Title," "Company Size," "Job Function," "Gender," and "Age," all of which can provide some interesting top-line insights into who is responding to your poll questions and how they are responding as their responses relate on these breakdowns. You can print your poll results, convert the page into a PDF, or manually type the results into a spreadsheet to keep track of your poll data. Polls are archived under **My Polls** on the LinkedIn Polls page.

If you are crowdsourcing within a group, you should treat it as a typical social networking forum where you can point to the polls or questions you've posed within LinkedIn to solicit additional responses. Then use the group to hold more in-depth discussions. Unfortunately, like Facebook, extracting the conversation content is limited to the basics, such as printing, copying and pasting, converting to a PDF, and screenshots.

Like Facebook and Twitter, LinkedIn can be used for crowdsourcing; unlike its counterparts, LinkedIn has some useful tools that can help streamline your crowdsourcing efforts, particularly when you're looking for input and opinions. Unfortunately, like Facebook and Twitter, extracting that data for analysis is mostly relegated to manual methods. If you are looking for input from professionals, LinkedIn beats Facebook hands down, and it is much easier to gather a crowd and get responses on LinkedIn than it is on Twitter.

The Least You Need to Know

- Business-minded crowds tend to be focused and behave in a professional manner because they are interacting with other professionals, often in their own industries.
- LinkedIn Answers lets you post questions to your contacts and receive the response messages in both your LinkedIn inbox and your e-mail inbox.
- You can send a basic poll to your contacts for free, but only to your first-degree contacts and not out to your peripheral network.
- Using LinkedIn Groups to crowdsource gives you a controlled space for your campaigns.

Harnessing Crowds for Work

In Part 4, you'll learn more about crowdsourcing sites and tools that help you get work done. I provide tips for choosing the right crowdsourcing platform based on your needs. I also cover crowd competitions, including design contests and creative collaboration marketplaces. Through these resources, you can tap into the talents of many or cast a wide net to find a few good workers to get something done such as website testing or video production.

Getting Crowds to Do Work

In This Chapter

- Using crowdworkers instead of automating tasks
- How to prepare to use crowdsourced labor sites
- Using popular crowdsourcing labor sites
- Picking the right site for the job

Crowdsourcing involves reaching out to people—usually outside your company or organization, but not always—to get something done. So does outsourcing. What's the difference?

When outsourcing your work, you hire a contractor to do a specific job or you work with a vendor who provides services through paid contractors or employees. Outsourced laborers can be paid per hour or per project or task.

In crowdsourcing, the crowdworkers are not usually part of an organized business entity. They're individuals who sign up at a crowdsourcing labor site to perform tasks independently. They aren't formal employees of those sites. Most crowdsourced labor—sometimes referred to as *cloud-sourced labor*—consists of tasks that are most often performed and managed online. The best tasks for crowd labor are microtasks, or very small tasks that can be performed as standalone tasks or as part of larger projects. You typically pay a crowdworker per deliverable or task completed, and in well-managed crowdsourcing work sites, several checks and balances assure accuracy of work completed.

> **DEFINITION**
>
> **Cloud-sourced labor** is done entirely online, or "in the cloud," often through specialized websites that assign, manage, and track work tasks and assets. Some companies specialize entirely in online services to manage their work processes.

Most sites that offer crowdsourced labor for microtasks charge on a per-task or per-piece basis, ranging from a few pennies to several dollars per result. Some of the more established crowdsourcing labor sites are CrowdFlower, Mechanical Turk, and Clickworker.com.

When Automation Won't Work

Crowdsourcing labor sites consist of web-based mechanisms that help you manage the work process. As a client or site user, you can submit work as "projects," "jobs," or "tasks"; upload work-related assets; and review work performed by workers who have applied to complete your projects.

Work performed through crowdsourcing labor sites are smaller, repetitive tasks that typically do not have to be performed by highly skilled workers, but aren't simple enough to be totally automated. The crowdsourcing site Mechanical Turk refers to a task that requires some degree of brain power as a Human Intelligence Task (HIT).

An example of a task you can completely automate with good results is tagging 1,000 photographs with the same tag, such as "animals." A task you can't automate is tagging 1,000 photographs with the correct species out of six on a list. The task isn't so difficult that it requires a degree in biology, but it does require some human review and consideration. A crowdworker would need to look at the reference photos and decide which photographs are lions, tigers, cheetahs, giraffes, elephants, or hippos. A person with basic skills is able to recognize a lion versus an elephant and tag photographs appropriately.

Another task you can't easily automate is verifying if websites on a long list are official corporate sites or web-page listings in a third-party directory. If the task was as straightforward as eliminating any website addresses with yellowpages.com in the URL, then it could be automated by running a script. But if each URL contains a different format and some official corporate sites don't contain the company's name in the URL or use the standard web address format of www.companyname.com, human intervention is required. The crowdworker would need to visit each site and look for reasonable clues that the site is either an official corporate website or a secondary listing.

Crowdsourced labor doesn't always require high-level skills, but in some cases, minimum skills in specialized areas can be important. For example, converting 200 images from a TIFF to a GIF file format may not require high-level Photoshop skills, but it does require access to image-editing software and knowledge of how to convert file formats. In cases where you need higher-skilled workers, you can apply a process called "expert sourcing," in which the crowd is more carefully vetted based on qualifications and skills.

Best Tasks for Crowdsourced Labor

Many tasks can be handled by myriad crowdsourcing or cloud-sourcing labor sites. The crowdworker must be able to perform the tasks online; the tasks should be basic enough to not require highly specialized skills; and the tasks should be achievable, verifiable, and measurable.

Here are some tasks that are well-suited for crowdsourced labor, with examples:

- Image tagging: Tagging photos based on subject matter.
- Image conversions: Converting PNG images to JPG images.
- Image optimization: Resizing images and remove excess borders.
- Database cleanup: Removing old contact information.
- Transcriptions: Transcribing podcasts or video content.
- Translations: Translating tweets to post on Twitter in other languages.
- Digitizing documents: Scanning receipts.
- File conversion: Converting Word documents into PDF files.
- Content moderation: Checking blog comments for profanity; removing and reporting spam.
- Content verification: Checking a list of company names and telephone numbers against the numbers listed on company websites.
- Content research: Finding the correct marketing contacts for companies on a list.
- Content categorization: Assigning categories to a list of blogs using pre-defined categories.
- Content creation: Writing a 150-word review of blogs from a list of blogs.

- Data collection: Copying and pasting biographical information for a list of famous people into a document.

- Sentiment rating: Marking Facebook comments as "Positive," "Negative," "Neutral," or "Not Sure."

- Relevance rating: Determining whether video titles are relevant to actual content contained in the videos.

- Quality rating: Determining whether the quality of audio files are "Excellent," "Good," "Fair," or "Poor."

Crowdsourced tasks should be concrete in scope, and the process for performing the tasks should be clear.

Preparing and Submitting Projects

Every crowdsourcing labor site is different in how it guides you through the process of posting your tasks to their system. There are some overarching similarities—a basic framework—for most of these sites because the more well-known ones tend to follow industry best practices. The best practices for crowdsourcing labor are still being refined.

On most sites, you name and describe your task, break the task down into smaller pieces that multiple workers can handle at once, specify the criteria for workers, and define the end result. Not all sites help you break down large projects into smaller tasks, so you may have to go through this process on your own before submitting tasks to a crowdsourcing labor site.

Listing Discrete Tasks

One important aspect of working successfully with crowdsourced labor is to break down your projects into smaller parts. Some sites assist with this breakdown either through a consulting service or through a questionnaire or application process that helps you think of your project in small parts. Some sites specify the types of tasks that can be done by their crowdworkers through their site. Others simply don't provide options for work they know their site or crowd can't do well.

Breaking down a project into smaller tasks takes some thought about the process and outcome. If you want to prepare 200 photographs for your web gallery, you first need to look at the steps it will take to complete this project. These steps might be:

1. Resizing images to 250×250 pixels.

2. Converting images from TIFF format to JPEG.

3. Renaming files based on a more descriptive filename format that you've defined.

4. Uploading and tagging photos based on criteria you set.

What starts out as a single project of preparing images for a web gallery turns into several discrete tasks. Of these tasks, you could combine steps 1 through 3, but that may require a more skilled worker. You should specify the skills needed in your job posting. The more specific you can get with your descriptions of each task, the more likely work outcomes will be accurate.

You could have workers perform each task separately, one worker resizing images and uploading them to a repository, another converting them and uploading them again, and a third renaming them. This may seem like more work—or "too many cooks"—but if you were to hire a person internally to do all this work, their fee would be commensurate with higher skills. By breaking down the project into smaller tasks, you can find workers willing and able to perform the simpler work for less pay. At any stage, there could also be overlap with workers performing tasks at the same time, shrinking the time to completion.

Specifying Skills Needed

Part of finding the right workers is picking the right site. If you're looking for workers who can help you with modifying images, you wouldn't go to a site that specializes in transcription or translation. If you're looking to get audio files transcribed or text translated, you wouldn't go to a site that doesn't specify that their workers can perform those kinds of tasks.

Depending on the crowdsourcing labor site you use, you may or may not be able to specify exact skills. In some cases, you select the type of task and the site's system will route the job to appropriately skilled individuals based on the task indicated. Other sites ask that you choose workers based on ratings or peer reviews.

If you're preparing 200 photographs for a web gallery and you are looking for one worker to perform all the tasks, you are likely seeking an individual with Photoshop skills. If you break down the tasks into multiple steps, however, you might be fine with one worker who knows how to size images, another who can convert images, and another who can rename images by following a pre-determined list that you provide. By breaking down tasks, you've also reduced the level of skills needed to perform those tasks.

Determining Preferred Outcomes

Whether you are having your in-house staff perform the work, hiring an outside consultant, outsourcing the work to another firm, or employing crowdsourcing to get the work done, only you know what kind of outcomes you'd like for your project. If you are choosing to crowdsource work, you most likely have tedious tasks, and it would be less cost-effective to have them done in-house. You can't expect that this low-level work will be performed by crowdworkers at the same skill level as your in-house, skilled staff.

The benefits of crowdsourcing certain tasks are sometimes the cost savings, sometimes the time savings, and sometimes both. The fewer mistakes that occur, the better your crowdsourcing experience will be overall, so take care to choose the right crowdsourcing tools that help minimize errors and be clear with your instructions every step of the way.

Some sites let you specify the percentage of accuracy you will tolerate. Is 85 percent accuracy okay or do you need 95 or 100 percent? Each percentage increase in accuracy can make a major difference depending on the task. In cases where sites let you specify accuracy, you can expect to pay more for higher accuracy ratings.

Set realistic expectations about the outcomes. Not every task is well suited for crowdsourcing.

> **PITFALLS**
>
> Don't try to force your project or task to fit into the crowdsourced labor model. When in doubt, contact the company and ask whether the site and its workers are right for your task.

CrowdFlower Pools Crowd Labor

CrowdFlower (crowdflower.com) accesses workers in over 70 countries, most sourced through other crowdsourcing labor sites such as Mechanical Turk, Samasource, and its own iPhone application called Give Work. Workers can choose to work on tasks any time of the day or night, and they can work simultaneously, which means multiple people can pick up different tasks in an overall project and work at the same time. This process can speed up task completion because the task gets channeled to thousands of workers instead of just a few.

How CrowdFlower Works

CrowdFlower uses statistical techniques to automatically monitor work quality. Part of CrowdFlower's quality assurance involves posting questions that have known answers, also referred to as "gold-standard data." Many fields use this gold standard statistical technique. This data can be used as checkpoints to rate and train workers.

In every project, the CrowdFlower system mixes in the known items with unknown items to determine how well a worker is performing a task as they complete the unknowns. If a worker makes a mistake on a known answer, the system immediately notifies the worker, which helps to train them. All workers in the system are continually monitored for accuracy.

When a worker completes a task, CrowdFlower provides you with a spreadsheet of results that you can sort based on a confidence score. The higher the confidence, the more likely a result is correct. 100 percent means that it is extremely likely the result is correct.

You can use CrowdFlower for smaller projects via their self-service website, or contact the company for enterprise-level work.

Self-Service Through CrowdFlower

CrowdFlower's Self Service tool allows you to easily design, test, and run jobs that yield quality results. You have many tools at your disposal, including two form editors, quality control tools, and a fully functional application programming interface (API) which is internal code for the site that gives programmers greater customization options. By partnering with multiple worker channels, CrowdFlower provides you with access to a workforce that runs 24/7.

> **DULY NOTED**
>
> You can access your own in-house team as your crowd labor pool using CrowdFlower's internal interface, which provides you and your workers with access to CrowdFlower's technology to assign, claim, and manage tasks.

Here are the basic steps for using the Self Service tool, after you register for free:

1. Upload your data. Some task types, such as surveys, do not require data upload.

2. Build the task interface. You have two options: the graphic editor for simpler tasks (such as ratings and text input), and the CrowdFlower Markup Language (CML) Editor for more complex tasks (such as identifying subjects of photographs and performing different tasks based on what is in each photograph).

3. Add gold. To ensure accuracy for your task, create gold-standard data that CrowdFlower can insert into the task with known answer checkpoints. This will train new users to provide the responses you expect and remove workers incapable of performing to your standards.

4. Define or calibrate your task. You determine how much you pay. CrowdFlower will suggest a payment amount, but you can decide to pay less or more based on the time it takes to complete the task.

5. Select worker channels. You can decide how far and wide to broadcast your task, such as running it on Mechanical Turk, Samasource, or Give Work.

6. Run your task. Once your task is broadcast to the crowdworkers and they sign on to perform it, you can view individual worker performances and see the rate at which they are completing the task.

When the job is complete, you can receive a spreadsheet of results in a variety of formats, including CSV. You can also receive your results in real time if you are using CrowdFlower's API, but the set-up requires a programmer to install.

Samasource Changes Lives

Samasource (samasource.com) has a mission to "reduce poverty among people in low-income communities around the world by providing dignified, technology-based work." The company sets out to bring quality work opportunities to remote areas and refugee sites throughout the world. Unlike most other crowdsourcing labor sites, Samasource operates as a nonprofit organization.

Services through Samasource include Samaguard, which provides moderation of image and text-based content; Samascribe, which provides audio and video time-stamped transcriptions; and Samaproof, which includes data mining, data enrichment, and business listings verification. Other services include digitization of receipts, books, and archival documents as well as text and numerical data entry.

Dedicated, full-time workers around the world access the Samasource online platform—called the SamaHub—from work delivery centers that are monitored by Samasource staff. Samasource integrates account managers and professionals into their work process to ensure quality, accuracy, and prompt turnaround times. Workers are managed and paid by Samasource Service Partners, including other non-profit organizations, grassroots businesses that have social missions, and educational institutions. Most of their partners are located in Africa and Asia, in areas where unemployment among skilled workers is often as high as 70 percent.

To date, Samasource has contracted over $1.5 million worth of work with both for-profit companies and large nonprofits. The company also accepts donations directly from their site. In partnership with CrowdFlower, Samasource has an iPhone application that lets users perform short on-screen tasks, which in turn helps to train workers at the world's largest refugee camp in Dadaab, Kenya.

Human Tasks on Amazon Mechanical Turk

Mechanical Turk was launched publicly by Amazon.com in 2005 as a "crowdsourcing Internet marketplace." To start using it, you can either log in with your existing Amazon account or create a new one. Once you're in the system as a requester, watch the video tutorial to get familiar with the site.

From Mechanical Turk, you can design your HIT, publish it, and manage it. To pay for your HITs, fund a prepaid Mechanical Turk account with either a credit card or bank account. The system won't let you proceed to enter and publish your first HIT until you upload funds into your account.

Getting Started with Mechanical Turk

From the **Resource Center** page, click on the **Design** tab to design your HIT template. You can also choose from sample HIT templates for tasks such as image tagging, data collection, surveys, product comparison, product categorization, and data correction. Choose a template that is close to your task and rename the template for your own administrative viewing so you can easily identify your task. Name your task and fill in a description that workers can view. This content helps workers decide whether they want to work on your task. Add keywords to your HIT so it shows up appropriately when workers search for particular tasks. Include your requester name in your keywords so, over time, workers can specifically find your tasks.

After you set up your HIT, set rules, including time allotted per assignment (to dictate how long a worker can hold on to your task) and an expiration date. You can target your HIT to workers with a high approval rating or publish it to the entire worker crowd. If you choose a higher approval rating, this will eliminate both workers who have not displayed top quality and new workers who haven't yet been rated.

You can also check a box labeled **Required for Preview**. This allows only those with the right qualifications to view your HIT details. The worker crowd at large can still see your HIT listed with a description, but only qualified workers can claim the task.

Launching Your Mechanical Turk Task

After you build the framework for your HIT, you can set the reward you are offering. The site sets five cents as the default amount. A higher amount can bring in workers more quickly. You can also request multiple workers for the same HIT to get more answers with a greater number of perspectives or for comparison purposes. Next, enter the amount of time you are allotting for the automatic approval of work, such as four days. This is a safeguard to make sure the worker gets paid. Otherwise, you have control over payment once you review the completed work.

If you know how to edit HTML, you can edit your HIT design template. You can modify the layout for your HIT, including the text and adding an embedded image or link. You can also create fields for worker responses. Preview your template as it will appear to the workers. When you save it, it is moved to the Publish page under the **Publish** tab, next to the **Design** tab. Give it a final review; if it looks correct, click **Next** for the Summary page, where you can review what you'll be charged for both Mechanical Turk fees and what you'll pay the worker or workers.

To review task status and the work performed, go to the **Manage** tab. Be prepared to review work within the time frame you set for your task and approve or reject it. If you don't take further action, the system will automatically approve and pay the worker.

Using Clickworker.com

Clickworker.com (clickworker.com/en) is a content-oriented site that specifically lists writing, translating, researching, and data processing as the work that can be done through their site. Based in Germany, Clickworker.com has been expanding its presence in the U.S. market.

You can place single text orders or multiple orders as you need work performed. Processing time varies depending on the type of task workers perform for you. The Clickworker.com site is partially self-service, but even if you place an order via a form, Clickworker.com staff will review your order for clarity and brevity and to break down the project into smaller tasks.

Services in Clickworker.com

Begin ordering work through Clickworker.com by reviewing their list of services, which are broken down into three main categories, with specific tasks listed for each category. Click on the appropriate task, and you're led either to an order form you can fill out or contact information for the company so you can explain your work request. For tasks with forms, Clickworker.com provides pricing up front. For those that don't, you can request information directly from the company.

Here is a breakdown of the services they list with a notation if there is a form or contact information:

Clickworker.com Services

Text and Content	Organization and Structuring	Research and Surveys
Text Creation (form)	Tagging (contact)	Web Research (contact)
Translations (form)	Categorization (contact)	Surveys (contact)
SEO Texts (form)		
Resume Check (form)		

Clickworker.com has a labor crowd of over 68,000 workers registered as independent contractors on their site.

Working Through Clickworker.com

The Clickworker.com process is similar to other crowdsourcing labor sites, walking you through a number of steps, from ordering work to reviewing completed work:

1. Place your order with work instructions. Select the level and type of quality control you want.

2. Clickworker.com converts your order into microtasks.

3. Clickworkers must qualify to work on your task based on relevant skills assessments.

4. Qualified Clickworkers log in to their workplace on the Clickworker.com site to process your task.

5. Quality control is performed by the Clickworker.com platform, based on the level you set when you placed your order.

6. Clickworker.com completes your order by converting completed microtasks into the overall completed project.

7. You can then download your completed order.

You can also use the Clickworker API, tapping into the system and Clickworkers directly, but this requires programming set-up. Payment is processed through PayPal, although you can also use a credit card through the PayPal interface.

Clickworker.com can get you a quick turnaround in a cost-effective manner, but both speed and cost depends on your specific tasks. Working with Clickworkers or other crowdsourced workers augments your capacity on demand.

DULY NOTED

Because you access Clickworker.com via the web, the site recommends using Microsoft Internet Explorer, Mozilla Firefox, or Apple Safari. You may need to download a new browser if you do not have one that's compatible.

When Crowdsourcing Doesn't Work

Before you begin your project on a crowdsourcing labor site, check to see what kind of guarantee or refund might be provided if the work is unacceptable. Most of these sites—if they don't offer refunds—have mechanisms to ensure that work is completed well. Those mechanisms may include automated checks and balances based on rating systems to help weed out workers generating lower quality.

Crowdsourcing can be an effective way to get tasks done, but in several situations, this kind of micro-labor process doesn't work well. If relationships are important to the work being done, you may be better off finding a site where you can have more day-to-day interaction, such as a freelance marketplace or an agency that uses crowdsourcing as part of its offerings. Both are business models in which you can benefit from crowds but also have a one-to-one relationship to have ongoing dialogue and control over work.

The more complex your work, the less likely it is that crowdsourcing through micro-labor will be effective, unless you can break down your project into small parts. The larger and more complex the project, the more challenging it is to break it down into parts. You also have the additional burden of tracking and managing many microtask projects and bringing them all together to fulfill the project as a whole.

When crowdsourcing micro-labor, it should be possible to complete and verify your work online. You should be able to determine whether work is done correctly or incorrectly and set up ways to verify work within the site's systems for the most efficient work process and outcome. By monitoring work progress, you can assess if your incentive is sufficient or if your directions are clear enough. You should also be able to change course midstream if things aren't going as well as you'd like.

The Least You Need to Know

- Work performed through crowdsourcing labor sites typically doesn't have to be performed by highly skilled workers.
- Select the type of task you need done or specify skills needed to complete the task to route your job to appropriately skilled individuals.
- Set realistic expectations about the outcomes. Not every task is well-suited for crowdsourcing.
- The more complex your work, the less likely crowdsourcing through micro-labor will be effective, unless you can break down your project into small parts.

Crowd Competitions

In This Chapter

- Using crowd competition sites
- Understanding crowd competition site pricing
- Holding your own crowd competition
- Considering legalities for online competitions

A recurring theme in many crowdsourcing activities is crowd competition, also referred to as a crowd contest, in which sites and companies present projects to a crowd to work on and offer a reward to the winning submission or submissions. Crowd competitions are also referred to as competitions, challenges, open calls, projects, and campaigns.

Technically, crowd competitions aren't your typical online contest. Rather, they function more like a request for proposals, or a pitch or bidding process. Someone gets the job or their work gets picked, and they receive some kind of consideration for their efforts.

Holding Competitions for Results

Competitions for crowdsourcing are common amongst designers, such as graphic artists. In design competitions, designers perform speculative work, or work "on spec," meaning they work on a design to near or full completion and submit their design in response to an open call. Programmers are familiar with the concept of crowd competitions and often participate in events such as "bug races" to identify software bugs. In many cases, programmers participate for the prestige.

DULY NOTED

In some circles, there is a backlash against speculative work called "no spec work." Some designers are against design competitions and the requirement that designers submit speculative work.

Either peers or other members of a design competition site vote on a designer's submitted work. A crowdsourcing service provider (CSP) may act as an intermediary and select the winning submission, or the company soliciting submissions may make the ultimate decision. In programming, programmers can submit code to identify bugs or bad code, including actual solutions to vexing coding errors.

You can organize your own crowd competitions, but if you don't have a large crowd already in place, you may end up spending most of your time, money, and resources publicizing your competition to garner interest. If you don't have an unlimited marketing budget, you may be better off submitting your projects to reputable competition sites that have built-in crowds awaiting assignments. Using crowdsourcing competition sites gives you a powerful creative engine driven by the site's back-end technology and tools and their active and engaged crowd. Still, holding your own competition from scratch is an option.

BEST PRACTICES

Mobile applications developer WinePicks used the creative crowdsourcing site Tongal to crowdsource concepts for a 30-second television commercial and then the actual commercial. The company received 206 submissions and spent a total of $15,000—a fraction of the cost of a television advertisement produced by a traditional advertising agency. The money covered awards to the top five pitches and the top five video submissions. The winning video's producer received about $4,800.

Projects for Competitions

Not everything you want done can or should be crowdsourced. Even if it is suitable for crowdsourcing, it might not work well as a competition or contest. Most successful competition sites focus on marketing, branding, design, coding, ideas, and innovation.

Even if you pick the right project for crowdsourcing, there are some common pitfalls that can make or break a crowdsourcing project:

- **Low prize money:** Each site has its own average range for prize or reward money and the amount should be commensurate to the project's complexity. Some sites let you lowball the crowd, while others set reasonable minimums. The latter sites are most likely more successful and reputable.

- **Crowd too small:** Not every online competition is run with a large and built-in community, so you're better off picking a competition site that already has a crowd.

- **Project too complicated:** Complex problems can be solved with crowdsourcing, but don't get your hopes up that a competition will solve everything. Temper your expectations.

- **Short turnaround time:** Competitions can deliver speedy results, but tight deadlines don't always mean submissions will come more quickly. If time is of the essence, you may not want to take a chance on a crowd competition.

Trying a Crowd Competition Site

Try starting a project on an existing competition site to get familiar with the process, before holding your own crowd competition from scratching. Find one that can help you with a smaller project.

As you go through crowd competition sites, you aren't entering these competitions; instead, you're providing projects for which the site's crowd members can enter submissions. Most crowd competition site activity is facilitated by behind-the-scenes technology to gather, sort, and manage the competition. An added benefit of participating in crowd competition sites is that the crowd gains exposure to your company and brand. The crowd can also help promote your brand to their social media connections as they promote their participation in your contest.

To find the right site to handle your project, conduct a web search of the following phrases (depending on your needs):

- Design competitions

- Idea competitions

- Innovation competitions

- Branding competitions

- Programming competitions

- Coding competitions

There are blogs that post information about various competitions, such as ideacrossing. com and dailycrowdsource.com. Perusing these blogs may lead you to a suitable site. Each crowd competition site has its own prize ranges; these can be influenced by the site's quality, the crowd's quality, and the job's complexity. Crowdsourcing simple ideas can be less costly than looking for a solution to a scientific problem.

Each crowd competition site has its own process for projects and submissions. Most consider the project provider to be the client, but in some cases, they use terms like "seeker." The site may call the person who submits a response to the project open call the worker, crowd member, or solver, or the site may refer to her or him according to skill set, such as designer, coder, or creative.

Using CrowdSPRING

CrowdSPRING is one of the largest creative communities, with over 75,000 designers and writers connected to their site. They claim you will receive over 110 entries for your project brief. This may sound impressive, but keep in mind you will have to review all those entries. They also offer a 100 percent satisfaction guarantee.

You start on the CrowdSPRING by posting a project. Your choices are Print Design (awards start at $300), Logo and Stationery ($300 minimum), Logo Design ($200 minimum), Company Naming ($200 minimum), or Small Website Design ($600 minimum).

CrowdSPRING offers three levels of service that come with an additional listing fee: Economy (a $39 listing fee), Standard (a $129 listing fee), and Pro (a $199 listing fee). The Pro level includes nondisclosure agreements, a private brief for approved creatives, and a minimum award of at least $1,000 (although this varies based on type of project). The Pro level provides add-on fee-based services inclusive in the price such as exclusion from search engines (an additional $29 for Economy or Standard levels) and basic or advanced promotions (normally $49 or $99 for Economy or Standard levels). The Pro level gives you more control over who sees and is invited to respond to your project.

Once you choose the type of project and level, you can name your project, specify your award (with an option to include a second award), choose an end date, choose optional features (such as search engine exclusion for $29), set entries to private ($49), and choose a promotional package (optional). Next, fill out the rest of your design brief, including target audience, style concept, and materials, which are files you want to upload and share. Finish your set-up by prepping a contract, completing your site registration, reviewing your brief, and submitting payment information. Then, watch the entries come in! Keep in mind that your participation in the review process will contribute to the overall success of your crowdsourcing campaign.

Using Guerra Creativa

Guerra Creativa calls their competitions "design contests." Their site helps you launch a variety of design contests and offers support and sites in English, Spanish, and Portuguese. They cover design including web, logo, stationery, Flash animation, 3D, icons and buttons, and banner ads. Guerra Creativa offers a simple process: set up your competition, evaluate entries, and pick a winner on their site.

They offer a 100 percent risk-free nonguaranteed competition, and will refund the listing price and prize money within 60 days of the close of your competition if you don't choose a submission. If you guarantee payment, you may see more submissions because it's more enticing to designers to know you are making a commitment to the competition. The site charges $19.50 for a private competition, which means it's viewable by only the site's community members; otherwise, your competition will be viewable by the public.

You can choose the duration of your competition and set the prize amount based on their pre-established pricing levels. For example, a logo design can start at $150, and the site specifies that you can expect about 25 design submissions at that price. For the standard level at $275, you can expect about 50 designs. For the premium level at $475, you can expect about 75 designs. You can also set a custom price, but you can't go below the minimum budget price for each type of design. As you choose the price level, the site automatically calculates a percentage fee on top of the design prize.

The rest of the submission process is similar to most other design competition sites. You fill out a design brief and launch your competition. And like other design sites, your participation and feedback is strongly encouraged to get the best results.

Sourcing Design, Getting Results

Software developer Tim Goggins was looking for some designs for his business. He'd worked with graphic designers before, but he was hoping for fresh ideas. He'd heard about crowdsourcing and turned to CrowdSPRING to get a website design. Satisfied with the results, he then submitted a project to get a logo and later an icon he needed to represent one of his software products. Each time, he carefully submitted clear specs that outlined and illustrated what he envisioned. Then, he waited as the submissions came in.

Goggins learned not to be discouraged when only a few initial submissions trickled in and the quality was low. He learned that the good designers tended to wait toward the end of a submissions process to learn from the feedback he gave to other designers. Inevitably, he found the design he wanted a few days before the end of each project. On only one occasion did he fail to find a suitable design—for a highly specialized interface for a shopping cart system. He was able to get a refund from the site, but Goggins remains enthusiastic about crowdsourcing artwork and plans to use this process anytime he needs a new design.

Using Squadhelp

Squadhelp's self-described mission is to "build an online community of experts who can help you market and grow your business at a fraction of the cost you would pay third party agencies." Squadhelp facilitates "branding and marketing contests"—their term—in the areas of domain names, viral video, viral marketing, SEO, usability and website testing, and article writing. The steps for the site are straightforward:

1. Choose your package. You can select a package based on the competition you want to run and your budget.

2. Describe your content. You can input your project description or upload a project brief. They have a budget level, premium level, and a level to set your own prize amount.

3. Select listing features. You can choose to bold your listing for $5, feature your listing for $10, make your listing private for $15, or feature your competition on the Squadhelp home page for $25.

4. Choose a payment amount and method of payment. You can make payments through the site using Visa, MasterCard, American Express, and PayPal, and all transactions are in U.S. dollars.

The site offers a 100 percent money-back guarantee if at the end of your project you do not like any of the submissions. If that's the case, you need to contact Squadhelp within 30 days of the end of the competition.

Using Prova

Prova is a site consisting of crowdsource advertising creatives. Through their competitions, Prova provides a long list of print, web, audio, and video deliverables. From billboard designs to business cards, audio books to instructional videos, Prova brings designers and developers together with clients—usually small businesses seeking quality creative work at an affordable price. Prova also refers to their process as a contest.

To use Prova, start out by filling in a creative brief outlining your industry, needs, advertisement goals, target audience, messaging, deadline, and other details that are important to convey to the design crowd. Then, pick your price. Competition prize amounts on this site range from $200 to $10,000, with the average being $300. Usually, the higher amounts encompass awards for several winning submissions.

Prova automatically tacks on a flat listing charge of $39.99, plus a percentage of the prize money you specify. You can also choose to enhance your Prova competition listing for a fee, such as $29.99 to make your listing private to the Prova community; $7.99 to bold your listing; $9.99 to highlight your listing; and $19.99 to include a private label for your competition, for a more branded appearance.

After you have launched your competition, interact with the designers, provide them with critical feedback, and request necessary modifications. You retain complete rights to the final design you pick. You pay Prova up front to launch your competition, but if you aren't completely satisfied with the submissions you receive, Prova will provide a full refund. To date, the company has received very few refund requests.

Setting Up a Competition

If you decide to hold your own crowd competition, consider the legal side of online competitions. Consult with a lawyer to make sure you cover yourself, especially considering each state has its own laws regarding online competitions.

Next, make sure you have the technical tools in place to manage the entire crowdsourcing process, including making the competition announcement, receiving submissions, assessing submissions, providing feedback, selecting the winning submission, and providing the winner with an appropriate reward. To pick the right tools, you need to establish what kind of crowd competition you want to run. Sourcing logo designs requires tools with different capacities than sourcing 30-second video spots, and sourcing answers or ideas doesn't require as much technology as anything involving file uploads and downloads.

Some crowdsourcing sites operate like a bidding process, in which crowd members bid on your project or make pitches, and don't have to submit completed work. In some cases, there is a seemingly fine line between crowdsourcing and putting out a request for proposal (RFP), which is a more traditional and straightforward process, usually conducted partly online and partly offline. You can dress up your RFP announcement as a crowd competition, but that may be misleading. Some of the tools you use to organize a crowdsourcing campaign may prove useful for an RFP process, but if the entire process doesn't take place online, then chances are you aren't crowdsourcing.

> **BEST PRACTICES**
>
> Don't think of crowdsourcing competitions as passive campaigns where you just put out a call for submissions and watch them come in. Your participation in the competition process may mean the difference between a successful campaign and one that falls flat.

Some crowd competition sites require that crowd members submit work speculatively for feedback from you, the client. In those cases you are encouraged to provide feedback on each submission and allow the crowd members to submit revisions. Other crowd competitions involve problem solving, and the first person to submit an answer that solves the problem wins the prize. In both cases, you pick the winning submission, which is essentially a finished product, whether a file or information. If this is the model you're looking to employ, then make sure you know the legal issues involved with calling your open call a competition.

Defining Your Project

Before you put out an open call for submissions, you need to clearly define what you're seeking and be able to articulate your request in a creative brief or project description. You may want to take a look at how crowd competition sites take project submissions and review some of their intake forms as a guide for detailing your own project.

More importantly, if you are running an online competition, you need to clearly lay out what criteria you will use to judge the competition and who will be judging. To avoid potential legal issues, you must show that there are specific judging criteria that you will follow so it is clear to the people submitting to the competition. Consult a lawyer for particulars on acceptable and unacceptable online competition practices.

If you are crowdsourcing design work, how you ultimately pick a particular logo design or ad banner is subjective, but you still need to specify some objective criteria. Receiving an answer to a problem is less subjective. In both cases, you can list your criteria in the creative or project brief and reiterate it in ground rules or guidelines you can post to your site.

How you define your project and state your desired outcome will shape the kinds of responses you'll get. How you participate during the steps of your competition will affect your outcome.

Setting Up the Mechanics

To manage your competition, you need to establish how you'll receive submissions and in what formats. In your project brief, outline the specifications for any materials submitted by designers. What you say up front may facilitate a successful crowdsourcing process, but the behind-the-scenes technology you use is equally important.

You can receive submissions in a number of ways that don't require major programming or building a custom site. Your options depend on the type of competition you are running and the kind of submissions you'll be receiving. If you'll be receiving large files, you'll want to use a service that allows you to receive and store those files. In the early days of the Internet, you might have used file transfer protocol (FTP) site, providing others with the address to upload files to a folder on your FTP server. These days, companies provide services that replace FTP so you can easily receive and store files without needing your own server.

FilesDIRECT lets you create a web page where you can direct competition participants. All they have to do is click on a button on that page, select the files from their computer, and then upload. The files are stored on the services' servers for you to access and retrieve. Check the file transfer limits and storage amounts for each paid level of service. For FilesDIRECT, costs are $18 per month for a 500 megabyte transfer limit and 10 gigabytes of storage, or for $80 per month you can have a 2.5 gigabytes transfer limit and 50 gigabytes of storage.

Similar FTP replacement services include SendYourFiles, which provides a dropbox where people can send large files to you, and SendThisFile, which offers a Filebox to receive large files. When you receive the files, you'll still have to download them to your computer, view them, and then provide feedback to each competition participant. You can also upload them to a forum where you can easily view and comment on them and where you can interact with the competition participants.

Corresponding with Submitters

You need a way to correspond with competition participants or submitters. E-mail may work to a certain extent, depending on the number of submissions and the need for dialogue. If you go the e-mail route, set up a new e-mail address and e-mail box that will allow you to keep all related correspondence in one place. Use an e-mail client that threads e-mail conversations together, such as Gmail or new versions of Outlook.

You can also capture the dialogue between you and the contestants through an online community or group site. You can invite people who have sent in submissions to the group. Then, you can create forums where you post submissions you've received and provide feedback for group members to see. You can use sites such as Google Groups or Grouply, or you can use sites where you can create private subgroups to give one-on-one feedback privately, such as Ning.

There is something to be said for keeping the submission and commenting process visible to at least the submitters, if not the public. On crowd competition sites, a lot of the value for you as the client and for the designers or people submitting comes from being able to see what others are submitting and the feedback you are giving.

Making the Payment

Payments on crowdsourcing competition sites are commonly made via PayPal, but there are other reliable forms of payment. If you're running an online crowd competition, be careful not to violate any federal or state laws regarding online competitions. There are laws and legal processes to protect consumers from being duped by fake online competitions and sweepstakes in states such as Florida and New York. First, establish with your lawyer whether your crowd competition falls under the laws of online competitions and discuss how to properly set it up—particularly the prize money—to avoid future problems.

When initiating a crowd competition, you're typically looking to engage someone to provide work for which you will compensate them, and yet you're choosing from a pool of submissions to obtain the best work. Crowd competition sites typically hold the money you've put forth for the winning submission or submissions, and then disperse it to the winner or winners once you've made your decision.

If you're holding the competition on your own, you need to somehow guarantee participants that you'll pay the award money to a winner as promised. Sometimes, you can build confidence by putting the money into an *escrow account*. Check with an accountant about how to properly set aside money so everyone knows you are legitimate.

> **DEFINITION**
>
> Putting money into **escrow** or in an **escrow account** is an arrangement wherein an independent and trusted third party receives and later disburses money for two or more parties involved in a transaction. This arrangement can give peace of mind to the party providing the service, and is used often by freelance sites like Elance (elance.com) and Guru (guru.com).

Consult a lawyer before announcing your crowd competition to make sure you are complying with all laws and that you properly demonstrate that the money you've promised as a prize will actually be paid out. You should also include statements of assurance and guarantee about payment on your site.

Promoting Your Competition

When you've worked out all the details for your online crowd competition, post your project brief in a number of formats for easy access:

- A page on your site
- A PDF document linked from your site
- A text announcement on your favorite social network sites
- A posting in appropriate online communities

For more information on promoting your competitions, see Chapter 6 for tips on how to invite people to join your crowd and refer back to Chapter 4 for additional do-it-yourself tips.

Competition Caveats

One of the biggest things to avoid running a crowd competition is getting bogged down by the mechanics and technical side of the competition. If you start feeling stressed over your competition from the start, you can always fall back on existing crowd competition sites to streamline your process.

Avoid starting a competition without having access to an active and engaged crowd, if you're not already hosting your own. Without a crowd, you could end up spending most of your efforts publicizing your competition to get a reasonable number of submissions. Having a small pool of submissions reduces your chance of receiving quality submissions.

Many people, particularly in the design industry, frown on the practice of requesting speculation work before hiring someone, but many people from around the world—including designers—participate willingly in this process. Programmers tend to participate often in competitions and enter them for the monetary rewards and the prestige amongst their peers. You can find debates online about this issue by searching the web for "no-spec movement."

Keeping in mind the potential issues surrounding holding and participating in crowd competitions, you can still use them to receive a variety of submissions from people with all levels of skills and talent. By casting a wide net and offering a prize, you can get work done or find the best worker for the job.

The Least You Need to Know

- Crowdsourcing competitions are common among designers such as graphic artists. Programmers are also familiar with the concept of crowd competitions, and often participate for the prestige.
- You can organize your own crowd competitions, but if you don't have a large crowd in place, you could spend most of your time, money, and resources publicizing your competition.
- Most successful competition sites cover marketing, branding, design, coding, ideas, and innovation.
- Consult with a lawyer to make sure you cover yourself legally, especially since each state has its own laws regarding online competitions.
- If you start feeling stressed over your competition, you can fall back on existing crowd competition sites to streamline your process.

Crowdsourcing Freelance Work and Consulting

In This Chapter

- Finding freelancers in the crowd
- Managing virtual freelance workers
- Working with agencies that crowdsource
- Getting the most out of freelance and creative crowdsourcing

Another type of crowdworker community is sometimes referred to as a freelancer marketplace. On sites like Elance, Guru, and oDesk, you can post your projects and receive bids from freelancers rather than actual work submissions. These differ from crowdsourced labor sites such as CrowdFlower and Mechanical Turk because the tasks are more complex and usually require higher skill levels. They also differ from crowd competition sites in that they don't require workers to submit work on spec; instead, they let them bid on projects.

Somewhere in between crowd competition sites and freelancer marketplaces are agencies that act as middlemen between you and the freelancing crowd. Each of these agencies has developed its own work process and way of leveraging communities of crowdworkers to produce work for a client.

Freelancer Marketplaces

Before crowdsourcing was even a buzzword—meaning pre-2006—there were sites that built up large communities of freelance workers and developed web-based systems to match clients with freelancers, commonly referred to as *freelancer marketplaces*. Like other crowd communities, where you can find someone to do work for you, these sites have active workers on the lookout for job opportunities. These sites let you reach out to these large crowds of workers with your job posting, making it more likely that it will be seen by more people—and more of the right people. This kind of pro-active outreach replaces the typical classified ad in a newspaper, which is far more passive.

> **DEFINITION**
>
> **Freelancer marketplaces** are websites that gather a large crowd of skilled workers and facilitate matching workers to jobs, along with vetting, hiring, managing, and payment.

Some freelancer marketplaces consider what they do crowdsourcing; others use the term outsourcing. In a way, they're a hybrid. You're technically outsourcing work to a freelancer or a virtual team, but to find your freelancer, you're posting your opportunities to an attentive and interactive crowd gathered for the specific purpose of matching workers with jobs. Freelancer marketplaces are all about finding the right person for each job, and the sites usually build into their systems features to help you vet, hire, manage, and pay the workers.

Freelancer marketplaces differ from crowdsourcing competitions or contest sites because they don't operate on a speculative model. They let you cast a wide net to get your job opportunity in front of many, but you must then go through a more traditional review process for the bids you receive, and then hire and pay the individual worker based on pre-established rates.

Steps to Crowdsourcing Freelancers

Elance, Guru, and oDesk each work off a similar framework for matching clients to freelancers and vice versa. Each system also has proprietary features. All three sites include mechanisms in their systems to handle monetary transactions to guarantee payment to the worker.

You can join any of these sites as a client or buyer and post a project. Soon after, you'll begin receiving bids, resumés, or some other kind of input from the community of freelancers in response to your post. You can then select the worker or workers of your choice, and in some cases manage the workers straight from the site. Then, review and accept the work and pay the worker. These sites let you specify industry experience and other skills required for your particular project, and even choose a location requirement, if necessary. Most work performed by these sites is done remotely.

Posting a Project

Most freelancer marketplaces start you off with a submission process to assist in posting your project to their crowd. Using Guru Employer, you start by selecting a skill category for your project ranging from technology to creative arts to business. Then you give your project a title and description, and attach any relevant files. You're prompted to also pick an estimated project budget from less than $250 to more than $25,000. Pick a skill category and up to two skill subcategories. You might pick public relations, with brand management and marketing communications as subcategories.

You can make your project public to everyone or to only Guru vendors who qualify, or you can make it viewable by invitation only. At this point, the Guru system lets you post your project if you're in a hurry, or you can continue with the application process to add other qualifications, such as onsite or offsite, duration, rate offered, and inputting any questions you want freelancers to answer in their bids. You can post to Guru for free, with no obligation to hire.

Elance starts in a similar way to Guru—naming your job and describing it. You then choose your job type, either hourly or with a fixed price. Then, select a category ranging from administrative support to writing and translation. You can also pick a subcategory and specific skills related to the job. Advanced criteria on Elance include job location, how long you want your post to remain online, a proposed start date, and job posting visibility options (including public or private). You can choose the option to make your listing accessible via search engines such as Google to have an even wider reach. After you fill out your job notice, you're led to a registration form to register as an employer on the Elance site. There is a one-time $10 activation fee to get started with an employer account.

On oDesk, you can search for contractors or post a job free of charge. You can also bring your own virtual team into the oDesk system or assemble a team from their community. oDesk starts you off with a form to open an account. The system walks you through describing your company first and then your job project. Like Guru and Elance, you name your project, describe it, pick a job type (hourly or fixed), attach related files, and specify preferred qualifications. oDesk includes the option to specify a worker's feedback score to narrow submissions to more qualified workers. You can then specify location, any tests they must have passed to work on your project, whether or not they must have a portfolio, their level of English, and how many hours they have billed on oDesk.

The oDesk system automatically tells you how many contractors on the system match your criteria as you select options. Depending on your criteria, you can go from tens of thousands of potential candidates to double digits. Once you verify your e-mail address, you can enter a credit card number to go through a final verification process, which you must complete before you can hire a contractor. Once you accept the oDesk agreement for using their service, oDesk will post your job and you can start looking out for proposals.

Managing Bids and Resumés

Guru lets you open your project announcement to everyone or keep it contained and private. There are over 250,000 active freelancers on the site, but you have the power to refine searches based on your criteria. You can tweak criteria as you go. Guru's site tools help you sort responses, and the sorting criteria Guru uses includes previous performance data based on proposal quality, earnings, and repeat business earned.

Elance has over 100,000 workers in their community. When you post your job and begin receiving proposals, you can interact with prospective service providers and interview them using voice or messaging built into the Elance system, or you can choose to meet with them offline.

On oDesk, you can keep track of your jobs and responses under the My Jobs tab. You can review active or completed contracts under the same tab. Your oDesk homepage is a dashboard view of notifications that track activity on your account, your job postings, your team members, and your payments.

Making Your Worker Selection

After you select your worker on Guru, click the **Award My Project Now** button. The system e-mails the freelancer and gives them the option to accept or reject the work. If they accept, they're added to your team on the site and their information is displayed under the Project Manager section of your Guru account. You're also notified via e-mail that they have accepted the project.

Before starting work with a freelancer on a freelancer marketplace, you need to put an agreement in place. Guru calls this a Project Agreement, and it consists of the project plan, milestones, and change orders (meaning how you plan to handle revisions on the project).

On Elance, you can review proposals from candidates that include a cost estimate. You can also compare worker profiles and their experience, ratings, credentials, and portfolios. When you're picking a worker, Elance recommends you review their skills, feedback from previous jobs, their portfolio, keywords that show a provider's areas of interest, and their summary (which provides additional professional background information). You can review applicants and then rate them as you go along to narrow down your choices. You can also ask providers questions and make a final choice.

Using oDesk, you can review applications by rates, qualification matches, reviews, cover letters, and contractor profiles. You can send out messages to start the interview process right through the site. When you make your choice, click the **Contact** button on a worker's profile to make an offer and decline the ones you don't want to hire. All interactions for tracking the hiring process are managed through the oDesk system.

Managing Your Freelancer

Guru has a section on their site called Project Manager, which—along with message boards—helps you keep track of your projects and workers. This section includes the finalized project agreement and a workroom where you can share files with your worker.

Elance has a similar area called Workroom where you can view and manage work in progress online, communicate in real time with workers, and hold live virtual meetings. The system lets you upload screenshots, files, and completed work in one place. The Workroom also provides alerts, status reports, and terms and milestones to keep your project on track. The Elance Work View software is a screenshot-streaming feature that lets you watch work in progress. Timesheets with screenshots are your way of verifying that workers are completing your work.

oDesk has a Team Room where you can review your team members, update them, group them into different teams, and view to see who has been working recently on one of your jobs. The Work Diary section is where your contractors log what they've been working on so you can manage your project. The Reports section offers Timelogs or reports that summarize payments and completed work each week. TimeAnalyze summarizes team hours and tasks. You can also assign task codes to tasks for better management and reporting.

oDesk has a desktop tool called oDesk Team that lets you see who on your team is working, what they are working on, and their activity level. You can use the application to chat via an instant messaging tool. Providers initiate time tracking as they work, and oDesk offers a system that can automatically take periodic screenshots to document work in progress.

Paying Your Virtual Worker

Guru's SafePay Escrow service offers a satisfaction guarantee. You only pay for work you've approved and accepted. Some freelancers may ask for a deposit up front; deposits are nonrefundable, however, and Guru leaves it to you to take on that financial risk. After you establish a relationship with a worker, you can choose to forego the escrow service. Guru takes a percentage fee from the worker based on what you've paid.

On Elance, you can approve work according to project milestones or use the system's Work View timesheets to assess work rendered before you trigger payment. For fixed-price projects, you can release payments based on achieved milestones. Elance also offers Elance Escrow service and has a satisfaction guarantee. In addition to handling payments, Elance takes care of workers' 1099 tax filings. After your project ends, you're asked to rate the work. The Elance rating system is critical to workers because it helps them get additional jobs on the system. Elance makes its money from service fees on the service provider side, meaning the worker pays a percentage of earnings to Elance. Elance also collects a small percentage of fees from third-party payment processors, such as credit card companies.

To pay a worker via oDesk, you must have a verified account. Hourly jobs are billed weekly. You can also opt to pay a weekly rate or break payments for fixed-price contracts into milestone payments. Some contractors request upfront payment on jobs, but this amount is nonrefundable. oDesk doesn't offer an escrow service, so fixed-price jobs can be risky for the contractor if you don't pay up front, or risky for you if you pay up front. oDesk takes a higher percentage of the payment made to contractors than its competitors.

Agencies That Crowdsource

Freelancer marketplaces are a hybrid of outsourcing and crowdsourcing. Another hybrid is agencies that offer services wherein part of their service is based on a crowdsourcing model. These companies are different from crowdsourced labor sites in that the crowds are highly skilled. The agencies offer creative crowdsourced solutions to clients, and can come in the form of ad agencies, marketing companies, and consulting firms. Each agency builds proprietary crowd communities and crowdsourcing processes into a part or parts of their work process. One example of a crowdsourced full-service marketing agency is blur Group, profiled in Chapter 5.

Creative crowdsourcing companies offer clients strategic planning and guidance. They may make the crowd visible to you or the crowd may be a seamless or invisible asset in the overall creative process. Crowdsourcing marketing and advertising services give you a larger number of outcomes or end products, versus working directly with a more traditional agency. In addition to more options and choices, you usually see deeper cost savings than you see when crowdsourcing work from virtual crowds.

Working with Victors & Spoils

Victors & Spoils (victorsandspoils.com) is an advertising agency with a goal of getting more people, and the best thinking, involved in the creative process. They use crowdsourcing principles, along with proprietary digital tools, to deliver work to you. Their community consists of 3,000 individuals worldwide who submit creative ideas to address client creative briefs.

The crowd brought together by Victors & Spoils consists of individuals who have a higher degree of training than crowd labor workers, and usually have some experience working in the advertising industry. They're skilled producers, art directors, product designers, and other creative types. The agency puts a framework around the crowd, including a proprietary reputation ranking system, to help them select the right crowd members for your project.

If you work with Victors & Spoils, the agency is hands-on and looks first to understand your brand and business challenges. The creative brief they craft with you describes your brand challenge and the brief either goes out to the whole crowd as an open call or Victors & Spoils pulls together a team from the larger crowd to participate directly on your project. The agency reviews solutions and directs the overall creative process for you. They can also break your project down into phases and might source work from different crowds for different phases of the process.

By stepping between you and the crowd, Victors & Spoils manages the large volume of responses and interaction required to properly source creative work from a crowd. Crowdsourcing helps them generate and deliver creative ideas in a fast and cost-efficient way. You pay for the ideas without the overhead you might pay when working with a traditional agency.

Working with Poptent

Poptent (poptent.net) is a social network that produces crowdsourced videos for online and offline use. The company connects major brand advertisers and advertising agencies with 20,000 independent video creators in more than 80 countries. Poptent videographers produce commercials and videos for other purposes at about a tenth of the cost of videos produced through traditional ad agencies and production houses. Their service fee and the cost of one video averages less than $35,000, compared to the industry standard of hundreds of thousands of dollars for a 30-second television commercial. Poptent has paid out nearly $1,000,000 in payments to videographers and filmmakers for accepted videos.

The company enlists the participation of videographers from their community to fulfill various production assignments. If you work with Poptent, you get the benefit of potentially hundreds of videographers accepting and participating in your project, with between 50 to 150 finished videos coming out of the process. You then narrow the selection down to two or three videos for use on television or online. You can use the final video produced via Poptent for your website, microsite, social networking sites like Facebook and YouTube, on television, in movie theaters, and on mobile devices.

After you sign a crowdsourcing contract with Poptent, the company creates a dedicated landing page on their site for your specific video assignment and to house the creative brief and any assets you provide to assist in the assignment. The assignment is then launched to the entire Poptent crowdsourcing community.

Videographers and filmmakers can accept your assignment, but they must agree to your rules and regulations. They then download and review the supplied assets and the creative brief. You can specify the time frame for your assignment between 30 and 45 days. After the videos produced are uploaded by creators, Poptent first reviews them and then shares them with you so you can make a final selection. After you pick the video you want, the creators of the selected video are paid.

Working with Crowdtap

Crowdtap (crowdtap.com/clients) is an online platform with an influential crowd offering insights into companies' products and services. The service was developed by an advertising and marketing agency, but the platform is self-service and the agency is hands-off. The crowd within Crowdtap is highly engaged and consists of pretty specific demographics, particularly the under-40 set with a large concentration of college students and moms. If you sign up to use Crowdtap, you can interact with potential consumers for research and learning and to help spread the word about your products and services via word of mouth and through social media.

Crowdtap puts a structure and system around consumer participation. The system is broken into actions under two major categories: Insights and Influence. On the Insights side, you can use the platform to learn, test, and co-create products and marketing using polls, feedback, and 7-day or 30-day discussions with a specific panel. Under Influence, you can leverage your crowd to engage in peer-to-peer marketing, such as viewing and sharing online content (videos and web pages). Crowdtap members earn cash for participation, and a percentage of their earnings go to a charity of their choice. These incentives help encourage quality crowd participation.

Some activities managed through Crowdtap actually take place offline but are tracked online, including "Sample and Share" as well as hosted parties held in consumers' homes. You can get your products directly into the hands of your crowd members who then pass them along to their networks, and all efforts are monitored by the Crowdtap system and reported on by the participating crowd. Pricing for Crowdtap's system and service is scalable and based on a per-action price—so, a cost per poll, a cost per person participating in a party, and so on. You can sign up and start tapping into the system without any sign-up fees or monthly costs.

Working with Tongal

Tongal (tongal.com) crowdsources collaborations for creative work—including video production—helping businesses transform their core consumers into creators. Tongal can help you tap into your fan following so consumers feel like they "co-own" your brand by being part of your creative process. Tongal works with you to understand your goals and then customizes a project or multiple projects to address those goals.

The Tongal site and technology works to break down big pieces of media, such as developing a 30-second television spot, into smaller creative components or phases. These components may include an idea, story, concept, video, or exhibition (where you generate views for your videos). Tongal helps you transfer the creative process into an online forum, bringing independent creatives together to work on different parts of your project based on their core competencies.

The first step of the Tongal process is ideation, in which contributors share and develop ideas. As the project "sponsor," you then choose the top five ideas and make them available to the crowd for development. The second step is production, in which the concepts are fleshed out into actual products, such as a 30-second television spot. The third step is test marketing, in which viewers predict what video will be successful based on a rating system. Finally, Tongal's process lets you leverage the Tongal community to help distribute the creative content produced via the site across the web and throughout social media.

Tongal differs from other creative competition sites in that it doesn't employ a winner-take-all model. Instead, five people from each stage of the process win and receive a monetary award for their efforts.

Working with GeniusRocket

Hundreds of vetted filmmakers, animators, and web and graphic designers have applied to be part of the GeniusRocket (geniusrocket.com) community to create rich media content, branding, and naming for companies through an online crowdsourcing platform. The company's executive management team reviews the creative portfolios of crowd participants on an ongoing basis. Clients range from small to large brands, as well as advertising agencies who tap into GeniusRocket's *curated* crowd to supplement their services. GeniusRocket has a no-spec-work philosophy and artists are compensated for every bit of work they render.

DEFINITION

Curated crowdsourcing involves a vetted crowd of pre-qualified members who participate on a project to guarantee a high level of output.

With the help of GeniusRocket's in-house creative team, you start a project by building a creative strategy brief, which the company refers to as a "Request for Brilliance." The brief describes your marketing communications or awareness goals, the target of your message, where you'll place the message, your competitors, your unique differences, and the tone or personality you wish to project. GeniusRocket handles all legal documents and administrates the transfer of intellectual property developed during the entire process.

Next, GeniusRocket recruits artists from within their creative community, matching skills and experience to your project. Next is the concept stage, wherein you and GeniusRocket review the submitted "conceptual ideas." Those you select advance to the storyboard and production round. All work at this stage is compensated based on your budget. If you so choose, you can bypass storyboarding to save time and money and proceed directly to production. You then get to review the near-finished products of the choices that made it this far and narrow them down to your final choice. Then you provide feedback for edits only on the product you've chosen.

Finally, you receive the end product and complete the purchase, along with all legal documentation. The entire process takes about 45 days. The GeniusRocket model builds in more opportunities for compensation for participating crowd members, which may foster greater motivation and quality.

Consulting Firms That Crowdsource

Not all creative crowdsourcing is of the artistic kind. Some companies provide business, marketing, and other strategic consulting services and incorporate crowd-sourcing to access more professional minds to work on the same assignment.

Working with Chaordix

Chaordix (chaordix.com) is an offshoot of parent company Cambrian House, which began in 2006 as a small group of individuals seeking good business ideas for investment opportunities. They launched a global community to identify web-based software ideas. The crowds submitted ideas, vetted them, and ranked them, so investors could understand what the crowd felt were the best ones.

Over time, Cambrian House decided to commercialize the technology and processes they had developed and formed Chaordix to tap into the wisdom of crowds. Chaordix combines services, insights, and technology to effectively leverage crowds. Services offered by Chaordix include planning and outcome assessment, crowd recruitment, community management, and an online platform and tools that foster collaborative innovation, market research, and brand management.

If you work with Chaordix, you gain access to their established crowd of over 50,000, or they can build a custom crowd for you using their fine-tuned search and outreach methods. After attracting the right crowd to your project, Chaordix manages and communicates with your crowd with an eye toward motivation and appropriate incentives to keep them participating. You can use the Chaordix platform—with your own branding, if you so choose—for both internal and external crowdsourcing.

Chaordix offers three models of crowdsourcing: secretive, in which individuals submit ideas privately to you; collaborative, in which participants submit ideas openly and the crowd helps to pick the winner; and panel selected, in which individuals submit ideas, the crowd helps to evolve them, and then a panel narrows down the finalists and the crowd picks the final winner.

Working with Whinot

Whinot (whinot.com) provides small-business consulting services by bringing together a community of skilled consultants to provide businesses with marketing services. Whinot projects start at $2,500. If you work with Whinot, the company starts by writing a project brief based on your marketing goals. They then broadcast the project brief to their virtual consultant community using private discussion boards. The consultants in the community brainstorm solutions for your project and ask you questions to make sure they are on the right track. Using a consultant voting process, the best ideas rise to the top.

You then pick the best pitches and select a few consultants to form your project team, narrowing the crowdsourcing process from a many-to-many relationship to a smaller consulting team of three to five members. The team uses collaborative tools, such as wikis, as they work together to develop a final product. Whinot can provide a project manager who's an independent consultant vetted by the company to manage the entire process for you.

Interactions between you and the consultants in the community can have varying degrees of visibility to ensure your privacy. In the Whinot model, the independent consultants work together rather than competing against each other. The value to you is that, instead of getting a few ideas, you end up with dozens from which to choose. Throughout the process, Whinot applies their crowdsourcing process and expertise to keep projects flowing and on track.

Getting Your Money's Worth

Whether you use a self-service site or work with an agency as the intermediary in your crowdsourcing creative process, there are some things you can do to help produce a more successful outcome.

Start with a clear creative brief. By knowing what you want or at least being able to articulate your expectations and give a specific assignment, you can equip the crowd with a road map to produce something relevant. Each site or agency should guide you to properly define your audience, your end product, and its intended use, and to develop any other descriptive information to direct the creators or consultants. In most cases, less information is better than more, as each crowd participant has to review the information you provide; too much information can be confusing.

Provide supporting documents and other assets such as logos, brand guidelines, examples of assets you like that other companies or organizations use, and any other reference materials to bolster your creative brief. Be ready to provide crowd participants with additional material as requested, but take care to stay on track with any further material you provide.

As in any crowdsourcing process that involves more subjective results, your participation is key. Poptent conducts "TownHall Discussions" with its participating creators so clients can openly communicate with their videographer community for more on-target results. Whinot facilitates an ongoing dialogue between clients and their consultant team using online messaging to make sure the process delivers what the client expects.

When crowdsourcing creative work, the client making a timely decision is better than belaboring the final review process. Crowd participants want to know if they're on track or are the "winning" creator. If so, they expect prompt payment. If not, they can move on to the next assignment. Creative crowd participants are fueled by feedback and constructive criticism even if they are not selected; this information helps them improve their chances of being selected in a future assignment.

The Least You Need to Know

- Use freelancer marketplaces when you need to tap into a large pool of potential candidates.
- Be prepared to manage a virtual worker or team when hiring through a freelancer marketplace.
- If you need guidance in working with a crowd for creative work, turn to an agency that offers crowdsourcing.
- The best results in any crowdsourcing effort start with a clear, concise creative or project brief.
- Plan to be very hands-on during your creative crowdsourcing process. It's not an automated process.

Crowds for Troubleshooting and Beta Testing

In This Chapter

- Preparing for beta testing by crowds
- Setting criteria for testers
- Formulating test format and questions
- Using companies that provide crowdsourced testing

Bringing on testing groups for websites and software is commonplace. Developers use people outside their immediate circle of programmers or staff who try to break their code or check for inconsistencies and errors as part of an overall quality-assurance process.

Diversity is important to carrying out effective testing. Depending on what you're testing, you may want testers who have different coding skills or varying speeds for their Internet connections, or different computer platforms and web browsers.

Preparing for Crowd Testing

Because a diverse group of testers is important for testing code—which can include the programming behind websites—a crowd of testers can be helpful in carrying out comprehensive tests. Testing code this way is referred to as usability testing, trouble-shooting, or *beta testing*, and the testers themselves are beta testers.

> **DEFINITION**
>
> **Beta testing** takes place before the release of a software product or launch of a website and occurs after more limited and private alpha testing to check for errors, discrepancies, and bugs has been completed.

Like most work you need done, crowdsourcing to test your website or other coded product requires advance preparation. Random crowd members may not have the skills, equipment, and connections needed to perform the work. Crowdsourcing other types of work can benefit from some variety, but usually relies less on technical specifics than beta testing.

Beta testing a website doesn't necessarily require a high level of programming proficiency, but the specifics of a tester's computer, connection, browser, and other technical specs can make a significant difference in identifying and fixing errors. Most website beta testers aren't coders; instead, they run the gamut of skill level and experience. Having coders testing your site can be a bonus, but it's not usually essential. Beta testing software, on the other hand, requires specialized technical skills.

Defining Your Needs

Planning your beta-testing project can make a big difference in the overall process and improve the outcome of the testing performed. Start by defining your needs. You may want to test many aspects of your site, from basic functions to more complex systems. Some things to test include the following:

- **Assess homepage load:** Determine the length of time and perceived length of time it takes the site's homepage to load.

- **Homepage clarity:** How clear is the homepage message, particularly for people not familiar with your company or organization?

- **Homepage effectiveness:** This is not a subjective analysis but a reporting of where each tester goes when they arrive at your site.

- **Embedded images:** Make sure all images load on each page.

- **Embedded links:** Make sure all links work and take the user to the appropriate page.

- **Communications features:** Test message boards and other features that allow visitors to communicate on the site.

- **Shopping cart function:** Testing the entire shopping process from selecting products to fulfilling orders.

Basic site testing involves both cursory and in-depth tracking and reporting of each tester's experience as they move through the site. Part of preparing for beta testing is defining the tasks you want your testers to perform on the different sections and with the different features of your site.

Specifying Skills and Resources

An important part of beta testing a website is to make sure the testers represent a diversified set of skills, connection speeds, browser types, and computer platforms and systems. Websites are usually available to the general public, so the potential audience for your site is diverse. You can narrow your tester criteria based on the audience you are targeting rather than the general Internet population. Don't be too narrow in your criteria or you may miss some important issues with your site that can be a barrier for future visitors.

Criteria you can consider for beta testing include ...

- **Computer operating system:** The most common systems are PC-compatible or Macintosh computers.

- **Central Processing Unit (CPU) specs:** You can specify or track each tester's computer hard drive memory, RAM, and CPU power to see how these affect the user experience.

- **Internet connection:** Broadband cable connections and Wi-Fi may be more common, but testing for the lowest common denominator via a dial-up connection can generate useful information about your site.

- **Browser type:** Some browsers such as Firefox and Google Chrome have cross-platform capabilities, but others are platform specific, such as Safari for Mac. Other browsers include Internet Explorer and Opera.

- **Internet proficiency:** You can specify Internet experience for your testers by level, such as beginner, intermediate, or advanced; you can also specify by time, such as less than two years online or two to five years online.

- **Technical skills:** Your typical website visitor may not have high-level technical skills, but having testers with a variety of skill levels can be beneficial to your testing process.

You can base other criteria on demographics such as language, location, age, gender, education, or even psychographics, such as habits, hobbies, and behaviors. Technical criteria can include very small tech variations, such as the types of plug-ins installed on browsers, browser preference settings, or installed software such as anti-virus applications.

If you already have a website and are beta testing a redesign, incorporate data from your previous web traffic logs to inform your testing criteria. For example, many web traffic analytics programs detect and report the computer systems and browsers used by the majority of visitors to your original site. Understanding that your audience mostly accesses your site via PC with Internet Explorer or Mac via Firefox can help you narrow down tester criteria. Don't limit yourself to just the specifications you see in your traffic analytics. Diversity can provide unexpected information that can help you identify potential site issues and improve your site.

DULY NOTED

Crowdsourcing doesn't change the basics of good software or website testing: clear instructions and communications and good project management are necessary to effectively crowdsource your beta testing.

Setting Testing Criteria

The choices you make for structuring your testing criteria can affect the complexity of testing and analyzing results. There isn't a single "correct" way of beta testing, but some best practices have been established. The testing process is also affected by the crowd of testers you need, the site features you are testing, and the overall goals for testing. For example, ensuring your site is accessible to sight-impaired visitors presents a different outcome than testing your shopping cart to make sure the transaction process is smooth and free of bugs.

A well-managed beta-testing process can consist of a formal process, with carefully defined steps and specific choices for testers to make; a loose process, with more open-ended questions that allow testers to be more free-form with their testing actions; or a combination of both. The more rigid and formalized your process, the more you limit the results you will get back from your testers. By guiding testers too closely, you may inadvertently affect the testing outcomes. Without some kind of structure, your testing can become chaotic and the results may be harder to organize and analyze.

As you beta test with a crowd, you can benefit from a balance of both formal and loose testing styles, particularly with large testing crowds. Beta testing should start with an explanation of what you are trying to test and what you'd like to achieve. Outline how a tester should perform the testing. There are concrete things that testers can test, and obtain measurable and actionable or quantitative results. Other things are more subjective, such as requesting the opinions of your testers based on their personal preferences. Qualitative data is harder to measure but can give you valuable insights to help you improve your site.

Performing Objective Testing

A basic way to test your site with a testing crowd is to ask testers to thoroughly comb your site to ensure that none of the embedded images and links are broken. This kind of testing is specific, measurable, and finite—as long as you have a set number of pages on your site or in the area you want tested. Your tester crowd can then go through your site, load images and click on links, record the URLs of the pages where there are errors, and make note of the exact errors. With that collective data— along with their connectivity, browser, and computer specs—you can direct your developer with a list of errors to fix.

Here are some sample steps to provide your beta-testing crowd that are relatively concrete and measurable:

Instructions

1. Go through the process of purchasing an item. Use your real address, but use the fake credit card number provided to you for testing purposes.

2. Start with selecting a product and specify more than one unit under quantity. Choose a color and size. Record your choices below.

3. Go to your shopping cart to verify that the products are in your cart, with the correct number of units, color, and size. Were the shopping cart contents correct? If no, specify exactly what was in your shopping cart.

4. Try to check out. Click the **Checkout** button and then fill out the shipping and billing information.

5. Was the form clear and easy to fill out? If no, what could be done to improve the form?

6. When you submitted your information, did the transaction continue to completion, did it stall out, or did it give you an error message? If you received an error message, please copy and paste the message you received.

Some of these are open-ended questions, but the answers are mostly looking for quantitative data with minimally subjective opinions mixed in. The answers are mostly yes or no; if no, the follow-up questions look for either concrete data, like an error message, or an opinion, such as, "What could be done to improve?"

Performing Subjective Testing

You can ask your beta-testing crowd to give you feedback on aspects of your site that are more intangible and based on opinion. This type of questioning produces qualitative data. You may test features such as your site's look and feel, navigation, content quality, information organization, and ease of use. You can ask open-ended questions, but the onus is on you to sort through and read long answers. You can instead use multiple-choice questions with fixed answers. This controls the variety of opinions testers share, which makes it easier for you to assess outcomes, but you might also miss some important information. That's why a mix of controlled and open-ended questions provides the most useful mix of data.

Here are some sample multiple-choice questions and answers:

Instructions

We are seeking feedback on our site redesign. Please answer the following questions honestly. Your identity will remain anonymous. You will be identified only by your computer, connectivity, and browser specifications.

1. How long have you been using the Internet?
a. Less than a year
b. One to three years
c. More than three years

2. As you arrive at the site, what is your first impression? Express what first comes to mind.

[Open paragraph field]

3. What do you think of the site colors? Pick all that apply.
a. Attractive
b. Unattractive
c. Distracting
d. Complementary

4. Review the content categories on the site's navigation buttons. How clear are the site categories?

a. Very clear

b. Relatively clear

c. Neutral

d. Not very clear

e. Unclear

5. Search for specific content on the site. How easy is it to find content on the site?

a. Very easy

b. Relatively easy

c. Neutral

d. Not very easy

e. Difficult

6. After using the site during testing, what are your suggestions for improving the site?

[Open paragraph field]

By mixing in some open-ended questions, you allow testers to provide you with information that may cover things that didn't occur to you when preparing the site and the beta-testing questions. Even though reports are subjective, and open-ended questions require more reading to find common threads, they may also provide surprising responses that can help you improve your site.

Finding a Crowd of Testers

Using an existing tester crowd through a self-service site or crowdsourcing service provider (CSP) can streamline your entire testing process. By turning to professionals in the crowdsourced testing space, you can bypass some of the challenges inherent to global beta testing, including managing disparate testers in different parts of the world and different time zones, communicating virtually without the benefit of face-to-face contact, protecting intellectual property, and carrying out quality assurance.

Some of the benefits of testing through well-organized and managed crowds include …

- **Lower testing costs:** By leveraging crowdsourced testing support, you can gather user input and feedback less expensively than outsourcing the work to a firm with employees. With an on-demand model, you pay only for the testing projects you need rather than paying ongoing salaries for on-staff testers.

- **Managing greater testing complexity:** Crowdsourcing can provide a wider set of platforms, software, and hardware, as well as other variables that can help produce better results.

- **Getting to market faster:** Crowdsourcing can help eliminate delays or staffing constraints that can hinder your time to market. You can get more testers—from dozens to hundreds—working on your testing project at once.

- **Higher quality and usability:** With more sophisticated consumers expecting high-quality, user-ready applications, crowdsourced testing can be closer to the quality of managed quality assurance than a more ad-hoc testing process.

By choosing a reputable crowdsourcing company with a proven track record of real-world customer successes, you may have a positive testing experience with higher quality outcomes. Many sites and CSPs provide a tester crowd, but each one may use different criteria for gathering, rating, and organizing testers. Look for ones that share with you the data gathered on testers, such as a tester's past performance or overall reputation within the testing community, so your tester crowd is better defined.

Website Usability Testing

Using an existing crowd to test your website may include different levels of service or may simply entail filling out an order form with your testing needs. A site like UserTesting.com charges per user and then gives you both written responses from the testers based on your testing questions and a Flash video of the user during the actual test, as they talk through their experience on your site.

Signing up at UserTesting.com's self-service site consists of a one-page sign-up sheet in which you furnish your site URL and a scenario or description of the type of experience you hope your site elicits. An example of a scenario might be "Imagine you are shopping for a birthday gift for your child," or "Imagine you are planning your family vacation to a tropical resort." The form gives you room for up to four tasks you can ask of testers, and each task should take no more than 15 minutes to complete. You can add up to four questions for the user to answer in writing after testing is complete. The site provides four default questions that you can use, modify, or entirely change:

1. What would have caused you to leave this site?

2. What other ideas do you have about how to improve this site?

3. What did you like about the site?

4. Anything else you would like to say to the owner of the site?

UserTesting.com claims you can start getting feedback within the hour, but if you narrow your tester audiences to a specific demographic, such as "moms with children under five," it will take longer. You can also invite your own tester crowd into the UserTesting.com testing environment if you prefer. Other usability testing crowds can be accessed via Squadhelp and a site called Feedback Army, which manages the testing process for you using Mechanical Turk workers.

Mobile Application Testing

There are tester crowds specifically gathered to test mobile applications. Mob4Hire (mob4hire.com) is one of them, and taps into a crowd of over 50,000 testers who have the variety of mobile devices, cellular networks, and technical expertise necessary to properly and immediately test applications. The crowd is also geographically dispersed to expand testing opportunities. The use of diverse mobile devices as well as the sheer numbers offered by Mob4Hire can create an ideal crowdsourcing environment, unlike straight web-based crowds.

Working with Mob4Hire, you can choose testers—referred to as "Mobsters" on the site—based on device, network, demographics, and country. Mobsters receive a test plan to follow and get paid for their work once the work has been confirmed. Tests and developers are rated after each project to keep tester quality high. Mob4Hire collects a fee for their service testing both the functional aspects of an application, to make sure it won't crash, and the usability of an application, to get input on how likely an application will be downloaded and used once it is released.

Crowdsourcing sites like uTest and TopCoder also offer testing for a wide array of mobile applications in addition to web-based testing services.

Software Testing

If you are developing software, you need crowds with higher-level skills and a stringent management process. uTest (utest.com) is a marketplace for software testing services with over 30,000 professional testers from 170 countries around the world. You can use uTest for web, desktop, and mobile application testing. You can handpick a testing team to match your user base. With their diverse community of professional testers, uTest helps companies test their applications across any and all criteria on an on-demand basis. The company gathers and stores individual tester data including basic demographics, hardware and software, and self-assessed skills and experience.

The uTest online platform includes a feature that lets you communicate with your tester team in real time. The company also assigns a dedicated project manager to help you handpick testers based on their particular criteria. The site also helps protect your intellectual property through careful tester selection and the use of nondisclosure agreements (NDA) with community members.

uTest emphasizes an organized skilled crowd rather than a loosely affiliated, unrated, and unprofiled crowd or mob. The company provides both monetary and reputation compensation to their testers. They also employ community recruitment and engagement, training and educational programs, social media integration, and public profiles and badges to stimulate participation.

Another software-testing crowd that can help on the development side for enterprise customers is TopCoder, a full-service "software factory." The company is involved from concept to delivery, including conceptualization, design, development, architecture, bug fixes on the software side, and even work on the graphics side (such as wireframes, storyboards, and logos). TopCoder applies a component-based methodology to build more complex applications, and they catalog previously built "generic" components, which can save you development time and costs. At every stage, TopCoder presents the work that testers must perform in competition form. The company also offers individuals who can act as project managers to assist you throughout the process.

Coders have been comfortable working in a virtual, open-source, and collaborative environment for years. As the crowdsourcing model continues to take hold, you're sure to see even more companies harnessing tester and coding crowds to offer scalable, on-demand, crowd-based tech solutions.

The Least You Need to Know

- Access testers with different coding skills or varying speeds for their Internet connections, different computer platforms, and web browsers.

- Prepare for beta testing by defining the tasks you want your testers to perform, based on the different sections and features of your site.

- Using an existing tester crowd through a self-service site or CSP can streamline your entire testing process.

- Choose a reputable crowdsourcing company with a proven track record of real-world customer successes for a better testing experience with higher-quality outcomes.

Crowdsourcing Customer Support

In This Chapter

- Using crowd input to build your FAQ resource
- Developing your FAQ page
- Getting your customers to help other customers
- Leveraging customer input to enhance customer service
- Using customer crowds during a crisis

If you offer products and services, your customers are often willing to provide you with feedback, but are you asking them for it? If so, how? In previous chapters, we discussed how to find, reach out to, and gather your existing and even potential customers as your crowd for a variety of reasons, from giving input on existing products to helping you come up with ideas for new products.

Learning from Your Crowd

Your customers are reaching out to you for help, to ask questions, and to provide feedback unsolicited. Are you listening? Are you responding? If not, they are most likely online talking about your products or services and sharing this information with their vast and growing networks. Customers now have unprecedented power to reach exponentially larger circles of friends, fans, followers, and connections with both positive and negative statements about your company.

Organically formed crowd communities are providing consumers with the power to talk candidly and publicly about the products and services they use. They can ask questions, get answers, give kudos, and air complaints. You can't control these crowds, but you can offer an alternative to these loose, disorganized forums.

Some companies offer platforms so you can proactively gather your customers together for customer support–driven conversations. If you don't have a customer service or technical support platform in place, your customers are already turning to their own online networks or other customer crowd communities to be heard and to seek help. Look for ways to bring your customers and their conversations under your purview for mutual benefit.

Building FAQs with Crowd Input

A good place to start sourcing your customer crowd for invaluable information is in the development of your company *FAQ* page, which stands for "frequently asked questions." Publishing an FAQ gives consumers a quick reference guide to get answers to commonly asked questions they, too, have. Crafting clear, succinct answers in anticipation of common questions is a great way to provide a first level of customer service.

 DEFINITION

FAQs—pronounced either "facks" or "eff ay cues"—are documents or information sections on your website that organize the questions most commonly asked by existing and prospective customers and that provide answers.

Having an FAQ in place also serves your internal team by having answers at the ready to alleviate response time. An FAQ can be a single- or multiple-page document or, for more complex issues, can be content stored in a searchable database. Source questions and possible answers from your customer crowd to build a more relevant document that addresses your customers' needs.

Compiling Common Questions

To write an FAQ, start with answers to questions you already know off the top of your head that you've heard repeatedly about your company and products or services. You can also gather questions over the phone or via e-mail from customer conversations. Consider putting a formal process into place to capture new questions, craft answers, and systematically add the information into your FAQ.

If you've gathered a crowd and are already surveying them, tap into them to find out what they consider important questions about what you offer, or even to share questions they had early on as a new customer. Your customer crowd can provide you with information you and your staff may have never considered, making your FAQ that much more useful to others.

Sourcing the Answers

You can craft the answers to the questions you've compiled in a number of ways. You or members of your team can draft answers based on company policies, best practices, and procedures. You can also turn to your customers for input. Sometimes, reaching out to your crowd provides a reality check that can bring new issues and information to light.

You can turn to your customer crowd in any number of forums, depending on what you have set up or what makes the most sense. For example, you can tap into your customers on Facebook or ask questions within a more private customer crowdsourcing community. There are also tools you can use to get input from your customers that may prove invaluable for building content for your FAQ, several of which are described later in this chapter.

Building Your FAQ

Your FAQ can exist as a single web page on your site or published anywhere you have an online presence, including a link on your blog, your Facebook page, your Twitter account, or anywhere your customers might interact with you. An FAQ can also be a robust, database-driven—and therefore seachable—area on your website. The key is that the content of your FAQ is vetted and edited by you versus being aggregated from a variety of sources.

As you assemble your FAQ, depending on the number of questions you have, you can list the questions and number them or break them up so they fall under categories and subcategories. You can use an outline format or a table of contents format to list the questions and make them live links to the answers. Following are some sample formats.

Version 1, for shorter FAQs:

What is our company?

Answer.

What products do we provide?

Answer.

What is our company return policy?

Answer.

Where will our company ship?

Answer.

What type of shipping options do we provide?

Answer.

Version 2, for longer FAQs; each question should be a link to the corresponding answer:

About Us

What is our company?

What products do we provide?

When were we founded?

Who is our team?

Purchasing Product

What products do we provide?

What is our company return policy?

Where will our company ship?

What type of shipping options do we provide?

Version 3, for longer FAQs:

1. Who are we?

1.1 Our company history

1.2 Our team bios

1.3 Our philosophy

2. What do we do?

2.1 Our products

2.2 Our services

2.3 Our work process

3. How to purchase our products.

3.1 Our catalog

3.2 Our shopping cart

3.3 Our retail store

The format to your FAQ can vary depending on the amount of content you include, but the content must be front and center and easy to access and understand.

PITFALLS

Don't make your FAQ hard to find. Make sure a link to it is visible on your site. Most sites publish it in the help section of their site or include it in their main navigation.

Getting Customers to Help Customers

It may sound like a recipe for chaos and disaster, but letting your avid and loyal customers help other customers can actually be an effective addition to your customer service offerings. Your customers are already a crowd, albeit loose and unmanaged, that is probably responsible for a great deal of word-of-mouth messaging about your company, products, and services on blogs and social networks. Tapping into the knowledge, interest, and enthusiasm of some of your customers to provide peer-to-peer customer support can help your company in a number of ways:

- Supplementing your current customer-support resources and reducing costs.

- Sourcing into the wisdom of your customer base.

- Leveraging the hands-on knowledge of your customers.

- Providing new insights into how customers perceive your products and services.

- Enhancing your effectiveness in supporting your customers.

- Increasing positive word of mouth for your company related to higher customer satisfaction.

The key to making customers part of your customer-support process is a robust platform to bring them together and oversee their efforts. You need to provide a more defined community for your customers to support one another beyond your Facebook page or the comments section of your blog.

Crowdsourcing Customer Service

Using crowdsourcing for customer support can be advantageous in several ways, including helping you reduce customer-support costs, strengthening your relationship with your customers, and even driving product improvements and innovation. More than anything, this kind of system helps close the feedback loop so customers feel they are being heard and their questions and complaints are taken seriously.

There are sites, software, and service providers available to help you harness your customer crowd and aggregate their feedback and input so you can put it to use. Use a system that is already well-established with a good track record. This alleviates the burden of custom-building a system.

You can modify and customize most systems to suit your needs, and many integrate with existing systems such as CRM Solutions and Salesforce. Make sure the system you choose enables you to moderate conversations to ensure the quality of the information shared.

Managing Customer-Support Communities

If you don't have a satisfactory customer-care process in place, your customers may go elsewhere for support, including social networks like Facebook and Twitter, or a site like Get Satisfaction (getsatisfaction.com).

Get Satisfaction gives your customers a place to voice their opinions—and complaints—about your company, products, or services. For a fee, you can actively build and take part in the conversations related to your company. The community is focused around four topic types:

1. **Ask a Question:** Customers can answer one another's questions, and you as a representative of your company can provide answers as well.

2. **Share an Idea:** Feedback from customers is aggregated to help you identify new ideas from your actual customers.

3. **Report a Problem:** Customers can search the community for solutions to their problems while giving you a heads up that something is wrong.

4. **Give Praise:** Your customers can give you kudos publicly.

The Get Satisfaction system helps to bring customer conversations together wherever your crowds gather, including your blog, Facebook, and Twitter. You can try the Get Satisfaction system for free for 15 days and choose from plans starting as low as $19 per month for a single moderator and $39 per month for three moderators, giving you the ability to provide one or several people with the administrative tools to manage your customer crowd community.

For a premium price, you can also add a custom Get Satisfaction tab to your Facebook page and have those conversations managed and integrated into your customer-service community system. This kind of integration enables you to avoid providing customer response or care via the less controlled environment of Facebook. The Get Satisfaction site also provides a "Plan Genie," where you can select a community-building plan based on your specific needs, such as the number of moderators you need, the degree of customization, your need for private communities, and your desire for deep analytics.

Crowdsourced Customer Feedback Tools

There are tools that help you harness your customer crowd to gather feedback. UserVoice (uservoice.com) and BearHug (bearhugapp.com) aren't specific crowd-sourcing applications, but they have crowdsourcing-like features. Both services allow you to harness input from your customers, including to help build your company FAQ, to aggregate product reviews, and to get actionable feedback.

UserVoice lets your customers submit, discuss, and vote on feedback about your company, products, and services. The system collects feedback and, based on customer voting, the best ideas are forwarded to you. When you act on ideas presented to you by UserVoice and your customers, an e-mail notification goes out to participants to close the feedback loop. This type of system empowers your customer to participate actively with your company in an online community setting rather than taking the passive feedback button approach.

BearHug lets you aggregate customer feedback, customer questions, and customer reviews. You can set up BearHug for your company, for each product you want to track, and to manage customer service. You can access a dashboard view that gives you a look at customer-related conversations and feedback for your company. You can then respond to customers through BearHug and, because all your responses to customers are fed through the BearHug system, you can see metrics for your company's average response time, with average customer ratings and overall customer satisfaction.

The BearHug modules that help you crowdsource and aggregate content and input from your customer crowd are "Answers," "First Rate," and "Overheard." Answers lets your customers ask questions and receive answers from you, as well as from other members of your customer community. You can moderate the crowdsourced questions and answers and publish them in the form of a rich FAQ that continues to grow over time.

Your customers can post reviews through the First Rate module, and you can moderate, publish, and syndicate those reviews on your site. The Overheard feature pulls in relevant mentions from Twitter, Yelp, Facebook, Flickr, and YouTube that you can review to better address issues that come up, even if they're posted on sites other than your own.

DULY NOTED

Technically, you can build an online community for your customers using any number of community-building tools including Ning, Grouply, and other networks mentioned in Chapter 4. Building a crowdsourcing platform from scratch can make it challenging to gather and organize crowd input.

Handling Customer Crises

There are upsides to crowdsourcing customer care in terms of leveraging your own customers to help you develop your FAQ, providing support to other customers, and giving input on your company, products, or services. But what happens if you experience a customer-care crisis? Can the crowd work against you?

The short answer is … yes and no. The longer answer is, yes, when something bad happens or someone has something bad to say, that information can spread rapidly around the Internet. Gone are the days of "private" feedback forms and e-mail with your customers. Instead, your customers are empowered with publishing tools like blogs, Facebook, and Twitter.

In the same way that a crowd can amplify bad news, however, with proper care and the right approach, you can turn the crowd around to help you work through a crisis. The most important thing to remember about a customer crisis is that you can more likely avoid it if you listen and pay attention to what your customers are saying. Use a tool that helps you manage your customer crowd and organize a response to issues in a timely—and public—manner to alleviate many potential problems.

When a problem does occur, immediately respond in an open and public way. Don't shy away from your crowd; reach out to them in the various forums where they've gathered. Keep your messages concise, consistent, nondefensive, and nonaccusatory, and directly address the issue. As a crisis is in full gear, you may receive a great deal of negative comments, feedback, and even publicity, but how you handle this pressure is part of turning your crowd around to help you defuse a situation.

Customers appreciate direct contact, rapid response, and at the very least, an acknowledgment of their situation. A properly managed customer crowd can become a key asset in your company's crisis-communications efforts. Above all, be honest with your crowd, and they'll reward you with their support.

Crowdsourcing customer support in any condition or situation is not meant to replace your main customer service system. Instead, it operates as an addition or enhancement to what you are doing. The crowd can help, but only you have the final word. Only you have the power to do the right thing with the information you gather from your customer crowd community.

The Least You Need to Know

- Customers now have unprecedented power to reach large circles of friends, fans, followers, and connections with both positive and negative statements about your company.

- Source questions and possible answers from your customer crowd to build more relevant support documents that address your customers' needs.

- Don't make your FAQ document hard to find. Make sure a link to your FAQ is visible on your site.

- The key to bringing customers together to become part of your customer-support process is a robust platform.

- If you don't have a satisfactory customer-care process in place, your customers may go elsewhere for their customer support, including social networks.

More Ways to Crowdsource

5

In Part 5, I'll introduce you to more options for crowdsourcing beyond performing technical tasks, from translation, to transcription, to traffic reports. You'll learn how major corporations leverage crowdsourcing for product ideas and innovations. I'll explain the ins and outs of crowdfunding for organizations, causes, creative projects, and companies. Finally, I'll show you how crowdsourcing is being used to help galvanize crowds to take actions that can have a positive impact in our communities and around the world.

Pushing the Envelope

In This Chapter

- Using additional applications of crowdsourcing
- Crowdsourcing through mobile devices
- Identifying corporate crowdsourcing programs

The types of crowdsourcing covered in this book fall under the main categories of work, input, and organizing. The sky's the limit in terms of how and to what end you apply crowdsourcing. You can gather and leverage crowds to perform tasks that address many different issues, problems, projects, and needs.

Crowdsourcing Miscellany

The key to crowdsourcing effectively is to know what specifically you're trying to achieve and to know where and how to tap into the right crowd for your project. There are many sites, companies, and even nonprofits forming around the concepts and principles of crowdsourcing.

Well-managed and reputable crowdsourcing sites assemble crowds and provide services to others using crowd power to deliver results. Rather than trying to harness your own crowd, you can instead use any of these sites and take advantage of their technology that streamlines the entire crowdsourcing process.

Translations from Crowds

Crowdsourcing translation can be challenging, but myGengo (mygengo.com) works to make online language translation easy, covering more than 12 languages via their site. Fill out a simple web form with the content you'd like translated—or upload it as a Word, Excel, or PowerPoint file—and provide any relevant comments. Then, submit it to the myGengo global network of translators. Within minutes, you will have your translation. The site offers a 100 percent guarantee.

The myGengo crowd is a network of over 1,300 translators from all over the world. Building a crowd of translators helps myGengo handle large volumes of content on demand and helps customers whose translation needs aren't constant enough to warrant hiring an on-site translator. Translators obtain work assignments on a first-come, first-served basis, and they proofread and peer-review one another's work. Translators can communicate with translation customers through the myGengo site.

For large businesses and developers, myGengo offers an application programming interface (API) to directly connect a company's website to myGengo's translators. For example, an online merchant can publish a new product listing and, within a few hours, receive the translated list back via their connection with myGengo.

myGengo tests its translators before they become part of the site's translating community. Because myGengo translation requires higher skills than other crowdsourced tasks, the company provides their crowd with rewards and incentives for good work. Rather than gathering temporary crowds, they look to cultivate long-term relationships with their crowd members while providing them with learning opportunities via myGengo.

PITFALLS

Avoid open translation projects with little or no vetting or results management; otherwise, you risk potentially embarrassing errors. Quality translation requires more oversight and skill than other types of crowdsourced work.

Crowd-Powered Transcription

CastingWords (castingwords.com) is a technology-oriented transcription and web-sourcing company that connects online workers with transcription work. The company's main offerings are transcription services, including a straightforward per-word pricing structure and higher prices for expedited services. Their typical customer is a podcaster who wants his podcast audio transcribed for online publication on a website or blog. If you use CastingWords' transcription services, transcripts are e-mailed to you or can be downloaded from their site. Transcripts can be delivered in plain-text, HTML, and Microsoft Word formats.

To deliver work, CastingWords uses a proprietary system and process that leverages Amazon's Mechanical Turk worker platform. They also provide consulting services to help companies get work done without having to navigate the Mechanical Turk site by using CastingWords' system as an intermediary. CastingWords acts as a quality assurance and project manager to the crowdsourcing process, and Mechanical Turk's site provides the workers.

Keyword Optimization

If you're paying for search-engine advertising through keywords, you can run your pay-per-click (PPC) campaign using the Trada crowdsourced marketplace. Paid search requires a large number of relevant keywords to be effective and can require constant attention to make sure your campaigns are optimized and effective. Trada has gathered a crowd of over 1,000 whom they certify as search experts—called "Optimizers"—to run campaigns with thousands of keywords and hundreds of ads appearing on Google, Yahoo!, and Bing search engines.

You can create a campaign specifying what you're selling and then establish your daily budget, maximum cost per click you're willing to pay, and the ad networks on which you want to advertise. You can also furnish information about the target cost per conversion, meaning how much you're willing to pay if someone doesn't just click on your ad but actually takes an action (such as purchasing your product).

After your campaign launches, you can review all the keywords and ads to make sure they accurately represent your business and objectives. PPC experts are paid when their efforts generate clicks or conversions. They earn their money by keeping the difference between what you said you were willing to pay for a click and conversion and what the keywords cost to generate the clicks or conversions on the ad networks.

Unusual Uses of Crowdsourcing

Crowdsourcing work, including creative work, is becoming more commonplace, but there are other uses of crowdsourcing that you might not think of because they aren't specifically covered by the larger crowdsourcing sites. The common denominator between these sites is that they use an Internet-based platform to bring together a crowd to perform specific tasks.

Tattoo Creation

There are numerous design competitions available online to crowdsource design work such as CrowdSPRING, Prova, 99designs, and Redesign Me (redesignme.com). One design competition site puts a twist in what members are designing on their site. CreateMyTattoo (createmytattoo.com) connects users with over 700 tattoo artists who compete to design a custom tattoo. The site guarantees you will receive at least 10 designs, or you can ask for your money back.

You start the design process by describing your custom tattoo idea and picking a prize amount to be paid to the winning tattoo artist. CreateMyTattoo then collects the money at that time. The minimum prize amount is $35. Once you start receiving designs, you're encouraged to participate in the design process by giving feedback.

The tattoo design contest runs for 14 days. When the contest time is over, you choose your favorite tattoo design, receive the completed design with a matching stencil, and the designer gets paid. You can then bring the stencil to any tattoo shop for rendering.

Group Buying

Groupon (groupon.com) is a daily deal site that offers deep discounts on products, services, and activities. The power of Groupon comes from harnessing crowd participation to trigger deals. Each potential deal package has a tipping point—that is, the number of people who need to sign up to make the promotion worthwhile for the business offering the deal. The deal isn't offered without the right number of people signing up for it. As soon as the right number of people sign up—and this differs for each deal—everyone's credit card is charged and they receive a digital voucher they can print and redeem before the promotion expiration date, usually six months to a year.

Crowdsourcing principles are incorporated into other aspects of the Groupon business model, in addition to deal participation. Customers can communicate on Groupon discussion boards, ask questions, and get input from the crowd (consisting of other Groupon users). Essentially, Groupon is crowdsourcing customer service. Groupon also depends on social networking and uses sharing of their deals via Facebook and Twitter; in this case, they're crowdsourcing marketing.

Without a crowd of enthusiastic deal seekers, Groupon would not reach the critical mass necessary to provide impressive deals to customers and significant customer growth opportunities for businesses. Groupon operates in over 130 cities in North America and continues to grow.

Traffic Reporting

Waze (waze.com) turns drivers into a crowd supplying traffic data. The tool is a free social mobile application that provides users with free turn-by-turn navigation based on the actual live conditions of the road, or "road intelligence" as the site calls it. Users also power the application to track road conditions in their local communities.

The service includes constantly updated road maps, traffic and accident alerts, and data to provide you with the fastest route to your destination. Map and traffic updates are automatically collected and generated as you drive around your area with Waze activated. Drivers can also report and update other users in their area with what is happening, as they see it on the road. This may include accidents, weather hazards, and even good deals on gasoline.

As a user-generated product, Waze depends on people using the application to work, so it may not be fully functional in your community. You can encourage local friends and colleagues to use the application to start the process.

More Mobile Crowdsourcing

Other crowdsourcing sites and projects leverage the prevalence of mobile devices in developing countries. Txteagle (txteagle.com) offers a virtual workforce with labor that users can crowdsource through their patent-pending platform using mobile phones. Workers are often in rural locations where jobs are scarce, but working via mobile phone is a viable option to earn money. Workers can earn either mobile money or airtime for the work they perform.

Txteagle focuses on projects that require deep local knowledge and insight in a given geography. The company has completed opinion and market research studies for the United Nations, brand engagement and education campaigns for global brands, and data gathering in dozens of countries for the World Bank and major investment firms.

Crowdsourcing to Save Lives

There are a number of examples of using mobile devices to crowdsource vigilance, from noting traffic jams to reporting on protests and street violence. Sproxil (sproxil. com) is a company that provides another type of crowdsourced vigilance that can supply life-saving intelligence.

Through Sproxil's services, pharmaceutical companies facing the problem of drug counterfeiting overseas have new ways of addressing the problem. The World Health Organization (WHO) estimates that up to 30 percent of medications on the market in developing countries in Africa are counterfeit. These fake drugs are said to account for hundreds of thousands of deaths due to people with life-threatening illnesses failing to get the medication they need.

The company has developed a scratch label for drug packaging to let customers provide data that can help companies pinpoint counterfeiting. Rather than taking a scattershot approach to combating drug counterfeiters through random checks around the world, Sproxil provides them with regional mapping of issues.

Pharmaceutical companies add a scratch-off label containing a hidden code to drug packaging. When a person purchases medication from their pharmacist, they scratch the label to reveal a code and text it to Sproxil. The customer immediately sees whether the code they've submitted signifies valid or fake medication. The pharmaceutical company gets a dashboard view of global intelligence showing where fake medication is showing, so they can better assess where there might be issues along their supply chains.

Corporate Crowdsourcing

Corporations didn't always reach outside their four walls to source innovation. Today, some of the largest corporations in the world use open innovation platforms to reach out to the general public to source new ideas and innovative solutions to everything from technology to products and product packaging to marketing and design.

Each corporation has its own process and criteria for submissions. Almost anyone has the opportunity to submit their ideas and potentially partner with these major companies to develop new products or improve existing ones. Each offers various levels of participation and partnership.

At the very least, you may see your idea become a reality in the marketplace, something you otherwise may not have been able to achieve. In some cases, you may be able to catapult your organization or company's growth by teaming up with a major corporation that can provide you with the funding, resources, and marketing muscle to perform at a level you couldn't reach alone.

DULY NOTED

If you plan on submitting ideas or solutions to a major corporation, you should first protect your innovation if it is protectable. Start with the U.S. Patent and Trademark Office's (USPTO) website at uspto.gov. Also, be sure to consult an intellectual-property (IP) lawyer.

Develop + Connect

Consumer product manufacturer Proctor and Gamble (P&G) is one of the first companies to experiment with open innovation, along with other corporations such as IBM and Eli Lilly. The company's research-and-development productivity was in a lull and the percentage of new products that met their financial objectives was stagnating. Suddenly, the smaller and more nimble entrepreneurial efforts were innovating new products all around them or licensing and even selling their intellectual property to bigger companies. Opportunities also existed through universities and government labs that wanted to form industry partnerships to turn their research into products and bring them to market.

In 2000, P&G's new CEO at the time, A. G. Lafley, challenged the company to totally reinvent their innovation business model. The resulting program—called Connect + Develop (pgconnectdevelop.com)—launched the next year to reach out to companies, individuals, government and contract labs, research and financial institutions, and universities for opportunities, solutions, and ideas. P&G also began leveraging the Internet, particularly through innovation networks such as NineSigma and InnoCentive. The goal: deliver 50 percent of the company's innovation through external collaboration. The company met that goal four years later.

An example of the technology sourced through their program is the anti-wrinkle peptide that ended up as the P&G product Olay Regenerist. The developers? A small cosmetics company in France. Another research-and-development business specializing in antimicrobial technologies, Syntopix, connected with P&G through an unsolicited submission on the Connect + Develop website and is helping the company to improve the efficacy of one of its major consumer health-care brands.

If you feel you or your organization has an innovation that might be of interest to P&G, the site gives the following criteria. Your innovation must meet one or more of them to be considered by P&G:

- "My innovation addresses a big, unmet consumer need."

- "My innovation offers a new benefit to an existing P&G category or brand."

- "My packaging solution has been demonstrated."

- "My technology is proven and can be quickly applied to a P&G consumer need."

- "I have a game-changing technology or approach."

At P&G, open innovation includes both inbound and outbound innovating and can encompass everything from trademarks and packaging to engineering, business services, and design, so it's not limited to technology.

My Starbucks Idea

In 2008, Starbucks created a social online community to source and vote on new ideas for their business and locations. The proprietary crowdsourcing platform, called My Starbucks Idea (mystarbucksidea.com), lets you join and then share your ideas—for recognition, not money—as well as contribute your opinions on other people's ideas. In turn, the company engages their customers in improving their offerings and builds an attentive base of customers ready to use, purchase, or benefit from the ideas that they implement.

If you have an idea for Starbucks, sign up for a free account and then submit it under My Idea. Give it a title and description and choose a category, such as "Atmosphere and Locations," "Frappuccino Beverages," or "Social Responsibility." You can also view ideas and give them the thumbs up or thumbs down so the best ideas rise to the top of the list.

Some of the "Ideas in Action" generated from the My Starbucks Idea crowd include suggestions for a recycling program at Starbucks locations, a request for more 24-hour Starbucks stores, and a brewed coffee and food express line to speed things up when customers aren't purchasing espresso drinks that take more time. In the fall of 2010, the company announced they had launched over 100 ideas submitted through the site. The number one idea was called Splash Sticks, a combination stirrer and plastic plug for to-go hot beverage cups to prevent splashing. These simple but useful gadgets can now be found in all Starbucks locations.

Innovating with Kraft

Kraft Food—the largest confectionery, food, and beverage corporation in the world—had hit a slump in 2006. Then-CEO Irene Rosenfeld is credited with launching the company's "Innovate with Kraft" (innovatewithkraft.com) program, which allows anyone to contribute product ideas.

One product that came out of the company's open innovation ethos was Bagel-fuls, a ready-to-heat bagel filled with Philadelphia cream cheese. The idea came from a bagel maker in Florida who had developed a tube-shaped bagel filled with cream cheese that he called a Bageler. He patented the process and then sent Kraft an unsolicited pitch, including a box of his innovation. Around the same time, Kraft researchers were facing a challenge trying to develop a similar product. The company struck a deal with the innovator, changed the name from the Bageler to Bagel-fuls, and began producing and distributing the product.

You can submit ideas to Kraft through the Innovate with Kraft website. The company encourages inventors and individuals to patent or otherwise protect their idea first before submitting it. According to the Innovate with Kraft site, if an idea is not protected or protectable through a patent or copyright, Kraft may, "at its sole discretion, grant you a nominal award. In no case will that nominal award exceed $5,000 U.S."

You can complete the Kraft submission process online through their form, and you can upload additional documents with the application, including a Submission Agreement with the legal terms of submitting an idea. Your submission package then goes to the right person at Kraft to assess the company's level of interest. Generally, you can expect a response within eight weeks, although it may take longer. Kraft does not commit to revealing any details of their evaluation. If they're interested in your idea, and you're interested in working with them, discussions begin to move the idea forward. You can negotiate compensation for protected ideas during this stage.

The company seeks innovations in the areas of technology, products, packaging, and processes through Innovate with Kraft, but the company also accepts recipe ideas that include Kraft products and ideas to improve or enhance products to create a better cooking or baking experience. Those ideas can be submitted via Kraftfoods.com. Those ideas aren't protectable and aren't compensated.

Dell IdeaStorm

Another company that developed a site to tap into their customers' product knowledge and ideas is the computer company Dell. Their IdeaStorm customer crowdsourcing platform was launched in 2007 after the company watched the dialogue directly with customers on their corporate blog Direct to Dell. In the first few weeks after it launched, the company received over 2,000 ideas. The company later launched StormSessions stemming from an IdeaStorm idea—to let Dell's development team ask questions directly to the IdeaStorm community during their design phase. The site also inspired Dell's EmployeeStorm to source innovation from everyone within Dell—not just from their research-and-development division.

In the Fall of 2010, users had contributed nearly 15,000 ideas via IdeaStorm with over 733,000 promoted, generating over 90,000 comments. At that time, Dell had implemented 427 of those ideas. One idea that Dell implemented is the company's involvement in Product (RED), a project designed to raise awareness and funding to help eliminate AIDS. Dell created a red Inspiron Mini and select red Dell All-In-One Printers, with a percentage of profits donated directly to the Global Fund to help eliminate AIDS in Africa. Another idea overwhelmingly supported by the IdeaStorm customer crowd and implemented by Dell was one point of contact for support, with faster response times. Your Tech Team now provides North American customers with one year of household support for Dell products.

You can sign up for a free account to participate in both IdeaStorm and StormSessions. You can view ideas, vote for them with a thumbs up or down, post your own ideas, and possibly see your ideas in action.

General Electric's Innovation Challenge

In the middle of 2010, General Electric (GE) put out a call for green innovations to "build the next-generation power grid." Several months later, GE—along with four venture capital partners (Emerald Technology Ventures, Foundation Capital, KPCB, and Rockport Capital)—announced they would be making 12 investments totaling

$55 million out of the nearly 4,000 concepts they received during the 10-week competition. The challenge was part of GE's $200 million Ecomagination competition (challenge.ecomagination.com). Winning ideas from the first round included energy storage, utility security, energy management software, and electric vehicle charging services.

Entries needed to include a clear, detailed proposal that described the technology. Entrants were required to indicate whether they had filed a patent application or had received a patent on their entry or any part of it.

Selected entrants were offered the opportunity to develop a commercial relationship with GE through investment, validation, distribution, development, and growth. People, companies, and organizations were invited to enter as many ideas as they wanted in the three categories: "Renewables," "Grid Efficiency," and "Eco Homes/ Eco Buildings." Check the GE Ecomagination website to learn when new challenges are launched.

Applying the Crowdsourcing Model

Regardless of the task at hand, chances are there's a way to source crowds to help. Not everything can be crowdsourced, but smaller parts of larger projects may be able to be handled through a crowdsourcing site or service. Some of these sites have defined limitations in terms of what work can be done through their systems, but others may be open to exploring new uses for their platforms and worker crowds.

Crowdsourcing as a work model continues to evolve, and companies and individuals continue to develop new technologies and apply them to processes to facilitate and manage crowd work. Mobile devices present myriad opportunities not yet discovered or fully formed, so don't discount opportunities to get work done via texting or other hand-held device applications.

You can also take a cue from major corporations who realized in the last few decades that a closed model of innovation is stifling and limiting. By opening their corporate gates to new ideas from small, nimble entrepreneurial efforts and other flexible entities and individuals, they breathed new life into their companies. Look at your own organization and explore how a more open-source model of idea creation and innovation can help you identify new opportunities and improve your existing processes and systems.

The Least You Need to Know

- The key to effective crowdsourcing is to know specifically what you are trying to achieve and where and how to tap into the right crowd.

- Rather than trying to harness your own crowd, consider a well-managed and reputable crowdsourcing site, to take advantage of their technology to streamline the entire crowdsourcing process.

- By partnering with a major corporation through their open innovation program, you may be able to catapult your organization or company's growth with that corporation's funding, resources, and marketing muscle behind you.

- If you plan on submitting ideas or solutions to a major corporation, you should first protect your innovation if it is protectable.

Fundraising from Crowds

In This Chapter

- Applying crowdsourcing to fundraising
- Articulating your fundraising needs
- Funding personal projects through crowds
- Finding crowds to invest in your company
- Managing money and donors

In the world of fundraising, whether for an organization or a company, there are benefits to reaching out to many people to ask that they contribute money. Fundraisers are applying the principles of crowdsourcing to raising funds, from donations to business capital.

When turning to crowds for money, it's important to have realistic expectations about the process. You also need a way to manage the funds and to understand the tax implications, especially if you're not running a nonprofit organization. Finally, you have to think of the crowd that is contributing to your project as donors and learn to manage those relationships beyond the moment they give.

Tapping into Crowds for Fundraising

A new term in fundraising—for both nonprofits and for-profit companies—is *crowdfunding*. Crowdfunding is a way to leverage your crowd and their connections to contribute money toward a specific project. Crowdfunding has been possible in recent years because of several factors.

- More people trust making payments online.

- Social networks allow an individual to communicate easily with his or her connections.

- Technology exists now that allows micropayments to occur securely.

- Online communities and crowds are able to more easily come together online for a mutual cause or purpose.

- Crowdfunding success stories are becoming more commonplace.

DEFINITIONS

Crowdfunding—also called crowd financing, micro-funding, and crowd-sourced capital—is an organized method of tapping into your network and their networks to raise money for an organization, project, or company.

How is crowdfunding different from traditional fundraising techniques? The main difference is that donations tend to be smaller and more numerous. Smaller donations are more manageable for most people and can often be pledged easily online through a secure payment system like PayPal. But sourcing money from more donors can be an administrative headache, so crowdfunding sites can help.

Crowdfunding turbo-charges traditional fundraising efforts, which until recently were predominantly offline efforts. Many nonprofits have a donate button on their websites, but few have fully incorporated all forms of digital communications into their fundraising efforts.

Crowdfunding isn't limited to organizations with a 501c3 nonprofit tax status. Individuals and even for-profit companies can use crowdsourcing to fund their projects or businesses. From a business standpoint, crowdfunding differs from traditional angel funding because funders are not taking an equity stake in the company; instead, funders are affiliated with the company in an informal way, with some kind of monetary exchange (depending on the deal structure). If you crowdfund, you need to give some kind of value and consideration to your contributors no matter how you structure a deal.

Articulating the Need

Crowdfunding requires the same amount of planning as crowdsourcing work. You start with articulating what you need. In crowdfunding, you not only need to be specific about what you are trying to fund (a book, a film, a new product prototype, a startup company, or a cause), but you also need to determine how much money you need. Work with a financial counselor to develop a profit/loss statement and help you run the numbers to project what you actually need.

As you articulate your need, the way you communicate your request is important. Tell your story in a compelling way. Inspire others to contribute to your project, cause, or company. Most crowdfunding sites force you to keep your request—known in the nonprofit world as the "ask"—very short and concise. Some encourage or require you to submit a video to communicate the need and articulate your ask.

Look for ways to create mutual benefit when asking for funds. Some people like to give out of the generosity in their hearts; others are looking for sound business investments. Still others simply want to do something that feels good or feels right to them.

Make sure your request is something many people can support—something suitable for crowdfunding in the first place. There are crowdfunding sites that let individuals ask for money for very personal things like getting out of debt or covering unexpected medical or dental bills, but most crowdfunding sites are looking for discrete projects with a beginning, middle, and end, so everyone benefits within the specified time frame and parameters of the campaign.

Sites for Crowdfunding

Many sites have processes and technical mechanisms to facilitate gathering monetary contributions in various sizes from many people. The goal of these sites is to simplify and streamline the process of crowdfunding, which can be onerous in terms of administration and legal and tax implications.

Crowdfunding sites run the gamut, from peer-to-peer lending to investment opportunities. Reputable crowdfunding sites have their own structure behind the scenes to ensure legal compliance and minimize fraud. They all have fairly straightforward processes to apply and access their tools for leveraging your own crowd and the general public to request funds and reward donors in both traditional and creative ways. Beware of sites with convoluted schemes, exorbitant fees, or no track record of funding success.

Peer-to-Peer Lending

You can crowdsource small loans from many individuals through sites that facilitate peer-to-peer lending; Kiva (kiva.org) is the pioneer for this lending model. Kiva's mission is to "connect people, through lending, for the sake of alleviating poverty." The recipients of Kiva microloans help fund microfinance institutions in developing countries and the United States to lend money to entrepreneurs and students.

If you are looking for loans from peers, a peer-to-peer lending site can help you tap into your connections and crowds at large. On Prosper (prosper.com), which focuses on personal loans, you as the Borrower must have good credit—meaning a credit score of 640 or more—to post a loan listing. You set the amount of money you want and the interest rate you are willing to pay. Lenders can each invest $25 or more toward your loan. They can also bid your rate down in the site's auction process.

Invested.in (invested.in) lets you either raise as much money as you can by a certain date or a fixed amount. They also offer a customizable and scalable platform for group fundraising sites and provide site hosting.

Funding Individual Projects

Kickstarter (kickstarter.com) is a funding platform for creative projects worldwide, including but not limited to music, film, art, technology, design, food, and publishing projects. The Kickstarter site has a number of examples of successful crowdfunding projects, including a film project called *Save Blue Like Jazz*, which had a target of $125,000 and raised $345,000, and a web technology project called Diaspora, which had a pledge goal of $10,000 and raised $200,641.

Starting a project on Kickstarter is free, and project creators keep 100 percent of their intellectual property. Kickstarter collects a 5 percent fee from the project's funding total if a project is successfully funded, and a 3 to 5 percent credit-processing fee is charged via Amazon, the site's payment processor. If a project doesn't reach its funding goals within the specified amount of time—meaning they don't receive enough pledges toward their goal amount—then contributors get a refund, the project creators are not paid, and the project is closed.

When raising funds through Kickstarter, setting realistic goals and reaching those funding goals is the key to success. Ninety-four percent of successful Kickstarter projects raise more than their funding goal. Kickstarter is not for funding charity projects or causes; instead, it focuses on creativity. The value of using a "social funding" site like Kickstarter is that, in addition to soliciting funds, you are tapping into your existing network and their contacts, gathering your crowd, and creating a base of people potentially interested in your finished project.

Part of the Kickstarter process is getting your project accepted after you submit your idea. You also have to create a promotional video to explain your project and determine a list of rewards or benefits for funders that correspond with different funding amounts.

Another global funding platform is IndieGogo (indiegogo.com). Their technology-based online platform helps anybody with an idea—creative, cause related, or entrepreneurial—to create a funding campaign, offer perks to their contributors, and get their idea funded. Over 12,000 projects from over 135 countries have raised millions of dollars on IndieGoGo.

Anyone can create a funding campaign on IndieGoGo. You establish a funding goal and deadline, pitch your idea, and offer unique or limited-edition perks to your contributors. After you've created your campaign and launched funding, you share your campaign broadly via your friends, family, and extended social network to stimulate contributions and word of mouth. Anyone can fund your campaign—not just people you know.

Another site, Spot.us (spot.us), fills a more specific crowdfunding niche by helping journalists fundraise via small contributions from people who are interested in seeing their story produced. Spot.us creates transparency and allows citizens to contribute to the process of news coverage rather than letting editorial control over news be limited to editors and publishers.

Other crowdfunding sites—such as SellaBand (sellaband.com) and ArtistShare (artistshare.net)—help musicians and artists raise money from fans.

DULY NOTED

Some individuals seek funding via micropatronage, wherein the general public directly supports the work of others by making donations through the Internet. This model has been employed by numerous bloggers who take microdonations to help fund their writing.

For-Profit Funding

ProFounder (profounder.com) is a crowdfunding site geared toward for-profit companies. Their site streamlines the administration of funds from many people and provides funds to either startups just getting off the ground or existing businesses looking to grow. To participate in ProFounder, you must be looking for less than $1 million in investment and be incorporated as an LLC or S or C corporation.

> **DULY NOTED**
>
> To limit your liability and protect yourself from possible legal disputes that can occur in investment situations, incorporate your company. In the United States, you can incorporate your company as an LLC, an S Corporation, or a C Corporation.

On ProFounder, you can raise funds in one of two ways: privately or publicly. Private fundraising means your request for support goes out to only people you know, such as family, friends, classmates, or clients. Public fundraising involves a public announcement, and anyone can participate, whether or not they have a connection to you.

To apply to ProFounder, start with a pitch by answering basic questions about your business, to craft a compelling offer to potential investors. Next, create a terms sheet; ProFounder makes this easy with template forms and compliance sheets to guide you through the process. The terms are based on a revenue share model, so investors don't get equity in your company; instead, they share in the revenues. For example, you can offer 2 percent of your revenue to investors over the next five years.

After you solidify your terms, you receive a destination page on the ProFounder site where you can invite your contacts to view your offer and the terms, and they can make pledges directly on the site. When you reach your funding goal, ProFounder oversees the signing of terms sheets and handles the administrative work of managing the deal, including bookkeeping, compliance issues (which can vary state by state), money transfers from investors, and later paying investors based on the deal terms. Your page on ProFounder remains open for all investors to see for total transparency.

If you choose to make your funding campaign public, your company's page on ProFounder is viewable by the public, and the terms limit how much investors can make back. In this arrangement, investors can only make back their investment amount and break even. This model is similar to the one on Kiva—the peer-to-peer lending site—uses.

If your company pays out investors before the terms of your deal run out, then the remainder of the money you've committed to the deal can be funneled to the nonprofit organization of your choice. For example, if you offer 2 percent of your revenues to investors over the next five years and everyone has been fully paid within two years, then 2 percent of your revenue will go to your selected nonprofit for the next three years. You can also give nonmonetary rewards to investors to make them feel like they're an ongoing part of what you are building.

Crowdfunding a Film: Life in Perpetual Beta

Melissa Pierce set out to make a film about the effects of technology—particularly the Internet—on our culture and ourselves. She had no experience making a film; she learned what she needed to know from online searches and used social networks to reach out to people to interview for the film.

To fund her film initially, she offered people inclusion in the film credits and a t-shirt in exchange for $30. She then heard about Kickstarter and signed up. She found the need to commit to a dollar amount and a time frame "nerve wracking," but she realized her fundraising efforts to date wouldn't cover sound technicians and camera crews. Although she felt the set-up process took a long time, from making decisions on what to write and what video to use to setting up the Amazon payment system that handles Kickstarter's transactions, her campaign was ready to go within a few weeks.

Overall, she enjoyed her first formal crowdfunding experience, but notes that a crowdfunding campaign is only as good as your social network and public relations campaign to drive people to participate. Melissa's Kickstarter initiative brought in $7,435 toward her film, slightly more than her goal of $7,000. Since receiving the funding, the film showed at several film festivals and won an award for merit at the Los Angeles Hollywood Film Festival. *Life in Perpetual Beta* is now a video series, and the first part is available for purchase on Amazon.com.

Sites to Support Causes

Social networks can be used to gather crowds to lead them to a fundraising campaign on another site or platform. An example of a social network add-on feature for fundraising is Causes, a third-party application for Facebook that lets you create campaigns and tie in transaction functionality to receive donations. You can add Causes to your Facebook page and use it to crowdsource signatures on electronic petitions or monetary contributions from your social networking crowd.

Crowdrise is a free-standing, cause-related crowdfunding site that incorporates social networking, and was founded by award-winning actor Edward Norton. The site focuses on volunteering and raising money for charity, taking an irreverent approach to help alleviate the awkwardness many people feel when asking for money.

You can sign up for a profile on Crowdrise, create a charitable page on the site, and start a fundraiser for any of the over one million charities. You can also contribute to someone else's project team to help them fundraise. You then ask for donations using the Share button on your project page, messaging your crowd via your social networks and e-mail. You can post your volunteer projects on Crowdrise or ask your friends to sponsor your volunteer projects to help you raise money for charity. Nonprofits can also use Crowdrise to raise money by turning their grassroots supporters into grassroots fundraisers.

> **DULY NOTED**
>
> In 2008, Barack Obama's campaign committee avoided using public campaign funds. Instead, they raised over $650 million, over half of it in micro-donations of under $200 contributed through the Internet.

Using Givezooks!

Givezooks! (givezooks.com) is a site that provides tools to manage your fundraising efforts and tap into your social networks. Nonprofits can use Givezooks! to reach their crowd networks and their crowd's friends and connections to help influence giving and encourage engagement. Givezooks! offers nonprofits several ways to source crowds for their causes: donor-driven crowdsourcing and nonprofit-driven crowdsourcing.

The Givezooks! site offers an organization donor-driven crowdsourcing tools—also known as peer-to-peer fundraising tools. The organization provides these tools to their current supporters to help them disseminate information along with requests to their social-networking contacts to donate to the organization they're supporting. Using the connectivity of social networking contacts, Givezooks! helps organizations spread the word to their own connections to generate an expanding ripple effect across wider and wider circles of contacts and potential donors.

Through nonprofit-driven crowdsourcing, an organization can easily integrate social fundraising into their traditional fundraising activities. With the Givezooks! system, organizations can create a branded campaign or annual fund, create a wish list of needs with specifics on costs and numbers needed, or hold an online fundraising event. These options tie into social networks, e-mail, and other web-based tools. Once a campaign is deployed, donor-driven crowdsourcing naturally occurs as participants continue to spread the word.

Organizations can track their campaigns and generate reports from the Givezooks! system. The company offers a variety of payment gateways, including PayPal, CyberSource, AmazonPayments, Authorize.net, and Sage.

Using DonorsChoose

DonorsChoose (donorschoose.org) is an online charity that aids you in helping students in need. Public school teachers post classroom project requests on DonorsChoose, with requests ranging from writing utensils to art supplies to musical instruments to microscope slides. Anyone can browse project requests and contribute any amount to any project. Once a project reaches its funding goal, the site delivers the requested materials to the school.

The site vets every request submitted by teachers, processes donor transactions using secure technology, purchases the actual materials, ships the items, and alerts the school principal when materials are on their way. Donors receive photographs of the project they've supported, as well as teacher and student letters with a report outlining how their money was spent.

Managing the Money Pipeline

If you're a nonprofit organization, you need to have systems in place to manage donations. Most crowdfunding systems that let you raise money from large numbers of people place a system between your funders and your normal fundraising channels, such as your bank account or PayPal account. These sites act as a layer to process contributions, making it easier for you to receive money.

If you're an individual who is raising funds for a creative project, there are fewer legal implications for you. But you must be careful with what you promise funders in return for their contributions. You shouldn't offer them money, because this can potentially put you in legal hot water. Plus, as an individual, you are not protected by any legal structure, such as an LLC or S or C Corporation. Most crowdfunding sites guide you to come up with nonmonetary rewards and recognition for your funders and supporters. Regardless of what a crowdfunding site claims or tells you to do, always check with your own accountant and lawyer to understand how to manage money coming in from a crowdfunding campaign.

To accept crowdfunded money, you usually need a bank account or a PayPal account. Different crowdfunding sites use different tools to collect and disburse funds. Some, like Kickstart, use an escrow account to hold funds until you reach your funding goal. If it isn't reached, that money is returned to the donors. A site like SocialWish sets up a merchant account for you and then provides you with a branded Visa card, putting the funds at your disposal.

Relationships with Donors

Any professional fundraiser will tell you that the key to successful fundraising is building relationships with people. Most savvy fundraisers don't just ask for money; they look for ways to make genuine connections with people and make their donors and potential donors feel like an integral part of something important.

Here are some steps for good donor management:

- Keep a detailed donor list with key information about each donor.

- Give kudos to donors in the way they prefer; some want to remain anonymous.

- Offer mutual benefits, rather than only informing a donor how the money will help you.

- Follow up to let donors know exactly how your organization used the money.

- Thank your donors!

Most nonprofit organizations have donor-management systems or software they use to keep track of who donated what, along with more personal information, similar to customer relationship management (CRM) software. Being able to focus on donors as individuals is an important part of major fundraising. In crowdfunding, it is more challenging to be so individualized, but most crowdfunding sites incorporate a system for donor management.

Crowdfunding sites help you create meaningful rewards, benefits, and packages for your donors, so they get a tangible return on their investment. In many cases, it is something as simple as a t-shirt or a copy of the completed film or book they helped to fund. In other cases, it is getting their money back or some other return on their investment.

Be careful to consult an accountant and a lawyer about the tax and legal implications of sourcing money through any crowdfunding site.

The Least You Need to Know

- You need a way to manage crowdsourced funds and to understand the tax implications of bringing them in, especially if you are not running a nonprofit organization.
- Work with your accountant and lawyer to best handle crowdsourced funds and to protect yourself from potential legal liabilities.
- Beware of crowdfunding sites with convoluted schemes or exorbitant fees, or without a track record of funding success.
- Keep a detailed donor list with key information about each donor, thank them, and give them recognition and some kind of return on their investment (especially nonmonetary).

Organizing for Crowd Action

In This Chapter

- Crowdsourcing for social change
- Addressing local issues with crowdsourcing tools
- Crowdsourcing tools for global innovation and support
- Moving beyond crowdsourcing tasks

There are many business applications for crowdsourcing. Nonprofit organizations can benefit from sourcing a crowd for funding and building awareness. This form of crowdsourcing is often referred to as "crowdsourcing for social change." Crowdsourcing principles can be used to bring people together to apply their thinking and actions to making positive change. As a result of successful crowdsourcing, change can happen in local communities or even around the world. Organizations are applying crowdsourcing to issues and problems faced in communities and harnessing the power of crowds to galvanize support.

Crowdsourcing for action involves a variety of basic interactive tools, including surveys and polls, voting, and building awareness, but it can also involve rapid development of open-source technology solutions to address urgent problems. The key to crowdsourcing for community and global action is a shared value system or a shared vision of an outcome that is to come from unified actions. If there is a problem, crowds that form must be united in working toward a common goal. This kind of crowd action starts with a compelling idea, and input from crowd members helps move a project, campaign, or solution forward.

Crowdsourcing Social Change

If you look at the many facets of crowdsourcing to get work done, to gather input and feedback, and to organize people for fundraising and action, there are common threads between seemingly unconnected efforts. Crowdsourcing involves first planning, then carrying out the actual campaign or project, and then performing an assessment.

Steps to crowdsourcing social change are similar to the steps for other types of crowdsourcing, but the content of those steps is different. Here are some questions to ask yourself to organize your efforts to harness crowd wisdom and actions to make a difference in your community and your world:

1. **What is the problem you are trying to solve or cause you want to support?** This question helps you articulate what you are trying to do.

2. **Who do you need to help?** This question helps you narrow down the skills you are seeking. Is it enough that your crowd is a body of individuals, or do you need individuals who have specific abilities or interests?

3. **Where can you find the right crowd to lend a hand?** This question helps you identify where you'll crowdsource. The most efficient places are websites with the express purpose of guiding you to an active crowd organized for a specific task or effort.

4. **What is the call to action?** This question tells the crowd what to do to address the problem or support the cause.

5. **How will you spread the word beyond your own crowd?** This question leads you to communications tools to spread the word about your project; most crowdsourcing sites for social change integrate with social networks.

6. **How can people take action?** For this question, chances are the crowdsourcing site or tool you are using provides mechanisms for people to join, share, contribute, or otherwise interact with you or your project to work toward an outcome.

7. **How will you measure outcomes?** The site you choose to use should help you measure the outcomes by providing dashboards and reporting features. If you are doing everything from scratch, you can compile results in spreadsheets or databases.

There are sites dedicated to bringing together crowds as specific as people in a single neighborhood to crowds as vast as the citizens of the world. They put tools into your hands as an individual activist, a nonprofit, or a business owner looking to align your company with a good cause. You can help provide solutions or be the solutions seeker. You can be part of a crowd for social change.

Civic Innovation Through Crowds

Cities and towns across the country are examining crowdsourcing as a new process for getting their citizens involved in projects that affect their environments and lives. Some communities run contests for ideas to improve their surroundings or resources. Others actively bring citizens together online to conduct ongoing crowdsourcing activities in public and private forums.

You can take part in making positive change happen in your neighborhood, city, or state through crowdsourcing sites such as Give a Minute and SeeClickFix. These sites provide technology platforms that can be accessed in multiple ways—via the web, mobile devices, e-mail, and other communications methods. Both residents and community leaders or officials can tap into the collective reports to take action, correct issues, or draw attention to a previously ignored situation.

Give a Minute: Empowering Residents

Give a Minute (giveaminute.info) gives city residents the opportunity to contribute ideas for improving their cities. The site has launched with Chicago and Memphis, with New York City and San Jose in the works. Residents can post their ideas to the site through a Twitter-like field at the top of the page. Ideas appear on the site as colorful sticky notes on a wall. You can also post ideas via text if you see something in a participating city that needs to be fixed or improved, such as identifying an empty lot where trees could be planted to improve the neighborhood.

The site plans to expand to take the aggregated crowd input and put contributors with similar ideas in touch with one another to work together to make things happen. They're also engaging community leaders on the site—people who can actually take ideas from residents and potentially do something about them. The project has developed Local Projects—a media design firm for museums and public spaces—in partnership with the civic innovation lab CEOs for Cities. Initial funding for the project came from the Rockefeller Foundation and Knight Foundation.

DULY NOTED

Crowdsourcing civic innovation and change can bring issues to light and apply pressure, but is only as effective as the city officials or people in positions with the power to implement the ideas and make change happen.

SeeClickFix: Engaging Citizens

SeeClickFix (seeclickfix.com) encourages citizens to report their concerns about their neighborhoods using their website, mobile applications, voice-mail, and widgets that can be embedded into websites and blogs, pulling in neighborhood maps and pinpointing problems. The site involves citizens, community groups, government, and the media to report and track nonemergency issues anywhere in the world. The site also runs analyses to see how cities around the world respond to citizen requests and reports.

The site taps into the crowd and aggregates input to provide on-the-scene intelligence that no single agency or organization can provide. Bringing issues to the attention of those who can take action and then seeing action taken empowers and engages citizens in new ways. Citizens can also alert others to a problem and set up watch areas to monitor the situation. This could include anything from broken windows and potholes to traffic issues and crime reports. You can help fix a problem by publicly broadcasting the issue to the appropriate parties for resolution. The crowd works together to raise the profile of key concerns or by taking collective and direct action.

Bristol, Connecticut, Sources Ideas

The city of Bristol, Connecticut (pop. 61,000), crowdsourced ideas for a local site revitalization project. The city had a vacant 17-acre former shopping mall site. The developer, Renaissance Downtowns, turned to "crowdsourced placemaking" company CoolTown Beta Communities (cooltownbeta.com), which specializes in gathering "beta communities" to come together to help innovate community-oriented places.

For Renaissance Downtown's Bristol redevelopment effort, CoolTown was brought in to help the developer crowdsource ideas to revitalize the site and to incorporate what the community actually wanted and needed. They were looking to create a sustainable, environmentally friendly local destination: a town center.

Community members joined the crowd to help develop a future neighborhood that focused on the "triple bottom line" of "people, planet, and profit." CoolTown used

Ning as the online space for gathering their community and incorporated their proprietary online tool, Bubbly (bubblyapp.com), to create a visual idea-sharing mechanism that let community members submit and rate ideas. The project sites are Bristol Rising (bristolrising.com) and Bristol Rising Survey (bristolrisingsurvey.com).

Since fall of 2010, over 240 residents were participating in the project, submitting and voting on ideas. Ideas that receive a minimum number of votes will be assessed for financial feasibility, then potentially move on to inclusion in the project's master plan. The project was still in progress in the spring of 2011.

Apps for Democracy: Sourcing Citizens

In 2009, Apps for Democracy sourced citizens of Washington, D.C., to come up with mobile and web applications to improve the city by running a competition awarding programmers for the best applications. Some of the winning applications included one that shows where crime happens in the D.C. area; one that pinpoints the location of broken parking meters; and one that locates the nearest metro station based on a person's iPhone GPS. The first edition of Apps for Democracy yielded 47 web, iPhone, and Facebook applications in 30 days at a fraction of what it would have cost the city to outsource the innovation and development work.

The program was run in cooperation with Washington, D.C., to involve citizens in the creation of the tools and applications they actually needed and would use. The public communicated what applications they wanted built, and then submitted their ideas through an online voting platform called Uservoice. Citizens then voted on the best ideas. The program offered between $20,000 and $30,000 in cash prizes to developers who built the top apps. Finally, the public voted for the "People's Choice Award" to select the best of the applications produced. The entire project was developed by iStrategyLabs, a digital agency, and the D.C. government's Office of the Chief Technology Officer.

Crowdsourcing Volunteers Through Sparked

If you are a nonprofit organization seeking volunteers to handle specific tasks, a for-profit company looking for volunteer opportunities for your staff, or an individual with professional skills and some time on your hand, Sparked (sparked.com) connects volunteers with volunteer work. If you access the site as an individual, you can choose the issues that interest you, such as animals, the environment, poverty, science, health, or justice.

Then you can specify your skills from a list ranging from graphic design to public relations to marketing, research, copywriting, and web development. Based on your choices, you then see how many people registered on the site as a *micro-volunteer* share your interests and how many challenges align with your interests. Log in to the site using your Facebook account or sign up manually. Once logged in, you can create a profile that lists the skills and causes you chose and will track the challenges you complete.

> **DEFINITIONS**
>
> **Micro-volunteering**—also called "e-volunteering" or "virtual volunteering"—occurs when a group of individuals complete tasks that are standalone or part of a greater project via the Internet using computers, smartphones, or other Internet-enabled devices.

Harnessing Global Crowd Power

Crowdsourcing for social change is happening at micro-levels in neighborhoods, but there are sites and projects that are farther reaching. The steps to tapping into the crowd are the same, but the tools used are scaled to manage larger and very dispersed crowds.

The very nature of crowdsourcing removes many of the barriers of organizing on a global scale through the use of the Internet and online tools. Crowdsourcing websites provide a structure for managing many people's input, which they can contribute at different times throughout the day and night due to time zone differences.

Crowdsourcing Global Philanthropy

Citizen Effect (citizeneffect.org) takes a crowdsourcing approach to philanthropy. Their site provides individuals with tools and networks to work with communities around the world to make a positive impact. When you sign up to the site, you are called a Citizen Philanthropist and you can choose your project and then tap into your social networks to rally support and build your partner community.

The site works with field partners who post projects from impoverished communities around the world. When you choose the project to support, you receive direct reports from the corresponding field partner to see the effects of your contributions. The Citizen Effect process is simple:

- Choose a project that aligns with your interests.

- Specify how you plan to raise funds.

- Tell your connections and ask for their support.

- Receive photos and videos about the tangible impact your contribution has had on a community.

The overall goal is to help partners build more sustainable communities abroad while promoting stronger civic-minded communities at home.

Another global crowdsourcing site for philanthropy is Jolkona Foundation (jolkona. com), which sets out to make it easy for individuals to contribute directly to low-cost, high-impact philanthropic opportunities around the world. Projects range from planting trees in Honduras to providing food and housing for an HIV-positive child in Cambodia, with 100 percent of your donation going to the project you've selected. Using their site, you can check on the progress of your current gift at any time, and you can keep track of past donations you've made.

Tracking Protests with CrowdVoice

Sometimes, crowdsourcing's power comes from the ability to source information from remote places and draw global attention to situations that might not otherwise be noticed. CrowdVoice (crowdvoice.org) is a user-powered service that crowdsources information about protests happening around the world. The platform brings together activists and journalists, and information about human rights abuses, demonstrations, and current events is chosen and approved by the community.

Topics and countries submitted range from "religious freedom in Uzbekistan" to "censorship in China" to "emergency law and police brutality in Egypt." Related information is then aggregated from news sources, blogs, video, and social networking sites. Anyone can contribute news, suggest new topics to cover, and approve what others have submitted.

CrowdVoice crowdsources submissions as well as moderation, editing, and sharing aspects of the content so the crowd is essentially building and maintaining the resource. All site visitors can easily approve or disapprove new content or add their own. Using crowdsourcing globally helps the CrowdVoice generate up-to-date and often overlooked news stories from local voices in other parts of the world, and empowers individuals to help build awareness of global events.

Crisis Support Using Ushahidi

Ushahidi (ushahidi.com), which means "testimony" in Swahili, is a crowdsourced communications platform that helps address communications challenges during natural disasters and crises that occur around the world. The site grew out of a project to map reports of violence in Kenya in 2008, tapping into the citizen crowd of 45,000 users throughout Kenya who reported incidences of violence and peace efforts through the website and their own mobile devices.

The data received through Ushahidi was turned into an actual map that served as an invaluable tool used by people on the ground and those trying to support them. Since then, the organization behind the site has grown from an ad-hoc team of volunteers to a cohesive organization with staff, developers, and volunteers working together to address crisis situations worldwide.

The site collects information from citizen crowds around the world to quickly produce visual and interactive mapping. Ushahidi not only allows rapid deployment and targeting of support, such as rescue workers in the Haiti and Chile earthquakes, it also allows individuals to share their stories with the world. The Ushahidi platform lets any person or organization use it and customize it to collect and visualize information.

Global Innovation on One Billion Minds

One Billion Minds (onebillionminds.com) is an online ecosystem that mobilizes individuals to create social impact in emerging countries. The site provides a crowdsourcing environment to bring together people from around the world to solve global problems through open innovation challenges addressing technology, design, science, and social issues. Companies and nonprofits who sign up as clients on the site can access both ideas and people outside of their own organizations to find solutions for real-life problems. The site brings together solution seekers and problem solvers to solve challenges surrounding issues such as poverty, food supply, sanitation, clean energy, and economics in the emerging world.

A clear example of the kind of work done through a site like One Billion Minds is the story of Mandar Thite, a 45-year-old engineer who developed a contraption to help his father scan and store broadsheet newspapers for later reading. Mandar hooked together a geared mechanism involving a cheap digital camera to scan and store with precision. Through the One Billion Minds ecosystem, Thite realized his innovation could actually be a useful, low-cost alternative to the commercially available large-format scanners and at a much more affordable price to people who could otherwise not afford such equipment.

Corporations and nonprofits connected to emerging countries post challenges to the site that can be solved by individuals from any part of the world. You can also sign up to be part of One Billion Minds' Fellows Program—it is a free membership to participate. You can then adopt a social innovation project, help spread the word about it, identify innovators, or develop your own idea and receive support from the crowd. You can also sign up to mentor an innovator who has an idea, but who needs guidance to develop it further. You can find innovators through the site or e-mail the company to be matched with one.

Innovation Support Through Ennovent

Ennovent (ennovent.com) is another for-profit company that focuses on supporting entrepreneurs who "advance innovations for sustainability at the base of the economic pyramid" in the areas of energy, food, water, education, and health. The company uses the crowdsourcing model to identify solutions that may exist in other parts of the world that can be applied to solve problems in India.

Through crowdsourcing, Ennovent looks for entrepreneurs who are creating new markets or changing existing markets using relatively simple, convenient, and low-cost innovations. Members of their crowd include representatives from nongovernmental organizations, for-profit companies, and universities. Crowd members help Ennovent identify and innovate products, processes, services, and business models.

Through Ennovent, a Seeker broadcasts a challenge. As a Connector, you help identify suitable Solvers or entrepreneurs with innovative solutions. You can also be one of the Solvers invited to submit a solution for consideration. If your solution is chosen by Ennovent's team, you can receive up to $500,000 in funding. Ennovent also offers a $3,000 reward to the Connector, the person that connected them to the Solver in the first place.

You can join Ennovent's network to be notified of specific "Challenges" and participate in their innovation process. The process—from posting a challenge to submitting a solution and selecting a winning innovation—can take six months or longer.

PITFALLS

Beware of crowdsourcing sites that purport to provide support to others and then seek large sums of money from you to join or participate. Most sites that use crowdsourcing for social change are free to join. Other than crowdfunding sites, no money changes hands, or you are compensated for your contributions and innovations.

Online Actions for Real Results

As with any crowdsourcing effort, to get to success you must start by knowing what problem you are trying to solve. Crowdsourcing an action involves gathering the right type of crowd—the one made up of people who share your interests or values and who understand the problem you've presented and who want to participate in addressing the problem.

You must know what kind of outcome you'd like to achieve, but leave room for innovation and transformation along the way. You'll soon discover that crowds can bring forth ideas and improve on processes to get you to an outcome you may not have anticipated, but one that solves the problem in a new way.

When engaging crowds in actions, have measurement tools in place to track and share progress. Action-oriented crowds want to be privy to outcomes and see progress. In many situations, final results can take months and even years to come to fruition. Part of the "payment" for participating in actions that result in change in communities or people's lives is the feeling that one's involvement really makes a difference.

The power of crowdsourcing can transform how we do business, how we address problems, and how we get things done. Sourcing a crowd is an opportunity to include diverse people with different backgrounds and disciplines, with varied experiences and education. Applied with care, crowdsourcing can have a positive impact on our communities and our world.

The Least You Need to Know

- The key to crowdsourcing for community and global action is a shared value system or a shared vision of an outcome that will come from unified actions.
- Steps to crowdsourcing social change are similar to the steps for other types of crowdsourcing, but the content of those steps is different.
- To facilitate a smooth process and clear outcomes, know what actions you want to happen before asking the crowd to get involved.
- When engaging crowds in actions, have measurement tools in place to track and share progress.

Glossary

alpha test   The first phase of checking a software product or website, usually private and launched on a smaller, controlled scale.

asynchronous   Not happening at the same time. Most crowdsourcing happens asynchronously, meaning your activities and the crowd's activities are not happening simultaneously.

beta test   The second phase of checking a product such as software or a website. This occurs after the alpha phase, during which paid or unpaid testers check the product for errors, bugs, and other issues.

bounty   A payment made by one party to another party. In crowdsourcing, a bounty may be referred to as a prize, award, reward, tip, fee, payment, or compensation.

civic innovation   The process of bringing together many stakeholders to generate new ideas in an organized fashion for improving cities or communities.

cloud-sourced labor   Work done entirely online, or "in the cloud," often through specialized websites that assign, manage, and track work tasks. Some companies specialize in online-based services to perform work.

cloudworking   Utilizing online-based systems and applications on secure servers to share resources, software, and information. The technical term for this arrangement is *cloud computing*. Also called *working in the cloud*.

co-creation   A form of product customization in which companies give consumers the tools, supplies, and resources to create a customized product or service. This term could also refer to a collaborative process of creation where a dispersed team comes together to produce something such as a video.

credibility score   Result of a rating system that measures the accuracy of a worker's work and presents a final number to help gauge the chances of accuracy and successful completion of work by that individual.

crowdfunding   An organized method of tapping into your network and your networks' contacts to raise money for an organization, project, or company. Also referred to as *crowd financing, micro-funding,* or *crowdsourced capital.*

crowdsourced service provider (CSP)   An agency or company that provides some or all of their services through crowdsourcing activities. Also called *crowdsourcing service provider.*

crowdworker   Someone who performs a task as part of a crowdsourced project or participates in a crowdsourcing campaign.

curated crowdsourcing   A vetted crowd of pre-qualified members who participate in a project to guarantee a higher level of output.

customer feedback loop   A mechanism set up to obtain feedback—both positive and negative—from customers. An organization or company can then make improvement modifications to a product or service, particularly in response to negative feedback.

design contest   Competitions on websites and within online communities among designers who compete by submitting designs. When a winning design is chosen, the contest host pays the designer. Also referred to as *crowd competitions.*

escrow or **escrow account**   An arrangement or repository in which an independent and trusted third party receives and later disburses money for two or more parties involved in a transaction.

expert-sourcing   Identifying and utilizing someone online with highly specialized skills or talents; similar to one-sourcing. *See* one-sourcing.

freelancer marketplaces   Websites that gather a very large crowd of skilled workers; facilitate matching workers to jobs; and carry out the vetting, hiring, managing, and payment process.

frequently asked questions (FAQs)   Documents or information sections on a website that organize the existing and prospective customers' most commonly asked questions, and provide answers.

gold standard   As a data-management term, refers to entering known or correct data in a system or process against which one can measure and assess the accuracy of answers. Connotes a standard of excellence. Traditionally refers to a monetary standard.

groupthink   A phenomenon in which the thoughts and ideas of people gathered together begin to conform; the individual's thoughts are influenced by the dynamics of the group rather than independent thinking.

human intelligence task (HIT)   A task that requires some degree of human brain power and cannot easily be automated.

iteration   A version of a process's step or phase. In design, each illustration's iteration is a different version with modifications determined throughout the process.

micro-labor   Work that is broken down into smaller parts or a work process that consists of tiny or compact tasks, usually performed to complete a bigger task or project.

micro-transactions   Financial exchanges that involve very small amounts of money. These transactions usually take place online. The online payments company PayPal, for example, defines a micropayment as anything under $12 U.S. Also called *micropayments*.

micro-volunteering   Occurs when a group of individuals completes either stand-alone tasks or tasks that are part of a greater project; these tasks are completed online without compensation. Also called *e-volunteering* or *virtual volunteering*.

microblog   A site such as Twitter where members can set up an account—usually for free—and post short messages to their friends, fans, followers, or the general public.

microtask   A small, discrete task that can be easily performed, usually repetitively.

mob-sourcing   Casting a random and wide net to engage a large number of people for a project that doesn't require specialized skills.

no spec work   The belief that a competition or process in which a person must submit completed work without a guarantee of payment is an unfair practice that takes advantage of the participant.

one-sourcing   Reaching out to online crowds to find a specific individual who has general skills for less skill-intensive tasks.

open innovation   The concept of organizations and companies going outside their traditional—and often internal—research and development channels to source ideas and solutions to advance the creation process.

open source   A philosophy and attitude of openness, with voluntary participation. An example of open source is when a company's code is open to other programmers to rework, enhance, and improve it, or to develop complementary products.

outsource   To contract work outside your organization. Crowdsourcing can be considered a form of outsourcing with specific parameters, such as being performed and managed by individuals online, and often consisting of smaller tasks and pools of workers.

peer review   When individuals within a group, online community, or crowd review and rate one another's work.

privacy policy   A written document published on a website, blog, or online community to detail how data about site visitors is collected, why the data is gathered, and how it will be used.

product development cycle   The process of developing a new product, from idea generation to market analysis to engineering to manufacturing.

qualitative   Data analysis that assesses the quality of something, usually involving approaches such as a narrative response to a question.

quality controls   Procedures or mechanisms put in place to assure accuracy and proper work completion or product manufacturing.

quantitative   Data analysis that assesses the quantity of something, usually involving numbers or percentages.

real time   A term referring to something that occurs online immediately and without delay. Instant messaging happens in real time, while e-mail does not. Actions that occur in close to real time are referred to as near real time.

redundancy   Duplication in a process or system. An example of this is in quality assurance, when several workers perform the same task to compare quality and assess accuracy.

response rate   The ratio of people who answer a survey during a survey process. Also can be referred to as *completion rate* or *return rate*.

security policy   A written document published on a website, blog, or online community that outlines what security measures have been taken to protect confidential information, including identifying any security software, securely configured hardware, and other security measures that the site manager is utilizing.

seeker   A term used for an individual searching for an idea or innovation, a solution to a problem, or an answer to a question.

self-service crowdsourcing   Using a site with an established crowd and an online platform with built-in tools to implement a crowdsourcing process, without a service provider's involvement.

social dashboard   A site, application, or tool to monitor and manage communications in multiple social networks, microblogs, and other social media sites.

social network   A website and often free service where members can set up profiles; connect with other site members; and post information privately and shared only with immediate connections, or shared publicly.

solver   Someone who participates in an innovation, idea generation, or crowdsourcing process to provide answers, solutions, or ideas. Can also be referred to as a *responder* or *submitter*.

status update   A message one posts to a social network to share information or communicate with others. Also called a *post* or simply an *update*.

team-sourcing   Using a vetting process to identify specific individuals in online crowds who can work with your team.

terms of service   Outlines responsibilities of a site or online community host, and the expectations of the user or site or community member. Specifies inappropriate actions, and details what actions would be taken for violations of the site's rules. Also called *terms of use*.

third-party application   Software or programming code that provides a function or feature for a site or network, but is created by an outside company.

tweetsourcing   Using Twitter, a microblog, to crowdsource information from one's followers.

validators   In crowdsourced work, the inclusion of automatic verification mechanisms for data, with standard formats such as e-mail addresses and phone numbers.

wide-sourcing   Another term for crowdsourcing or reaching out to many, usually with some process and order.

widget   A small piece of code placed on a website or blog that pulls content dynamically from another source and appears as an icon or badge. Widgets provide a function; for example, a Facebook widget provides an easy way for someone to like a Facebook page from another site or blog and can display both a list of recent updates and photographs of a handful of fans of the page.

wiki   A collaborative website built with contributions from the community or with crowdsourced content; Wikipedia is an example of one such site.

Crowdsourcing Resources

The following are websites for different areas of crowdsourcing to check out.

Crowdsourced Service Providers and Agencies

blur Group (blurgroup.com)   A full-service, integrated creative agency that leverages crowdsourcing to enhance creative thinking and augment creative output.

Chaordix (chaordix.com)   Provides planning and outcome assessment, crowd recruitment, community management, and an online platform and tools for collaborative innovation, market research, and brand management.

Clickadvisor (clickadvisor.com)   An online consumer-research agency specializing in co-creation and innovation for consumer brands using consumer crowds.

GeniusRocket (geniusrocket.com)   Offers curated crowdsourcing to create rich media content, branding, and naming for companies through an online crowdsourcing platform.

Poptent (poptent.net)   A social network that produces crowdsourced videos for both online and offline use.

Spigit (spigit.com)   Provides software to companies for innovation and "collective idea management," both internally with employees and externally with customers and business partners.

Tongal (tongal.com)   Crowdsources collaboration for creative work including video production, helping businesses transform their core consumers into creators.

Whinot (whinot.com)   Offers small-business consulting services and marketing services by bringing together a community of skilled consultants.

Answer Sites

Aardvark (vark.com)   A peer-to-peer answer site that uses both e-mail and instant messaging to distribute questions and disseminate answers.

Answerbag (answerbag.com)   A general topic answer site open to the public. Requires that individuals set up a free account.

Answers.com (answers.com)   A highly trafficked site that gives you the option of getting answers from web-based reference sites or their Wikianswers online community.

ChaCha (chacha.com)   Pays guides to answer questions via text messaging and phone.

Facebook Questions (facebook.com/questions)   Facebook's version of public and peer-to-peer questions and answers.

LinkedIn Answers (linkedin.com/answers)   LinkedIn's version of peer-to-peer and public questions and answers, with an emphasis on answers from your own connections.

Mahalo Answers (mahalo.com/answers)   Crowd answer site that pays responders in virtual currency (Mahalo Dollars) that can be converted into real currency.

Quora (quora.com)   A newer entry into the answer site space, founded by a former Facebook employee. The site is growing rapidly, partly due to its powerful, integrated technology platform but also the high-profile tech industry crowd it has attracted from the start.

WikiAnswers (wiki.answers.com)   The online answer community for Answers.com.

Yahoo! Answers (answers.yahoo.com)   Crowd answer site owned by Yahoo!

Co-Creation and Customer Participation Products

Blank Label (blank-label.com)   A site where customers can design their own dress shirts for men.

Chocri (createmychocolate.com)   A site where customers can select ingredients—from dried strawberries to bacon bits to gold flakes—to add to chocolate bars that they can then purchase.

Design a Tea (designatea.com)   A site where customers can pick a base tea and add their favorite flavors to create a custom blend.

FashionPlaytes (fashionplaytes.com)   Girls select from different design elements to customize clothing that they—or their parents—can buy.

Furniture4Home (furniture4home.net)   Customers vote on new products on the website, before they are manufactured.

Made.com (made.com)   A site where customers vote on new products on the website before they are manufactured.

ModCloth (modcloth.com)   Customers pre-order and fund up-and-coming designers' collections, putting the consumer in the role of "fashion buyer."

Threadless (threadless.com)   An online community that designs t-shirts, votes for favorites, and purchases the produced t-shirts.

Crowd Action and Activism

Bristol Rising (bristolrising.com)   The crowdsourcing civic project of Bristol, Connecticut, where residents are suggesting city projects for an undeveloped former shopping mall site.

Citizen Effect (citizeneffect.org)   Provides individuals with tools and networks to work with communities around the world to make a positive impact through crowdfunding.

CrowdVoice (crowdvoice.org)   A user-powered service that crowdsources information about protests happening around the world.

Give a Minute (giveaminute.info)   A site that empowers city residents in Chicago and Memphis to post ideas for city improvements. The site shows plans of expanding to New York City and San Jose.

One Billion Minds (onebillionminds.com)   An online network and platform that mobilizes individuals to create social impact in emerging countries.

SeeClickFix (seeclickfix.com)   Encourages citizens to report concerns about their neighborhoods using the web, mobile applications, voice-mail, and widgets that produce neighborhood maps that pinpoint problems.

Sparked (sparked.com)   Brings people together on their website to connect volunteers with volunteer work.

Spot.us (spot.us)   Lets individuals or groups share the cost in reporting news in their community by commissioning freelance journalists to write news stories. Referred to as "crowdfunded" news.

Ushahidi (ushahidi.com)   Crowdsourced communications platform that helps address communications challenges during natural disasters and crises that occur around the world.

Crowd Design and Creative

99designs (99designs.com)   A crowd design competition site for logos, brochures, print, t-shirts, banner ads, websites, icons, business cards, and WordPress themes.

CrowdSPRING (crowdspring.com)   One of the largest crowd communities of creative individuals, with over 75,000 designers and writers connected to their site and design competitions for print design, logos, stationery, company naming, and small website design.

Guerra Creativa (en.guerra-creativa.com)   Design contest site for logos, web design, stationery design, business logos, flash, or 3D design.

Logo Arena (logoarena.com)   Design competition site focused on logo design.

Naming Force (namingforce.com)   Creative competition site for business names, website names, and product names.

Prova (prova.com)   Advertisement design contests, including logos, postcards, packaging, and websites.

Quirky (quirky.com)   Brings two brand-new consumer products to market each week, co-created by the company's global community and their own expert product design staff.

Squadhelp (squadhelp.com)   Freelance competitions for company names, taglines, slogans, website and usability testing, article writing, content design, logo designs, and search engine optimization (SEO) analysis.

Zooppa (zooppa.com)   Global social network for creative talent for user-generated video, print, and banner advertising for leading brands.

Crowd Testing and Troubleshooting

TopCoder (topcoder.com)   Competitive software design and development community with online computer programming competitions.

UserTesting.com (usertesting.com)   Low-cost usability testing website where you pay per site tester.

uTest (utest.com)   Marketplace for software testing services, with over 30,000 quality assurance (QA) professionals from more than 150 countries.

Crowdsourcing Feedback and Input

Crowdtap (crowdtap.com/clients)   An online crowdsourcing platform with an influential crowd offering insights into companies' products and services.

Evly (evly.com)   Platform for building a free website integrating crowdsourcing tools, social media, and e-commerce.

UserVoice (uservoice.com)   Provides tools for companies to allow their customers to submit, discuss, and vote on feedback.

Crowdfunding and Crowd Fundraising

ArtistShare (artistshare.net)   Allows fans to fund musicians and other creative artists.

DonorsChoose (donorschoose.org)   Online charity to help raise funds for students in need through school donations.

Givezooks! (givezooks.com)   Online social fundraising platform that helps non-profit organizations increase charitable giving within local communities by leveraging their social network contacts.

IndieGoGo (indiegogo.com)   Helps anybody with an idea—creative, cause related, or entrepreneurial—to create a funding campaign, offer perks to their contributors, and get their idea funded.

Invested.in (invested.in)   Interactive platform enabling users to leverage their social network contacts to raise financial capital.

Kickstarter (kickstarter.com)   Funding platform for creative projects worldwide, including, but not limited to, music, film, art, technology, design, food, and publishing.

ProFounder (profounder.com)   Crowdfunding site geared toward for-profit companies.

Prosper (prosper.com)   Focuses on crowdfunding personal loans for people with good credit.

SellaBand (sellaband.com)   A music website that helps artists raise money from their fans and the SellaBand community to record a professional album.

Crowdsourcing Work

Clickworker.com (clickworker.com/en)   A Germany-based crowd labor site with over 68,000 workers performing tasks, including writing and tagging content, organizing data, and researching.

CloudCrowd (cloudcrowd.com)   Helps companies break down large projects into smaller tasks, including translation, editing, data entry, image processing, Internet research, and content creation.

CrowdFlower (crowdflower.com)   Accesses workers in over 70 countries through other crowdsourced labor sites such as Mechanical Turk, Samasource, Gambit, and its own iPhone app called Give Work.

LiveOps (liveops.com)   Virtual call center outsourcing with trained at-home agents handling inbound and outbound calls.

Mechanical Turk (mturk.com)   Micro-labor site owned by Amazon.com.

myGengo (mygengo.com)   Crowdsourcing translation site.

Samasource (samasource.com)   Nonprofit crowdsourcing site with a mission to "reduce poverty among people in low-income communities around the world by providing dignified, technology-based work."

Freelancer Marketplaces

Elance (elance.com)   Freelancer marketplace for skilled programmers, designers, writers, translators, marketers, researchers, and administrative contractors.

Guru (guru.com)   Online marketplace for accessing freelance programmers, web developers, graphic designers, and writers.

oDesk (odesk.com)   Global service marketplace for small- and medium-sized businesses for hiring, managing, and paying remote freelancers or teams.

vWorker (vworker.com)   Formerly Rentacoder.com, an international marketplace connecting employers and entrepreneurs with virtual workers.

Ideas and Innovation

Cofundos (cofundos.org)   A platform for open-source software innovation and development.

Ennovent (ennovent.com)   Seeks solutions for sustainable development in energy, food, water, health, and education in rural and remote India.

Hypios (hypios.com)   Helps companies solve their research and development problems by organizing online competitions with thousands of solvers from around the world.

IdeaConnection (ideaconnection.com)   Open innovation challenge site for new inventions, innovations, and products.

IdeaOffer (ideaoffer.com)   Competition site that pays for winning ideas.

InnoCentive (winnocentive.com)   Online platform for open innovation, crowdsourcing, and innovation contests.

NineSigma (ninesigma.com)   Open innovation service provider, connecting clients with a global network of innovation experts.

Monitoring and Management Tools

BearHug (bearhugapp.com)   Customer care and support application that lets you aggregate customer feedback, customer questions, and customer reviews.

HootSuite (hootsuite.com)   Web-based and mobile social media dashboard application for managing multiple social networking accounts.

Radian6 (radian6.com)   Provides enterprise-level, fee-based solution and strategic services for monitoring social media channels.

Seesmic (seesmic.com)   Social-media management client for desktop computers and mobile devices to oversee and post to Twitter, Facebook, LinkedIn, and other popular social media channels. Recently began offering a web-based version.

Sprout Social (sproutsocial.com)   Provides a web-based tool to help you listen, grow, and manage your social networks. Offers a free trial.

TweetDeck (tweetdeck.com)   Desktop and mobile application for managing Twitter, Facebook, and LinkedIn, among others.

Online Collaborative and Community Tools

Basecamp (basecamphq.com)   Web-based project management and collaboration tool with to-do lists, file uploads, messaging, scheduling, and milestones.

Evly (evly.com)   Free, web-based service for creating custom social-networking sites specifically for crowdsourcing activities such as gathering input and crowd voting.

FilesDIRECT (filesdirect.com)   Service that lets you send and receive large files online without using FTP or e-mail.

Glasscubes (glasscubes.com)   Online project management and virtual workspace for teams.

Grouply (grouply.com)   This site lets you set up online communities and groups for free.

KickApps (kickapps.com)   Online community builder incorporating custom social networking, message boards, video sharing, widgets, and user-generated content.

Ning (ning.com)   Online fee-based service for creating, customizing, and sharing a social network.

SendThisFile (sendthisfile.com)   Service for sending and receiving large files without e-mail attachments or software to install.

SendYourFiles (sendyourfiles.com)   Service to back up, share, and send large files, including video, music, and other files.

Wall.fm (wall.fm)   Simple social networking site builder with free themes, photo and video upload, blogs, groups, and other features.

Web2PDF (web2pdfconvert.com)   Site that lets you instantly convert a web page into a PDF file.

Zoho (zoho.com)   Online web applications for productivity and collaboration, including a project management tool.

Polling Tools

PollDaddy (polldaddy.com)   Online survey generator with integration options for other sites, including WordPress blogs, Facebook, and Ning.

QuizSnack (quizsnack.com)   Online poll and survey software for creating and publishing questionnaires.

Survey Gizmo (surveygizmo.com)   Online survey software tool.

SurveyMonkey (surveymonkey.com)   Free online questionnaire and survey site.

TwtSurvey (twtsurvey.com)   Free and fee-based surveys and polls with Twitter integration.

Zoomerang (zoomerang.com)   Online survey software tool with reporting and advanced survey logic.

Social Networks

Facebook (facebook.com)   The most trafficked social network that connects people with friends and others.

LinkedIn (linkedin.com)   Professional, business-oriented networking site.

Twitter (twitter.com)   Microblogging site with social networking aspects for sharing and consuming information.

Index

Numbers

projects
access, 224
posting, 223-224
workers
managing, 225
paying, 226
Project Agreements, 224
selecting, 224
freelancer marketplaces, 221
workers
frequently asked questions, 145
FTC and Netflix, 99
fundraising, 271
social networks, 137

G

gaming money, 18
gardens, online communities as, 70
GE (General Electric), 268
general topic answer sites, 125-127
GeniusRocket, 230
Ghidinelli, Brian, 19
Give a Minute, 285
Givezooks! fundraising, 278-279
Glasscubes, 48
global philanthropy, 288-291
goal setting, 26
common business goals, 26
Goggins, Tim, design sourcing, 214
Goodie Two Shoes wine, 98
goods crowdsourcing, 97-98
Google Answers, 121
Google Forms, 40-42

Google Groups, 81-83
Google Spreadsheets, 40
Google Talk, 113
group buying, 262
Grouply, 83-85
Groupon, 262
groups
LinkedIn, 187
announcements, 189
publicizing, 189
setup, 188-189
groupthink, 115-117
Guerra Creativa, 213
guidelines for communities, 73-74
Guru, 221
SafePay Escrow service, 226
worker selection, 224
workers
managers, 225
paying, 226

H

HIT (Human Intelligence Task), 196
Mechanical Turk, 203
homebound workers, 20
HootSuite, 174
Howe, Jeff, 3
Hypios, 130

I

iChat, 113
idea crowdsourcing
legal issues, 103
marketing, 104

idea generation sites, 99
IdeaOffer, 101-102
legal issues, 103
marketing, 104
product development, 100
idea sourcing, 100
IdeaOffer, 101-102
product development, 100
IdeaConnection, 129-130
IdeaOffer, 101-102
ideas on new products, 96
IdeaStorm, 268
image conversion, 197
image optimization, 197
image tagging, 197
in-kind incentives, 22-23
incentives, 22, 146
in-kind, 22-23
monetary, 22
income, 18
IndieGo fundraising, 275
information, customers helping customers, 251
InnoCentive, 129
innovations for sustainability, 291
input, 10-11
crowdsourcing, 4
customers, 103
prior to manufacture, 103
FAQ building, 248-251
social networks, coaxing, 145
input on products, 94-95
feedback loop, 96
focus groups, 94
improving existing, 96
new products, 96
prior to manufacture, 103
when to ask, 95-96